SMART MAMA'S GREEN GUIDE

SMART MAMA'S GREEN GUIDE

SIMPLE STEPS TO REDUCE YOUR CHILD'S TOXIC CHEMICAL EXPOSURE

JENNIFER TAGGART

CENTER STREET™

New York Boston Nashville

The information herein is not intended to replace the services of trained health professionals, or be a substitute for medical advice. You are advised to consult with your health care professional with regard to matters relating to your health and the health of your children, and in particular regarding matters that may require diagnosis or medical attention.

Center Street
Hachette Book Group
237 Park Avenue
New York, NY 10017

Visit our Web site at www.centerstreet.com.

Center Street is a division of Hachette Book Group, Inc.
The Center Street name and logo are trademarks of the Hachette Book Group, Inc.

Printed in the United States of America

First edition: June 2009
10 9 8 7 6 5 4 3 2 1

Library of Congress Cataloging-in-Publication Data

Taggart, Jennifer.
Smart mama's green guide : simple steps to reduce your child's toxic chemical exposure / Jennifer Taggart.—1st ed.
p. cm.
ISBN 978-1-59995-151-5
1. Toxicology—Popular works. 2. Environmental toxicology—Popular works. 3. Poisons—Safety measures—Popular works. 4. Children—Health and hygiene—Popular works. I. Title.
RA1213.T34 2009
615.9'02—dc22 2009001166

To my father-in-law, William Hoyer Welcher.
Thank you for always being ready to help.
We miss you.

Contents

Foreword

by Devra Davis

When my children were little, I was the community head-lice inspector and lead inspector. This was not because I had any special training in the area, but because the District of Columbia, where my young urban family lived in the 1980s, did not have anyone paid to do this work at the time. Sad to say that some thirty years later, many localities still lack the resources and expertise to provide help to parents of young children, especially to those who are most in need of it—the poor and those without the ability to bring in expert consultants.

One has to ask why we transfer property throughout our nation with certificates that the homes are free of termites and their roofs will not cave in, but do not always certify whether or not they are safe places for our children to live—that they don't contain asbestos, lead, or persistent toxic agents, like PCBs or pesticides. Of course, those who rent where they live have even less access to such information. Our homes remain our castles, the places where we bathe, clothe, feed, and take care of our children. But, as Jennifer Taggart reminds us in this well-written compendium, our homes and the environments into which we bring our children can be sources of hidden dangers.

Though the first environment of our babies is the only one that we can control, even that control is not as complete as pregnant women may believe. You can control what you eat and your good and bad habits, but you can't control the residues in your body that will flow through your growing baby. As Jennifer Taggart shows us in this beautifully written book, our babies are being born already polluted, because most of us contain chemicals in our bodies that did not exist even three decades ago. What all this means for our health is a subject of intense scientific debate, but the facts are clear. If we want our children to have the right to be as healthy as possible, we need to become informed about those things around them that we can control. We start, naturally, with the mother, who becomes the first fortress of human life. Cleaning up workplaces and homes for moms and dads has to be understood as a fundamental need for any society that prides itself on taking good care of its children.

My dad used to say a consultant is a man with a briefcase and a suit who comes from 200 miles away. Nowadays, the Internet has changed—mostly for the better—our ability to get information about the environmental hazards that can affect all of us. We don't need to call on men or women to travel long distances to help us understand how to improve our lives. We just need to read this book and learn of the many resources available to us to get informed about how to lower modern risks.

Anyone thinking about getting pregnant or who has small children will find this book of value. Of course, pregnancy should be thought about and not entered into as some omigosh experience after a forgetful night. The fact is that many more pregnancies in this nation and throughout the world are not carefully planned, but are the result of unexpected and sometimes unwelcome experiences. This book uses the candid, well-crafted stories of Jennifer to take us through the joys and fears of the pregnant and new-mom experience to the sobering realities of discovery that our charming world—the world of well-built, carefully constructed woods and homes—can contain hazards to our children and grandchildren. It provides a guide for many of the dangers that can be addressed.

The modern world is full of miraculous benefits. We have phones that keep us connected across the seas and with remote areas of the globe. We have cosmetics that can plump up our sagging faces and droopy bodies. We have lightweight toys with which to entertain our children and a dizzying array of mechanical sounds and devices to lull and soothe our infants and toddlers into states of relaxation—or is it overstimulation? Some of these remarkable developments themselves come with added prices that are not always apparent.

Read this book if you care about the future of our children. Read this book if someone you love is about to become a parent. Jennifer understands that nobody can do it all, but everybody can do something to keep the environments of their children safer.

Acknowledgments

This book is part of my journey to living a healthier, greener lifestyle. During my journey, many have assisted me. Mom, thank you for reading me Dr. Seuss's *The Lorax*. You were green in the 1970s without even realizing it. Thank you also for buying me Rachel Carson's *Silent Spring*, the beginning of my journey. Sis, thank you for telling me to write the damn book already and for patiently listening to all the information and statistics that I know you did *not* find interesting. And to my grandmother, who inspires me to be a better person and to live a better life.

Corky Harvey at The Pump Station: thank you for encouraging me to teach The Smart Mama class after I kept interrupting your new-mom class with information on chemical exposures, and Carol Patton for always being a smiling face.

To Christopher Gavigan, Natalie Cadranel, Mandy Geisler, and Janelle Sorensen at Healthy Child Healthy World: keep fighting the fight.

To the gang at Demetriou, Del Guercio, Springer & Francis, thanks for welcoming me back to the fold and giving me the opportunity to complete this work. Heather, thank you for your attention to detail and willingness to help out.

To the women of the Green Moms Carnival, thank you for inspiring me and teaching me. You are the most amazing group of intelligent, outspoken, inspirational women. Lynn at OrganicMania: thank you for putting us together. Beth at Fake Plastic Fish: I am in awe. Jess at the Green Phone Booth: you are my soul sister. Sommer of Green and Clean Mom: I wish I had your sass.

Thank you also to Christina C. I really needed your help! Thank you to Jill, my BFF. And Erica, thanks for patiently reading sections even though it was the last thing you wanted to do after work.

To my editor Christina Boys, it was a bumpy road getting to you but well worth the wait. Thank you for your able assistance and patience. To the most responsive agent in the world, ever, Sharlene Martin, thank you for believing in me and encouraging me to sit tight.

To my husband: I couldn't have completed this book without your help. Thank you for encouraging my passion, even if it meant putting up with some spectacularly unsuccessful attempts at making my own household cleaners. Again, I'm sorry about ruining all of those dishes!

Finally, to Cole Griffin and Kylie Ruth Welcher. Without you, this book would never have been written. I hope my journey to make the world a little safer for you helps others make the world a little bit safer for their children.

Introduction

While I was pregnant and waiting to welcome my son to the world, I wanted everything to be perfect for him. I nested feverishly to make a warm, inviting haven. Granted, it was a little difficult because we were living in a ramshackle, tear-down house. It was in a great location (the only thing to recommend it), and we'd just purchased it with the plan of building our dream home. The timing, of course, was my husband's idea, and he went out of town when we had to move, so I was stuck moving, pregnant, with my father-in-law. The new home only had a subfloor (we had to pull up the flooring because of the overwhelming, fetid urine odor from feral cats), windows that didn't close (vines had twisted and pushed their way in from the outside), and a leaky roof that required numerous pots to catch drops when it rained. But I perservered, and used the depressing circumstances of our living arrangements as an excuse to shop. (As if I really needed an excuse to shop.)

From before trying to get pregnant, I thought I was fairly "non-toxic." I had eliminated mercury-contaminated fish from my diet. I steered clear of scented products, and used natural cleaners. I was more than a little annoying—I had a penchant for smugly spouting off the hazards of common foods and activities.

But in my effort to get pregnant, I suffered two miscarriages. I was devastated (and also wondered why, if it was so difficult to get and stay pregnant, I had wasted all the money and aggravation on birth control). My research into why I had suffered those unexplained miscarriages suggested that environmental factors could have played a role. So I tried to do even more to eliminate chemicals. I switched to a stainless-steel water bottle (no BPA for this chick), limited my soy intake (phytoestrogens), and replaced many of my personal care products. Having decided finally to get pregnant, I was committed to it, and I was probably pathologically vigilant. I ate organic foods, studiously avoided environmental tobacco smoke, and stopped heating in plastics. But when I started taking barely warm showers to reduce my exposure to trihalomethanes (by-products of chlorine disinfection), my husband, of course, concluded that I was treading into the nutty zone.

Once I knew my son was on the way and we had moved into our new home, I nested with the best of them. I tried to make the "nursery" charming even though it was just a corner of the living room. I hunted down the perfect black, white, and green crib bedding set to match my chosen theme, and cajoled my mom into painting Dr. Seuss characters on the walls. I shopped for cute outfits, fun toys, the right pacifier, and the best baby bottles.

While shopping for my son, I tried to be eco-smart. I tried to pick products that were greener and healthier than conventional products. I was focused on less toxic products because of my concern about children's environmental health. My environmental legal practice focuses on consumer product labeling and Proposition 65 compliance. Before becoming a lawyer, I was an environmental engineer. My background compelled me to go a less toxic route — the more you know about what is in most products, the less you want to use them.

However, my quest to find less toxic products was difficult in 2002. Selection was limited—going green wasn't cool quite yet. Information was often hard to find. I had to contact manufacturers directly, and frequently the information just wasn't available. Or I was assured ingredients were safe, even though I had a sneaking suspicion that wasn't the whole truth.

Then I was in a car accident at twenty-nine weeks and went in to preterm labor. The doctors put me on magnesium sulfate to stop the contractions, and steroids to develop my son's lungs just in case. The next six weeks had me mostly on bed rest and I cradled my belly and the life within, urgently chanting to him to grow and be healthy.

At thirty-five weeks, Cole Griffin was welcomed to the world, five weeks early but healthy. With his sweet smile, I fell instantly in love and wanted to hand him the world, the moon, and the stars. I knew it was my job to give him a safe haven so he could thrive and develop to his fullest potential. A fiercely protective maternal instinct kicked in. I suddenly understood how a mother could lift a car off her child, or face down a grizzly bear, or do any of the amazingly heroic things mothers do. I would do the same. I would lay down my life for him without hesitation.

With his first breath, I became even more of a worrier. I was shocked by the intensity of my vigilance once I became a mom. I think every new parent looks at his or her new baby and worries. *Is he healthy? Is it okay that his head is squashed?* We can't help it. Why else do we ask whether there are ten fingers and ten toes?

As I drove home, I worried about a crazy driver hitting us. And then it hit me.

I was *responsible* for this small life.

All of my worrying in the abstract about whether I was exposing this fetus to mercury, phthalates, lead, or a host of other chemicals became very real. Here was this five-pound baby, already with a body burden of toxic chemicals. It was my job to protect him, and I already hadn't done a very good job. Had I already doomed him?

Well, I probably hadn't doomed him. But I did start second-guessing every single thing I had done, used, or eaten while I was pregnant.

It is true. Hidden dangers do lurk everywhere—there is an entire secret world of unpronounceable chemicals. Yes, they may potentially harm your child, even the things that are specifically designed for babies.

I'm not trying to tell you that the mere presence of these chemicals dooms our children. The actual risk posed by the chemicals may be small. But, although small, it may be a risk that you don't want to take for your children. If I'm willing to die for my children, wouldn't that mean that I would do anything to protect them from toxic chemicals if a reasonable probability exists that they might do harm? Why shouldn't I choose to be safe rather than sorry? The increased risk of cancer from the carcinogen found in some baby shampoos may be relatively small, but why take that risk when shampoos exist *without* that chemical? And that is my point. Some politicians, bureaucrats, and scientists want to wait to regulate until we have certainty that a particular chemical in a particular product in fact causes harm. But I don't need to have certainty if a reasonable chance exists that something could hurt my child. I'll choose an alternate while the rest of the world debates the issue.

And, really, why should any of us be guinea pigs to determine whether any chemical is safe or not?

Without a doubt, the information is overwhelming. The statistics are downright frightening. Seventy percent of birth defects have no known cause, and environmental exposures may play a large role. Pesticide use in the home and garden is linked to significant increased risks of leukemia and autism spectrum disorder (ASD). The rising incidence of a host of childhood diseases has been linked to the prevalence of chemicals in our environment.

There is a lot to worry about. But pathological vigilance isn't required to reduce your child's exposure to toxic chemicals. And it is never too late to take a few easy steps to make your child's environment healthier. Armed with a little bit of information, you can control what comes into your home, limit exposure to toxic chemicals, and make informed choices.

You may be thinking to yourself, *Sounds good, but I don't have the time or the energy or the money to make my home completely non-toxic, cook organic dinners every night, or make my own non-toxic art materials.* Relax. This is a book for those of us without a staff. Trust me, a working mom with what always seems to be too much to do. As my sister succinctly quipped, this book will help you hug a tree without getting dirty.

In these pages you'll find the information you need to create the world you want, and a safe, healthy place for your children and your children's children. And that's the point — to give you an opportunity to make more informed choices. You don't have to do everything in this book, just pick a few simple steps. And then a couple more. And then a couple more.

I'll be honest. Even if you wanted to, you can't stop all of the toxic chemical exposures. We need a significant change in our policies to change the world. And contrary to popular belief as evident from advertisers hawking all things green, I don't think we can shop our way to a better world (as much as I love to shop). But I do think our consumer choices have a big impact. Certainly the reports of retailers pulling polycarbonate plastic baby bottles off the shelves because of concerned consumers wanting bottles without bisphenol A illustrates that our shopping does influence. And I do think it is unfair that we have to follow a list of dos and don'ts to have a healthy home environment.

I believe that small changes make a difference. I believe that the small changes add up. I believe that we are all connected to each other and this world. Perhaps because we are connected, it is foolish to think that we can be healthy in an unhealthy world by making individual changes in our lifestyles and improving our individual buying habits. But I believe I should try. I believe that while I don't make our policies, I can shape them. I believe that by making my home safer for my children, I make the world a little bit safer for every living thing.

And I believe *you* can change *your* world.

SMART MAMA'S
GREEN GUIDE

Chapter 1

Toxic Chemicals Permeate Our Modern Lives

A true conservationist is a man who knows that the world is not given by his fathers but borrowed from his children.
—John James Audubon

I think we all generally feel that exposure to toxic chemicals isn't good. The strong smell of paint stripper just doesn't seem to be particularly healthy. We might not know precisely why they are bad, but we instinctively and intuitively know that if toxic chemical exposures aren't good for us, then they can't be good for our kids, either.

So if we have a general understanding that toxic chemical exposures aren't healthy for us, why do we blissfully ignore the toxic chemicals that are found in our homes, our schools, and the products that we use every day? A recent study confirmed that while we are all concerned about toxic chemicals in the environment, most of us don't realize that our greatest exposure to such chemicals is in our homes, mostly from our household cleaners, beauty care products, and other common household items. So why do we ignore these exposures? At least part of the answer, I think, is that it is easier just not to question our easy-clean, easy-care, disposable lifestyles. Unfortunately, the result is a body burden of toxic chemicals. That's right—we all carry around lead, mercury, flame retardants, bisphenol A (BPA), DDT, PCBs, and others.

By the way, I think one of the most annoying and frustrating parts of trying to eliminate toxic chemical exposures is the alphabet soup of acronyms and long chemical names. Did any of us really like chemistry in school? Unless you are truly an eco-geek, who really wants to know the difference between diisodcyl-phthalate (DIDP) and diisononyl-phthalate (DINP)? So if you can't or don't want to keep it straight, just check out the nifty acronym list in Appendix B.

Common Household Toxic Chemicals

Chemical	Health Effects*	Common Exposure Sources
Bisphenol A (BPA)	Birth defects; hormone disruptor	Polycarbonate plastic; canned foods and beverages
Lead	Toxic to brain and nervous system; decreased IQ; aggression and hyperactivity disorders	Lead-based paint; household dust; outdoor soils; consumer products
Mercury	Toxic to brain and nervous system	Consumption of contaminated fish and shellfish
Perchlorate	Interferes with iodine uptake of thyroid gland, which regulates hormones necessary for proper development	Drinking water; consumption of irrigated crops; milk
Phthalates	Hormone disruptor; birth defects; reproductive disease; reduced sperm counts; heart disease; diabetes	Polyvinyl chloride plastic; household cleaners and other products with synthetic fragrance; cosmetics; food packaging
Polybrominated diphenyl ethers (PBDEs)	Interfere with brain development and may be linked to hyperactivity; toxic to reproductive system	Flame retardants used in electronics, polyurethane foam in upholstered furniture and mattresses, blackout drapes and textiles that off-gas and can be found in household dust and food
Triclosan	Toxic to liver; disrupts thyroid hormone system (necessary for development); may cause cancer	Antibacterial agent used in liquid soap, beauty products, and cleaning products

* Based upon animal and/or human studies.

If you're not familiar with all (or any) of these toxic chemicals, don't worry. That's why you're reading this book, and we're going to cover all of them, including easy steps you can take to reduce your family's exposure.

But first let's cover some eye-opening information about toxic chemicals in the world we live in.

A Brief Glossary of Toxicology Terms

A **carcinogen** is a chemical that can cause cancer.

A **developmental toxicant** is a chemical that can produce adverse health effects prior to conception, during pregnancy, and during childhood. The adverse health effects can manifest themselves in a variety of ways, including death, stillbirths, malformations, reduced birth weight, mental retardation, sensory loss, growth alteration, and/or functional deficit.

A **neurotoxin** is a chemical that affects the nervous system, and can adversely affect intelligence, cause memory deficits, and result in cognitive and behavioral problems and sexual dysfunction, among other problems.

A **reproductive toxicant** is a chemical that adversely affects the male or female reproductive system.

A **teratogen** is a chemical that specifically causes birth defects.

Chemical Body Burden

We all carry around a chemical body burden. What does that mean? Your chemical body burden refers to the total amount of toxic chemicals present in your body at any one time. You may well feel violated by the thought of all these chemicals in your body. Some of the women who have participated in various body-burden monitoring studies have expressed shock and outrage after finding out their bodies harbored DDT, despite the fact that it was banned thirty years ago; mercury, despite having eliminated highly contaminated fish from their diets; flame retardants; and a host of other chemicals. Even those who led relatively "clean, green" lives found that their bodies were repositories for numerous chemicals.

One of the first biomonitoring studies in 2003 found that participants had an average body burden of:

- 53 carcinogens;
- 62 neurotoxins;
- 58 chemicals that interfere with the hormone system;
- 55 chemicals that are associated with birth defects or developmental delays;
- 55 chemicals toxic to the reproductive system;
- 53 chemicals toxic to the immune system.[1]

Charlotte Brody, executive director of Commonweal, mother of two, environmental health activist, and the "Godmother of Green Health Care," felt violated upon learning of the results from her body-burden testing. While she admits that she "wasn't one of these wavy gravy groovy people who didn't think I had chemicals in me," she was nonetheless surprised by her results. Her test results showed that she was carrying eighty-five toxic chemicals, including PCBs, mercury, lead, and pesticides. The pesticides were the most surprising. She had never used them.

In a follow-up conversation, she added, "My body-burden testing shows that we can't buy our way out of the problem of toxic chemicals. There are things that we can do to reduce our exposures: eat fish that are low in mercury and choose organic when you can. Don't use herbicides and pesticides. Take off your shoes before you walk in the house and clean with non-toxic products. But, as my results show, we also need a government that will protect us from the exposures we can't avoid by ourselves. We need new laws that will create less toxic products and practices."[2]

Before you panic—don't. The mere presence of toxic chemicals in your body does not mean that they have caused or are causing harm. Yes, it does mean that your baby can be exposed to your chemical body burden or, for males, that the quality and quantity of sperm can be altered. And fetuses are particularly susceptible to harm from exposure to toxic chemicals. But it doesn't mean that harm has occurred.

We are all exposed to chemicals, many of them toxic, every day. Of course, we can't live without chemicals. Water is a chemical. Lots of chemicals are good. And being man-made versus naturally occurring can't tell you whether a chemical is "toxic" or not.

A **chemical** is generally defined as a substance with a definite composition. A common example is pure water. Water is always composed of two hydrogen atoms and a single oxygen atom, whether it is collected from a lake or synthesized in a laboratory.

A **toxic substance** is generally a chemical or mixture that may be harmful to human health or the environment. Toxic chemicals or mixtures can occur naturally or can be man-made.

A chemical can be toxic whether it is man-made or occurs naturally. Lead is a naturally occurring chemical, but it is toxic. And some chemicals may be okay in one application, but not in another. For example, polycarbonate plastic is used to make helmets, and it seems unlikely that there is any risk of exposure.

However, use that same polycarbonate plastic to make baby bottles, and you have the risk of the baby bottles leaching BPA into formula or breast milk.

Can any particular environmental exposure be linked to a particular disease or condition? Not with the information we have. Yet it is clear that some chemicals in our environment can cause harm. No one debates the adverse health effects of lead, and though it is a naturally occurring chemical, its widespread presence in our environment is a result of our use.

As Ana Soto, a Tufts University professor of cell biology, said in response to a list of 216 chemicals linked to breast cancer in laboratory animal studies, "When you look at their list of chemicals, we are exposed to all of it. We know that humans are exposed to mixtures, and studying mixtures is very difficult. We will never have the whole picture, and it will take many, many years to collect epidemiological evidence, so we should take some preventive measures now."[3] I agree.

So, how exposed are you? Take the quiz. I dare you.

1. Was your home built before 1978? If yes, it is likely that you are exposed to lead paint and lead-contaminated dust.
2. Do you use any folk or herbal remedies? If yes, you should consider that some can be contaminated with lead, mercury, and arsenic.
3. Do you know what's in your drinking water? Not just from the source, but from your pipes, fittings, and faucets? If your pipes were installed before 1986, it is possible that they leach lead into the water they carry. Even today, federal law permits piping to contain up to 8 percent lead.
4. Do you drink water from a water cooler with a five-gallon plastic bottle? If so, the bottle may be polycarbonate plastic and leach BPA. If you have a filter for your water, when was the last time you changed the filter? And do you know what it is certified to remove?
5. Do you eat meat? Meat products can be contaminated with chemicals that accumulate in fat, such as dioxins and PCBs, and we can be exposed to these chemicals when we eat meat or dairy products.
6. Do you eat fish? Contaminated fish and shellfish are our primary route of mercury exposure. Also, just like meat products, fish, especially fish at the top of the food chain, can be contaminated with dioxins, PCBs, and flame retardants.

7. How many personal care products did you use today and what's in those products? Did you use shampoo, conditioner, soap, a shaving product, body lotion, facial moisturizer, hairstyling product(s), sunscreen, perfume, toner, makeup, night cream, or bubble bath? Any or all of these products can have ingredients that are toxic, such as formaldehyde contributors (forrmaldehyde is a carcinogen) and hormone-disrupting phthalates.

8. How many cleaning products did you use today? Do you know what is in those cleaning products? All-purpose cleaner, dish soap, glass cleaner, furniture polish, stainless-steel cleaner, or tub-and-tile cleaner? What about air fresheners? Conventional cleaning products can contain a number of nasty chemicals that can pollute indoor air and potentially cause adverse health effects.

9. Did you use any household pesticides, in the home or garden or on any pet? Weed killer, ant spray, indoor fogger, flying insect spray, or anything else? Pesticides can increase the risk of childhood leukemia and have been linked to autism spectrum disorders.

10. How many electronic products do you have in your home and your office? What about upholstered furniture? Are they made of polyurethane foam? Do you have a conventional mattress? Electronic products, upholstered goods, and mattresses have flame retardants added to them, which off-gas chemicals that can affect brain and nervous-system development.

Considering all the toxic chemicals around us, can we really do anything to reduce our exposure? Chemicals are integrated into our modern life. We spray them in our homes to freshen our air, we squirt them on our floors to clean, coat our clothing and fabrics with them to repel stains, and slather them on our bodies to moisturize and firm. We thrive in our non-stick, disposable, easy-care lives. Considering that the chemical industry took off just after World War II, it is staggering how relatively new chemicals have permeated our lifestyles. How we find them indispensable. How we can't imagine doing without them. They have made our lives easier, more hygienic, lightweight, and efficient. But, that old adage is true: There's no such thing as a free lunch. Some of those chemicals that make our lives so much easier do harm.

Who Is Minding the Store?

Whenever I give lectures about being green, people are always amazed by the fact that there are toxic chemicals in the products we buy. Most of us believe that the products we buy are safe, and that they are rigorously tested to address safety concerns before they are placed on store shelves. In a survey of Maine residents, a 56 percent majority of those polled agreed with the statement that "currently, the government carefully tests chemicals used in all major consumer products to make sure they are safe for people to use."[4] National surveys report similar results.

But it isn't true. Consumer products are not, for the most part, subject to pre-market approval by any regulatory agency or independent body. Why aren't all the products we buy "safe"? There are many reasons, but I think it boils down to the fact that our regulatory schemes are founded on the principle that a chemical or product is not regulated or controlled until it is established that a substantial risk of harm exists. That's simplifying it a bit, but it sums up the problem. So let's look at what each of the key government agencies is empowered to do.

Environmental Protection Agency

The independent federal U.S. Environmental Protection Agency (EPA) is vested with the power to regulate air and water pollution, solid wastes, pesticides, radiation, and toxic substances. It is primarily responsible for enforcing environmental laws. You may be most familiar with the EPA's work under the Superfund (otherwise known as the Comprehensive Environmental Response, Compensation and Liability Act, or CERCLA). CERCLA was enacted to address hazardous substance release sites, which are known as Superfund sites. The EPA is also responsible for a number of other important federal environmental laws, including the Clean Air Act, the Clean Water Act, the Safe Drinking Water Act, and the Emergency Planning and Community Right-to-Know Act.

The EPA is also responsible for implementing and enforcing the Toxic Substances Control Act of 1976 (TSCA).[5] TSCA is the primary federal law for regulating chemicals used in the United States. TSCA authorizes the EPA to gather information on chemicals. The current TSCA inventory, a list of the chemicals in use in the United States, has over 82,000 chemical substances.[6] Each year, around 1,000 new chemicals are introduced.

When the EPA started to review chemicals under TSCA in 1979, all chemicals in use at the time, around 62,000 chemicals, were grandfathered in under this program and exempted from review under TSCA. For those grandfathered chemicals—those that were already in use in 1979—the EPA cannot request information about the chemical's safety unless it can establish that the chemical poses an unreasonable risk or a high exposure. This has significant implications for determining the safety of the products we use. Of the "high volume" chemicals produced today—those chemicals produced in the U.S. in amounts of more than a million pounds per year—92 percent were grandfathered in under TSCA.

Because EPA's authority is so limited for grandfathered chemicals, it has only used its authority to require testing for fewer than 200 out of the 62,000 grandfathered chemicals.[7] And then, to take the next step and actually restrict a grandfathered chemical, the EPA has to show that the chemical "presents or will present an unreasonable risk," that the benefits of regulating the chemical outweigh the risks of not regulating the chemical, and that the restriction is the least burdensome means of reducing the risk to acceptable levels.[8] This is an extremely difficult burden for the EPA to carry. In fact, when the EPA sought to restrict the use of asbestos, it spent ten years developing the ban, supported by a record of 45,000 pages. Yet, following a legal challenge, the EPA's regulation was thrown out by the court because the court found that the EPA did not carry its burden under TSCA.[9] Because of the difficulty of meeting this high standard, the EPA has only restricted *five* chemicals since TSCA's enactment. Only five! Although, to be fair, I should point out that EPA has worked with industry and developed some voluntary initiatives.

TSCA also regulates new chemicals. But the EPA hasn't effectively used TSCA to evaluate and regulate chemical risks.[10] TSCA does not require companies to develop information on new chemicals (chemicals introduced after the EPA began reviewing chemicals under TSCA in 1979) before they are placed into commerce. The result? According to the EPA, 85 percent of the new chemicals registered under TSCA lack any data on health effects. Of the 82,000 chemicals on the TSCA inventory, less than 10 percent have been reviewed for toxic effects.

While TSCA places the burden on the EPA to establish a chemical poses an unreasonable risk before it will control production or use, the European Union (EU) regulates chemicals differently. The EU's Registration, Evaluation and Authorization of Chemicals (REACH) law generally places the burden on the chemical companies to ensure that chemicals do not pose risks to human health or the environment before they are used.

Consumer Product Safety Commission

The independent federal agency the U.S. Consumer Product Safety Commission (CPSC) is tasked with protecting consumers "against unreasonable risks of injuries associated with consumer products." It has authority over a wide variety of consumer products. The CPSC's job is enormous: it has jurisdiction over more than 15,000 consumer products and is charged with protecting us from fire, electrical, mechanical, and chemical hazards, and other consumer product hazards that can result in injury.

Even though the CPSC is the federal regulatory agency charged with protecting us against hazards in consumer products, its authority is more limited than you would expect. But that is changing. Dubbed the "year of the recall," 2007 tarnished the CPSC's image. In 2007, the CPSC issued recalls for sixty-one toys, an increase of more than 30 percent over 2006. These recalls, many involving favorite characters such as Thomas the Train, gave the CPSC unwanted national attention, although those in the field were well aware of the agency's limitations before the numerous recalls.

Following the recalls, Congress passed legislation to improve the CPSC and consumer product legislation. And the CPSC needed it. Its budget in 1973, the year it was formed, was $140.5 million (in today's dollars). In 2007, its budget was $62.4 million. In 1973, the CPSC had 786 full-time employees. In 2007, the CPSC had 420 full-time employees.

Reform legislation was signed into law in August 2008. Known as the Consumer Product Safety Improvement Act of 2008, the new law makes sweeping changes in the regulation of children's products, including imposing the first national maximum limit for lead in children's products, including toys (as opposed to just paints and coatings), lowering the limit for lead allowed in paints and coatings, and banning children's toys and child-care articles containing certain phthalates. The law also provides the CPSC with significant additional resources, including increased staffing, increased funding, and additional laboratory resources.

Food and Drug Administration

The FDA is responsible for over-the-counter and prescription drugs and medical devices, biologics, food (except for meat, poultry, egg products, and the labeling of alcoholic beverages and tobacco) and food additives, radiological products, and cosmetics. For this book, how the FDA oversees personal care products is the most relevant. (The FDA's regulation of personal care products is discussed in Chapter 9.)

The FDA is also responsible for food-contact substances. Food-contact substances are those items that are not directly added to food, but are in contact with food, such as packaging materials. If a manufacturer proposes a new food-contact substance, or a new use of an existing food-contact substance, the manufacturer must give the FDA notice of the new substance or new use of an existing substance unless existing regulations already cover the situation or the substance or use is considered "Generally Recognized as Safe" (GRAS).

This voluntary GRAS notification program was proposed in 1997 when the FDA abolished its existing approval procedure because it lacked the resources to review and approve all the petitions. Under the GRAS notification process, a manufacturer informs the FDA that it has determined that a substance or use is GRAS, as opposed to petitioning the FDA to approve that the use or substance is GRAS. As explained by the FDA, if the manufacturer's determination is correct, the use or the substance is not subject to any legal requirement for FDA review and approval. In fact, since the GRAS notification process is voluntary, a manufacturer may market the substance or use without informing the FDA if the manufacturer determines it is GRAS or, if the FDA is so informed, while the FDA is reviewing that information. So, as long as a *manufacturer* determines that its *own* food-contact substance or use is Generally Recognized as Safe, it can go ahead and market it without any input from the FDA whatsoever. Sounds crazy, doesn't it?

So what does "safe" mean in this context? Well, the governing regulations don't really provide much clarity. According to the implementing regulations, the term "safe" means "that there is a reasonable certainty in the minds of competent scientists that the substance is not harmful under the intended conditions of use. It is impossible in the present state of scientific knowledge to establish with complete certainty the absolute harmlessness of the use of any substance. Safety may be determined by scientific procedures or by general recognition of safety."[11] In other words, safe does not mean that no risk exists or that the substance is absolutely harmless. It means that competent scientists are pretty sure that the substance will not cause harm based upon available information. But, as we have already discussed, most chemicals do not have sufficient information or data to really evaluate safety, so all that is really meant is that a group of scientists think that the substance is safe as far as they can tell.

United States Department of Agriculture

The United States Department of Agriculture (USDA) is responsible for overseeing the safety of our meat, poultry, and egg products. The USDA also implements the National Organic Program (NOP). The NOP implements and administers national production, handling, and labeling standards for organic agricultural products. The term "agricultural product" means any agricultural commodity or product, whether raw or processed, including any commodity or product derived from livestock, that is marketed in the United States for human or livestock consumption.[12] In other words, the NOP covers any product derived from plants or animals, including processed products, so its jurisdiction includes everything from fresh fruits and vegetables to bread to personal care products.

This I Believe

Steven G. Gilbert, Ph.D., DABT

Brains, our minds included, are the most marvelous, mysterious, and complex creations known. Early on I stumbled on the question of what separates the mind from the brain, what makes us who we are. It was a short step to wondering how the brain was created and how it worked to shape the mind of each of us. At birth the human brain weighs about 350 grams and by adulthood it has quadrupled in size to about 1,300 grams. Hard to imagine but at its peak the brain is developing at a rate of 250,000 neurons per minute on the way to 100 billion neurons, give or take a few million. Each neuron connects with other neurons with up to 10,000 connections per neuron. In essence, "connections are us." Indeed the neuron and its connections are fundamental to the nature of all living things.

My interest in the brain and its influence on the mind led me to investigate chemicals that disrupt the development of neurons or upset the connections and communication between neurons. This led me to the field of toxicology and years of research that showed that even very low levels of some chemicals can affect the brain. Even though the brain seems well protected in its bony shell, experience and research document that the developing brain is very vulnerable to chemical exposures. Pregnant women or mothers exposed to mercury or lead or drinking alcohol during pregnancy clearly leads to subtle damage to the brain, thus affecting the mind. As a scientist, I conducted research that showed that even very low levels of a chemical can affect the developing brain. The chemicals were damaging the neurons and changing the connections, altering one's mind. These changes reduce a child's ability to learn and remember, thus robbing a child and society of their full potential.

I believe that all living things have a right to an environment that allows them to reach and maintain their full potential. The salmon have a biological need and a right to get upstream to bear their young so they too may reach their potential. Each of us, especially our leaders, has an ethical responsibility to ensure that offspring of all species can grow and develop in an environment that is not robbing them of their potential. It is no longer a question whether or not exposure to chemicals damages the developing infant. The research has largely been done. We have the knowledge and now must face the challenge of turning this knowledge into action.

I love science and research and believe it can provide the answers and direction we need to make decisions that ensure a sustainable future. However, science cannot achieve protection of children alone. Research has lost its appeal for me; I have now turned toward finding ways to apply the knowledge we have and to find ways to communicate this knowledge to help others make informed choices. I believe that it is my responsibility to share the knowledge I have, to help ensure the potential of our children and our future.

Steven G. Gilbert, Ph.D., DABT, is the director and founder of the Institute of Neurotoxicology and Neurological Disorders (INND) in Seattle, Washington, a non-profit institute dedicated to research and education in the neurosciences. Dr. Gilbert has a Ph.D. in toxicology from the University of Rochester, Rochester, New York, and is a diplomat of the American Board of Toxicology. He is an affiliate associate professor in the Department of Environmental and Occupational Health Sciences, University of Washington, Seattle, and an affiliate associate professor, Interdisciplinary Arts & Sciences, University of Washington, Bothell. He is also the author of A Small Dose of Toxicology *and has authored or co-authored over forty peer-reviewed publications as well as numerous abstracts, and several book chapters and articles.*

Chapter 2

Kids: Toxic Chemical Exposures and Risks

In order to talk about simple steps to reduce exposure, it is helpful to understand a bit about how kids are exposed and why they are at greater risk of adverse health effects as a result of their exposure. But before we can do that, we need to discuss briefly the health-risk-assessment process. Yes, I know, it sounds boring. But it is the premise upon which our scheme for regulating toxic chemicals is based. Once you understand the strengths, as well as the limitations, of the risk assessment process, you can make informed choices. Plus, you will sound really smart when you argue whether it makes sense to buy phthalate-free baby products.

Health Risk Assessments

Health risk assessments are used to determine whether a particular chemical poses a risk to human health and, if it does, under what circumstances. Here's the basic formula:

$$\text{Risk} = \text{Hazard} + \text{Exposure}$$

The highest risk is assigned to the chemical with a high potential hazard and a high likelihood of exposure. The health risk assessment is a tool to answer the questions: Does exposure to a chemical cause health effects? How much does a person need to be exposed to before experiencing health effects? What are the potential health effects?

In the health-risk-assessment process, data from human studies and laboratory animals is used to determine the potential health effects of exposure. Laboratory animal studies are primarily used because the effects of few chemicals have been studied in humans. The human studies that do exist are mostly limited to workplace exposures and, thus, do not include infants and children. But animal studies have their own limitations. Scientists have to determine whether a chemical's health effects as shown in laboratory animals will be similar to the health effects demonstrated in humans, or if some difference or differences between the species will change the outcome in humans. Scientists make assumptions when translating the laboratory animal data to human exposure. These assumptions introduce uncertainty in the health-risk-assessment process. If the assumptions are wrong, then the health risk assessment is also invalid. Another problem with lab studies is that cumulative, aggregate exposures from multiple sources, like those experienced in the real world, are generally not considered. How mixtures of chemicals affect us is similarly not considered.

Cumulative risk is the risk of a common toxic effect associated with exposure at the same time by all relevant pathways and routes of exposure to a group of chemicals that share a common mechanism of toxicity.

Aggregate exposure is the sum total of all exposure to a particular compound or group of compounds through inhalation, ingestion, or dermal contact.

Our real-life exposures are to mixtures of chemicals, from multiple sources, over periods of time. Many of these chemicals have a common mechanism of toxicity. This means that risk assessments just don't tell the story. It defies common sense to think that we can be exposed to mixtures of many chemicals from many sources and yet think we are safe because risk assessments, frequently funded by industry, done for an individual chemical, often from a single source of exposure, concluded that that chemical was safe. For example, the FDA's decision to deem bisphenol A (BPA) in baby bottles safe has been criticized because it fails to take into account the *cumulative risk* of exposure from other sources of BPA, such as baby formula, which increases a baby's *aggregate exposure.*

And then you consider our kids. Few chemicals are regulated or controlled with the purpose of protecting kids, the notable exceptions being mercury and lead (and even the regulations for mercury and lead are challenged by some as not protective enough of our most vulnerable population). Infants and children are sensitive populations, but most risk assessments and most regulations aren't geared to protect them.

> *"We're conducting a vast toxicological experiment and we are using our children as experimental animals."*
>
> —Philip Landrigan, M.D., *Trade Secrets: A Moyers Report*

There's no way around it. A lot of uncertainty exists about the risks of toxic chemical exposures. But this book is here to help. Though our knowledge is incomplete, our children are here, growing and thriving. And you and I want to do everything we can to help them grow and thrive in good health.

Toxicology Basics

Toxicology may seem even more boring than health risk assessments but, trust me, with a little bit of understanding of toxicology basics, you can sound extremely smart at any cocktail party—if you have time to go to a cocktail party. Okay, so you can show up any of the other moms at Mommy and Me. They will be convinced that you are the most put-together mom—not only are you bonding well with your baby but you have time to read.

Traditionally, in toxicology, you examine the relationship between a dose (how much) of a chemical and the resulting response. The response is usually a particular adverse outcome. This is called the dose–response relationship.

Generally, it is true that the greater the dose, the greater the response. This is one of the more fundamental principles of toxicology: "The dose makes the poison."[1] That may sound complicated, but it isn't really. You probably evaluate the dose–response relationship every day. "If I eat one piece of pizza, I'll be fine. If I eat the entire pizza, I'll end up with a stomachache (and an extra inch or two on my hips)." See what I mean about sounding smart? Instead of saying that you are figuring out whether the piece of cake is in your diet, you can say that you are calculating the dose–response relationship.

So how do you figure out the dose? Sometimes it is fairly easy. If a chemical is ingested, the dose is generally calculated as the amount of chemical ingested per unit of body weight. So, using our pizza example, the dose would be one eight-ounce slice of pizza per body weight of 150 pounds. If a chemical is inhaled, then determining the dose is a little more complicated. You need to determine the concentration of the chemical in the air, the amount of air inhaled by the individual, the length of time the individual is exposed to that chemical (the duration of the exposure), and the individual's body weight.

In the risk assessment process, you are usually considering an adverse outcome (or outcomes). For example, a toxicologist may look at how much of a chemical a person needs to be exposed to before he dies. Or the risk assessment process may examine how changing the dose changes the outcome so that a range of adverse responses can be evaluated.

Another central concept in toxicology is exposure. Basically, this is how an individual comes into contact with the chemical. The routes of exposures to chemicals are inhalation, ingestion, skin absorption (dermal exposure), and injection.

Inhaling chemicals allows them to contact our nasal passages, airways, and our lungs. Our lungs are designed to facilitate absorption of oxygen, so they are rich with blood. This allows the rapid absorption of chemicals directly into the bloodstream.

Ingesting contaminants present in our food, water, and (for infants, who like to put everything in their mouths) household dust allows them to be absorbed by the stomach and intestines.

Absorbing occurs when chemicals come in contact with our skin; it is also called dermal exposure. Most chemicals are readily absorbed through the skin, and skin exposure can be a more significant route of exposure than inhalation. We are exposed to chemicals when we apply lotions, sunscreens, and other personal care products directly to our skin, or when chemicals from household cleaners and air fresheners settle on our skin.

Injection is another route of exposure, although typically not a relevant exposure mechanism for fetuses, infants, and small children, except exposure as a result of maternal injection of medicines or recreational drugs. However, of course, the debate over the safety of vaccinations stems from an exposure by injection. Many parents and some child-health advocates contend that children develop autism after being exposed to the mercury-containing preservative thimerosal in some vaccines.

In addition to the route of exposure, the frequency and duration of the exposure are factors. Duration is how long we are exposed to a chemical, and frequency is the amount of time between exposures. These two factors together determine the degree of exposure. Acute exposure, for instance, is an exposure of a short duration, sometimes just one or two times, whereas chronic exposure is exposure over a long period of time, perhaps even a lifetime.

For all of the routes of exposure, the risk assessor must determine how much of the chemical of concern is absorbed or retained by the body. If the body doesn't absorb the chemical, then no exposure occurs. So, to continue with our pizza example, if I take a bite of the pizza but spit it out, I won't absorb much of it. Absorption rates can significantly affect the evaluation of potential risk of an adverse health effect. Lead is a good example to illustrate the importance of absorption. When adults ingest lead (say, from drinking water that contains lead leached from lead pipes), they absorb into their bodies around 10 percent of the lead, while the rest passes through their system. However, infants and pregnant women may absorb as much as 50 percent of the lead they ingest.[2] So the exposure of infants is much higher than the exposure of adults for the same glass of lead-contaminated water.

How the body metabolizes chemicals—or processes them—is another factor. Our bodies have developed defense systems that can change some substances into different chemicals, known as metabolites, which are usually less toxic or more easily excreted from the body. The liver is the primary organ that produces enzymes to metabolize toxic agents. How the body metabolizes a chemical is important in evaluating the risk to children from an exposure because they can metabolize chemicals differently than adults. For example, it is believed that adults metabolize most bisphenol A (BPA) relatively rapidly. However, infants do not have the necessary enzyme to metabolize BPA until about three months, and even then only at a rate of about 25 percent of the level of an adult. So infants' exposure to BPA may be much more significant because they are not able to metabolize it.

Some chemicals aren't excreted very well from our bodies. These chemicals tend to accumulate, usually in our fatty tissues. This is called bioaccumulation, the increase in concentration of a chemical in an organism over time.

Distribution of the chemical in the body also plays a role. And no, I'm not making reference to the pizza ending up on my hips, although that's close. A chemical's distribution, or where and how the body stores a chemical, is important. Let's use lead again as an example. Lead usually ends up in our bones and is stored there. It remains in the bones until a heavy demand for calcium occurs, at which time our blood will mobilize the lead stored in our bones along with the calcium. This can occur during pregnancy, for example, and your stored lifetime burden of lead can be passed across the placenta to your developing baby. We'll talk more about this in Chapter 4.

Exposure during Pregnancy

> *"For the first time in the history of the world, every human being is now subjected to contact with dangerous chemicals, from the moment of conception until death."*
>
> — Rachel Carson, *Silent Spring*

When you are pregnant is the only time you will have virtually complete control over your baby's exposure to toxic chemicals. Your toxic chemical body burden when you get pregnant will dictate your baby's initial exposure to toxic chemicals. That existing body burden plus what you eat, drink, breathe, and put on your skin while you are pregnant will make up the environment in which your baby will grow. At no other time will you have such complete control over the chemicals to which your baby is exposed.

Babies are welcomed to the world with a chemical body burden because of exposures to toxic chemicals in utero. They are exposed in the womb because we are all exposed to chemicals, and many of those chemicals cross the placenta. In fact, before a baby is born, he gets quite a dose of potentially toxic chemicals—more than 250 industrial chemicals. The Environmental Working Group (EWG) conducted a study of umbilical-cord blood from ten randomly selected babies born in August and September 2004.[3] The blood was analyzed for 413 industrial chemicals. Out of the 413 chemicals, 287 chemicals were detected. Of those 287 chemicals:

- 180 cause cancer in humans or animals;
- 218 are toxic to the brain and nervous system;
- 208 cause birth defects or abnormal development in animal tests; and
- 212 have been banned for thirty or more years.

And although those results are scary, what I find even more frightening about the study is that just over one hundred of the chemicals were detected in *every single* umbilical-cord blood sample, including mercury. Methylmercury is toxic to fetal brain development. Other studies have similarly confirmed the presence of toxic chemicals in umbilical-cord blood.[4]

When you are pregnant, your baby starts off getting nutrients, oxygen, and hormone signals from you. Simply put, your baby's first environment is you. If you reduce your toxic chemical body burden, then you will reduce your baby's exposure from the very beginning. If you are pregnant and reading this, congratulations. Welcome to parenthood! You have an amazing opportunity to protect your baby-to-be against toxic chemicals. If you already have given birth, you can still defend your children against the world by eliminating or reducing their toxic chemical exposures. Don't feel that it is too late, and don't panic about all the exposures that have already occurred. It is never too late. Every step helps. Just consider that a study of school-age children showed that in only *five days* after switching their diet to organic, their pesticide body burden was reduced.[5]

How can you reduce toxic chemical exposure in the fetal environment? To answer that, we need to talk briefly about fetal physiology—the fetus, the umbilical cord, and the placenta, and how they work together. Before your eyes glaze over, this is just a simple discussion to provide a framework to discuss how a fetus is exposed to toxic chemicals. And it is truly amazing when you stop to think about it.

Several days after conception, the fertilized egg implants itself in the mother's uterus. The implanted embryo starts to get its nourishment from the uterus's rich lining. Its cells begin to divide into two groups: one group will form the baby, and the other group will form the placenta. The fetus is connected to the placenta by the umbilical cord. The mother feeds the fetus and removes its waste through the placenta and umbilical cord.

A fetus does not produce most antibodies. Instead, the placenta passes antibodies from the mother to the fetus, and gives the baby immunity that continues into the baby's first three months or so after birth. The blood of the fetus and the blood of the mother do not mix. Instead, the fetal blood is contained in fine capillaries that reach into a pool of the mother's blood in the placenta. Once the exchange of nutrients, oxygen, and antibodies occurs, the now replenished fetal blood moves through the capillaries into the umbilical vein and travels through the umbilical cord to the fetus.

The placenta functions as an immunological barrier, protecting the fetus by suppressing the mother's immune response to the "foreign" tissue, the fetus. The placenta also produces and secretes four main kinds of hormones: estrogen, progesterone, human placental lacotgen, and human chorionic gonadotropin (hCG). You are probably familiar with hCG if you took a home pregnancy test—the presence of hCG in urine is what turns the stick blue.

Okay, lesson over. I always visualize the exchange across the placenta as the roots of a floating water lily seeking sustenance from the pond waters below. For me, the image evokes the primal waters of life. The imagery seems most apt when you consider the effects of toxic chemical exposures. If the pond waters are contaminated with toxic chemicals, then the water lily also becomes contaminated.

The placenta protects the fetus by acting as a barrier to filter out some, but not all, substances. It is fairly well known that the placenta does not act as a barrier to alcohol, certain viruses, and certain chemicals associated with smoking cigarettes. Historically, it was believed that the placenta would serve as a barrier against fetal exposure to toxic chemicals, but, unfortunately, the opposite is true. Most chemicals can cross the placenta.[6] As a result, whenever a mother is exposed to toxic chemicals, her fetus is most likely exposed as well.

The rapid growth and development of the fetus in utero is remarkable, and unmatched later in life. With respect to environmental hazards, the most vulnerable time in human life may well be fetal and early postnatal development.[7]

We still have a lot to learn about how a particular mother's exposure to toxic chemicals influences fetal development. The relationship between a toxic chemical dose and the resulting response (the dose–response relationship) is well understood for only a handful of chemicals. Moreover, except for an extremely limited number of chemicals, how maternal environmental exposure to a particular toxic chemical translates to a fetal dose is not yet well understood. Many factors influence what will happen, including the toxic chemical itself, the dose, and the fetal development stage. Also, the route of maternal exposure, the length of maternal exposure, the rate of maternal absorption of the chemical, and maternal elimination of the chemical are all factors that influence the amount of the toxic chemical to which the fetus is exposed. For most environmental toxic chemical exposures, the complexity of these factors means that scientists are only just beginning to understand how chemical exposures affect fetal development, if at all.

Nonetheless, scientists agree that exposure to a toxic chemical during a critical developmental window may cause disease or disability. The complicated series of development events that changes an egg and a sperm into a baby offers a variety of time-specific targets for toxicity.[8] For example, a critical phase where structural malformation may occur is during organ development, which occurs between twenty to seventy days post-conception.[9] As we previously discussed, a basic toxicology principle is the dose–response relationship. The oft-quoted principle is "The dose makes the poison." But for fetal development, it seems that the dose and the *timing* make the poison.[10]

It is important to discover these critical windows in fetal development and how the windows influence the adverse health effect of a toxic chemical exposure.[11] According to Ted Schettler, M.D., "Even a relatively small exposure to a toxic chemical during a window of vulnerability can have a permanent impact that might not occur if the same exposure happened at another time."[12] For example, in rat embryos, birth defects occur when embryos are exposed to carbendazim, a fungicide, in mid- to late pregnancy, but the same exposure early in pregnancy does not show the same effect. Scientists are studying the effects of toxic chemical exposures at various stages of fetal development and looking to identify these critical windows of development.[13] If they can figure out these windows, we may be able to create effective prevention strategies.

Unfortunately, many of these critical windows occur very early in the pregnancy, some before you may even know you are pregnant. What does that mean? You can screw up before you even know you got it right. And that's just downright scary.

Okay, now that I've scared you about all the harm you might have done, don't be overwhelmed by maternal guilt. And don't jump to the conclusion that you have already doomed your baby. The mere presence of these chemicals in maternal or umbilical-cord blood does not mean that harm has occurred as a result of the exposure. But what these studies and others like it demonstrate is that we are all exposed to chemicals, and mothers can pass along chemicals to their babies.

So what can you do? You can't control all of your exposures, but you can control more than you think. If you reduce or eliminate the toxic chemicals you eat, drink, breathe, and put on your skin, you will also reduce or eliminate the toxic chemicals to which your fetus is exposed. In each section of this book, I highlight simple steps you can take to reduce exposure to common toxic chemicals before and during pregnancy.

Children's Exposure

After birth, children are exposed to chemicals just as adults are, via inhalation, ingestion, and dermal exposure. However, a child's exposure to toxic chemicals is usually more significant than an adult's exposure because of physical and other differences.

Children are not "little adults." Children breathe more air on a body-weight basis than adults, so they get higher doses of contaminants on a body-weight basis than adults breathing the same air. An infant has a minute ventilation rate (the amount of air inhaled in one minute) three times an adult's, and a six-year-old has double that of an adult.[14] Children consume more food on a body-weight basis, and have a faster metabolism. They have a larger skin-surface area in relation to body weight, and have a different body composition. They experience rapid growth not seen in later life. Many of their systems are immature when born, including their immune system, and may be more susceptible to harm.

Infants are exposed to toxic chemicals present in the air in their homes, day-care centers, religious centers, and any other buildings where they spend time. Of course, they are also exposed to toxic chemicals in outdoor air. However, indoor air-pollution concentrations can be significantly higher than outdoor air-contaminant levels because our homes are more airtight, trapping pollutants from commonly used products and activities. Cleaning products, beauty products, paints and coatings, off-gassing from building materials and flooring, chemicals used in hobbies, pesticides, air fresheners, cooking, and heating all contribute to indoor air pollution. It is estimated that infants spend as much as 95 percent of their time indoors, so their primary exposure is to indoor air.

Infants eat three or four times as much food as adults on a body-weight basis, and children eat two to three times as much food as adults. However, although they consume more calories on a body-weight basis, their diet isn't as varied.[15] Because infants and toddlers consume fewer distinct foods, it is important to consider the contribution of chemicals in the foods they actually eat. If any particular food a child consumes has elevated contamination levels, the child's exposure is likely higher due to the restricted variety of his or her diet. For example, children tend to eat significantly more apples and apple products than adults. Children between the ages of five and nineteen months consume an average of 19 grams of apples and apple products per kilogram of body weight per day, as compared with adults, who consume only 2 grams of apples or apple products per kilogram of body weight per day.

Children also drink more than adults. Infants drink five to seven times more liquid than adults on a body-weight basis. An infant living on breast milk or formula consumes about one-seventh of its body weight each day. In a 155-pound adult, this would correspond to a little more than 2½ gallons. As a result, any contaminant present in water (to make up formula) or breast milk will be consumed in higher quantities per unit of body weight. Children drink between 2½ and 3½ times more than adults.

Children have a greater skin surface area in relationship to their body weight as compared with adults. This means that their insides are large compared to their outside. An infant's surface-area-to-volume ratio is three times that of an adult, and a toddler's is twice that of an adult. As a result, body lotions and other personal care products applied to the skin and other dermal exposures may result in a more significant exposure for children. Children also tend to have more cuts, abrasions, and rashes, which can lead to greater exposure. Finally, a newborn's skin is thinner than an adult's skin, as much as 30 percent thinner, which can result in a much greater penetration of chemicals applied to the skin for newborns.

While it seems unlikely, several examples exist of chemical exposure through the skin. For example, an epidemic of babies suffered from potentially fatal blue baby syndrome (methemoglobinemia) as a result of dermal exposure. The source? Aniline dye. The aniline dye was used to print the name of the laundry service on cloth diapers used for the babies.[16] Today, skin reactions have been reported from the relatively new "tagless" tags, leading to the FDA issuing an advisory and at least one lawsuit.

Kids are also potentially exposed to more toxic chemicals than adults because of their behavior. They mouth everything, from their hands and feet to random objects that strike their fancy. By this mouthing activity—hand to mouth, object to mouth, hand to object to mouth—kids, especially children between the ages of one and three, ingest everything, including dirt, dust, surface coatings, and associated chemicals, from pesticides to lead. The average child ingests twice as much soil as an adult from these behaviors. A child in the upper percentile can ingest eight times more soil than an adult.

The combination of a child's mouthing activity and increased susceptibility can result in significant exposure that might not be significant to an adult. For example, an infant was poisoned by diazinon, a pesticide, applied by an unlicensed pest control company. The infant was the only family member who displayed any symptoms because of the infant's susceptibility and behavior.

You can't stop this mouthing activity—it is how children explore their world. It is an immutable law of childhood that a baby will find the most objectionable object possible and put it in her mouth. No one in my family smokes, but our house is near a local surfing spot and favored hiking trail, resulting in our street being a parking lot. Of course, playing out front, my daughter has attempted to put cigarette butts, old chewing gum, and some even more disturbing items in her mouth.

Children also breathe in a different zone compared to adults. The air closest to the ground tends to be the most contaminated air in the home. Measurements taken inside homes after pesticide applications find that concentrations are always highest closest to the floor, where children spend more time.

Spending such a great deal of time on the floor can also expose children to any contaminants present on the floor, including those tracked into the home from outside. Babies and toddlers also tend to pick up and mouth items lying on the floor, exposing them to a host of contaminants.

General Health Risks of Exposure

So children are exposed in utero, by ingestion, via inhalation, and through dermal exposure. But what is the risk of a particular disease or disability as a result of these exposures? That is difficult to predict.

Children are potentially at greater risk than adults because their neurological, immunological, respiratory, digestive, and other physical systems are still developing. For example, the blood brain barrier—a structure that protects against unwanted chemicals in the blood getting into the central nervous system—isn't fully developed until about six months after birth. This puts babies at risk for chemicals that target the brain because they lack the insulating barrier that adults have. This rapid growth and development demands enhanced absorption of nutrients, which means that children are at risk for greater exposure.

Timing of the exposure is also critical. After birth, children continue to grow by increasing the number of cells (although this is much more rapid in the fetus) and also by cells differentiating into the types of structures they will be and functions they will handle. Chemicals can interfere and disrupt these processes. Animal studies have shown that chemical exposures that occur when growth happens by increasing the number of cells have very different health consequences than the same exposure when this growth is not occurring.[17] Similarly, chemical exposures that interrupt the cell differentiation process can have profound effects. The differentiation process—how cells know what they will be—is accomplished by hormones telling the cells what to do. If this process is interrupted by an exposure to an endocrine (or hormone) disruptor, the cell may not develop properly. Laboratory animal studies have shown that exposures to endocrine disruptors in the newborn can dramatically affect sexual organ development.

In humans, the potential health risks to various developing systems as a result of exposures to toxic chemicals are not yet well understood. But we've recognized that exposure to lead in the first five years of life is much more significant than exposure later in life. Also, the National Research Council concluded with respect to pesticides that, absent data to the contrary, "there should be a presumption of greater toxicity to infants and children."[18]

Scientists are just beginning to understand how toxic chemicals may interact with one another to cause adverse health effects, how genetic factors may make some people more susceptible to toxic chemical exposures, and how toxic chemicals may interact with other conditions, such as hypothyroidism or stress, to magnify adverse health effects.

It cannot be denied that environmental contaminants are threatening our children:

- Between 1975 and 2002, the annual incidence of cancer in children increased 28 percent, from 129 cases per million children to 166 cases per million children (although cancer mortality decreased).[19]
- Exposure to household pesticides is associated with an elevated risk of childhood leukemia, by as much as three to nine times, with exposures to insecticides early in life more significant than later exposures in terms of increased cancer risk, and the highest risk associated with exposure to insecticides during pregnancy.[20]
- One out of every six children has a developmental disability.
- Environmental causes play a role in at least 28 percent of childhood developmental disabilities.
- The prevalence of asthma among American children increased 75 percent between 1980 and 1994.[21]
- Asthma is the leading serious chronic disease in children in the United States. In 2005, an estimated 6.5 million children under age eighteen (almost 1.4 million under age five) currently had asthma, 3.8 million of whom had an asthma attack in the past year. Many others have "hidden" or undiagnosed asthma.[22]

Several environmental pollutants are known to exacerbate asthma, and common indoor air pollutants, including some volatile organic compounds and pesticides, may play a role in asthma.

For certain exposures and resulting diseases, scientists have quantified the increased risk resulting from the exposure. For example, babies who are born to mothers who smoked during pregnancy and are exposed to environmental tobacco smoke after birth are at a three to four times greater risk of dying of sudden infant death syndrome. For other exposures, scientists have not yet identified whether a risk exists, quantified the risk, or determined what the adverse health effects might be.

In terms of cancer, the United States Environmental Protection Agency (EPA) estimates that exposure to carcinogens between birth and two years of age increases cancer risk. The EPA has developed exposure factors to estimate cancer risk that include a tenfold adjustment for exposures between birth and two years of age over adult exposure.[23] The adjustment for children after two years through less than sixteen years of age is a factor of three, that is an increased cancer risk three times that of an adult.[24] The EPA notes, however, that children going through puberty may be more susceptible to the effects of certain carcinogens.[25]

We know more about environmental toxins than ever before—so much information is a blessing, and, I know, a curse. How do you sort through it all? This book is here to help. As much as we all try, we can't be perfect parents. But we can make our children's world a little healthier and a little safer.

We all want the best for our children and we want to give them every opportunity to thrive. So it only makes sense to eliminate toxic chemicals, especially if there are simple steps and easily available alternates. Be warned: You are not going to be able to eliminate all of your baby's exposures to toxic chemicals because we live in a world surrounded by chemicals. But you can make a good start.

You may have already started. Many are questioning the presence of these chemicals in our environment, in our bodies, and in our children's bodies. A shift seems to be under way. The news stories about contaminated pet foods and medications, lead in our toys and lipsticks, and phthalates and 1,4-dioxane in baby shampoo and other personal care products have brought the issue to our attention. And people are starting to consider how their personal choices factor into the presence of toxic chemicals in our environment. In mommy blogs and discussion boards many more posts and discussions concern toxic chemical exposure, from advice on the most effective non-toxic cleaners to safer personal care products.

Sandra Steingraber writes in her compelling book, *Living Downstream,* "Many people are now asking how we can remain alive and secure in an increasingly toxic environment. They ask how we can claim liberty when our own bodies—as well as those of our children—have become repositories for harmful chemicals that others, without our explicit consent, have introduced into the air, food, water and soil." I quibble with her statement because I think we have indeed consented by not questioning what is in what we buy, by not questioning assurances of safety, and by not demanding safe products, clean water, and healthy air.

The answers aren't easy. There is still a lot we just don't know. Sometimes there isn't research available to help us tell whether something is safe or not. Sometimes the research is incomplete. Sometimes the equipment isn't adequate to test. Still, a growing consensus exists that we need to evaluate the chronic low-dose, multi-source, multi-chemical exposures and how they may interact together so we can effectively determine the potential health risks faced by our children. And, you—and I—want to make our world as safe as possible for our children.

With a few simple steps, we can start.

Chapter 3

This Is the House That Jack Built: Whole House Issues

Now that we know it's up to us to make our homes safe for our kids, let's get to what we can do. We'll start with the broadest subject: "whole house" exposures. Whole house means just what it says, an exposure that can be found throughout the house, not one linked to any particular source or activity in the house, like food in the kitchen. Radon, gas, mold, asbestos, and environmental tobacco smoke are the whole house issues, and we'll address each one in this chapter. Lead is also a whole house issue, but we'll get to that in Chapter 4.

Radon

Had I ever been asked about the number-one cause of lung cancer among nonsmokers, I would have guessed secondhand smoke (or environmental tobacco smoke). I think most of us would. It might surprise you, therefore, that the EPA estimates that radon is the *number-one* cause of lung cancer among nonsmokers.[1] It surprised me. I didn't think anything at all about radon until a home inspector brought it up before we bought our current home. I'd always thought that the problem of radon gas was limited to certain mountainous regions, surely not the coast in Southern California. In any event, it turns out secondhand smoke is the third leading cause, after smoking and radon, for lung cancer.[2]

Another cause for concern is that recent research suggests that children who live in homes with high radon levels may have an increased risk of developing childhood acute lymphoblastic leukemia (ALL). The research found that children exposed to "intermediate" levels of radon had a 21 percent higher risk of developing ALL as compared to children exposed to the lowest levels. Children exposed to the highest levels of radon relative to those with the least exposure had a 63 percent greater risk of developing ALL.

In fact, of all the potential environmental contaminants, radon might be the one to pose the greatest risk of cancer. The good news is it is one of the easiest environmental exposures to address. You can readily test for it in your home, and eliminating or significantly reducing the exposure is pretty easy. But first let's look at what radon is and how it gets into your house.

> *"Indoor radon gas is a national health problem. Radon causes thousands of deaths each year. Millions of homes have elevated radon levels. Homes should be tested for radon. When elevated levels are confirmed, the problem should be corrected."*
>
> — Richard H. Carmona, U.S. Surgeon General's Health Advisory, January 13, 2005

What the heck is radon? Radon is an odorless, tasteless, invisible gas produced by the decay of radium. Radium, in turn, is produced by the decay of naturally occurring uranium present in soil, rock, and groundwater.[3] Generally, the uranium content of a soil will be around the same as that of the rock from which the soil was derived, although some rocks have greater uranium levels. Correspondingly, their associated soils will have higher levels as well. Certain areas in the United States have a higher potential to have elevated radon levels because rocks with higher uranium levels are located in those areas.

As a gas, radon can escape rocks and soils by moving through soil pore spaces and rock fractures to make its way into the atmosphere. Outside, radon gas isn't a problem because it disperses. Typically, the concentration of radon in outdoor air is 0.4 picoCuries per liter of air (pCi/L).[4]

But radon in homes can be a problem. Your home's air pressure is usually lower than air pressure in the soil around your home, so your house can suck in radon like a vacuum through cracks, utility entries, seams, and other openings in the foundation, as well as from uncovered soil in crawl spaces. Radon can be a problem indoors because it can build up to unhealthy levels. It is a very heavy gas, so it tends to accumulate in basements or at the floor level.

Because radon is odorless and colorless, it has been called the silent killer. Not only are there no signs that radon is present in your home, there are no signs that you are being exposed. It causes no symptoms that you might notice and the harmful effects are delayed many years. Once exposed, there is no treatment.

Radon can also enter your home through your water if the water supply contains dissolved radon. Radon enters water as bubbles from radium decaying next to the water. These bubbles easily escape when the water is agitated, so most surface water supplies have low radon concentrations. You also ingest some radon when you ingest water. However, the risk of lung cancer resulting from inhaling radon is far greater than the risk of stomach cancer from ingesting water with radon in it.

If your home's water supply is from a municipal system, the mixing, treatment, and long residence time (the time it takes the water to make it from the treatment plant to your home) result in dilution and release of radon. By the time it reaches your tap, it is highly unlikely that you will have radon present, unless it is a very small public municipal system. However, a home that is supplied by a private groundwater well may have radon enter the home from the well water. But radon in water can be readily treated.

If radon gas is present in your home, every time you inhale you get a dose of radioactivity in your lungs. Radon gas decays. When radon decays, small radioactive particles are released. Once radon is inhaled into the lungs, the tiny radon particles damage the cells that line the lung. These particles release small bursts of energy as they decay. These small bursts of ionizing radiation can affect DNA, leading to mutations that may turn cancerous. The latency period for developing lung cancer from radon exposure is twenty to thirty years.

Thus, exposure to radon increases the risk of developing lung cancer. Tom Kelly, director of the EPA's Indoor Environments Division, states, "We know that radon is a carcinogen. This research confirms that breathing low levels of radon can lead to lung cancer."[5] The EPA states that radon results in the lung cancer deaths of approximately 21,000 persons per year.[6]

The increased risk of lung cancer from radon exposure is greater if you smoke. But even if you don't smoke, elevated concentrations of radon in the home pose a fairly significant increased risk of cancer. For a home with 4 pCi/L, the lifetime risk of cancer is 7.3 out of 1,000 persons. That is really high, surprisingly high, especially when you compare it with the 1 in 1,000,000 risk factor generally used to regulate contaminants in our environment. "Scientists are more certain about radon risks than from most other cancer-causing substances."[7]

Per Person Lifetime Risk of Lung Cancer Death from Radon Exposure in Homes[8]

Radon Level (pCi/L)	Non-Smokers (Never Smoked)	Smokers
8	15 out of 1,000	120 out of 1,000
4	7.3 out of 1,000	62 out of 1,000
2	3.7 out of 1,000	32 out of 1,000

No scientific studies have been completed to determine whether children are at a higher risk from radon than adults. However, some children's health advocates have suggested that children may be more sensitive because they have higher respiratory rates than adults. Also, as discussed previously, the EPA has determined that exposure to carcinogens in the first two years of life is more significant, and a factor of 10 should be applied. Data generated from Japanese atomic bomb survivors suggests that exposure before the age of twenty years may have more significant health effects than exposure later in life. The American Academy of Pediatrics concludes that "until further data are available, it seems prudent to assume that the risks to children are at least as large as those determined in occupational studies."[9]

The EPA has developed a map that generally predicts radon levels in three areas of the United States. But I have to emphasize that you cannot use the geologic potential to determine the actual radon levels in your home. Some overlying soils with low uranium levels nonetheless have high radon levels, and vice versa. You must test your house to determine actual radon levels.

SMART MAMA SCARY FACT

One out of fifteen homes have radon levels above the EPA's recommended radon action level of 4 pCi/L.

The good news? It is easy and relatively inexpensive to test for radon. You can purchase do-it-yourself kits from your local hardware store or online. If you have a radon problem, it is also relatively inexpensive to fix.

Radon Gas: Smart Mama's Simple Steps to Reduce Exposure

Test Your Home. You can purchase an inexpensive do-it-yourself kit from a hardware store or online. Short-term and long-term test kits exist. A short-term test is typically exposed to your home's air two to seven days before being sent to a lab, and long-term tests are usually exposed ninety days. The National Safety Council offers short-term test kits for $9.95 and long-term test kits for $20.00. Many states offer free test kits for their residents. If you buy a kit from a hardware store or online, make sure the test kit is state certified. A study by *Consumer Reports* found long-term tests more reliable than short-term test kits. Radon levels can vary day to day, so a ninety-day exposure period gives a more accurate reading of a home's average radon level. Of the seven short-term kits tested by *Consumer Reports,* only the RTCA charcoal canister was accurate enough for *Consumer Reports* to recommend. Two of the kits, AccuStar's Short Term LS Radon Test Kit CLS 100i and Kidde's Radon Detection Kit 442020, underreported radon levels by almost 40 percent! Of long-term test kits, *Consumer Reports* recommends, and found most accurate, AccuStar's Alpha Track Test Kit AT100. Of course, follow the instructions, including maintaining closed house conditions. You can also hire a trained contractor to test your home. Contact your state's radon office for a list of qualified contractors or check the EPA Web site at www.epa.gov/radon.

Check your day care or school. If your child is in a day care or school, ask if the building has been checked for radon. A lot of times day cares are in the basements of buildings, and bottom-level rooms and basements are more likely to have high radon levels than other rooms. Of course, keep in mind that the lung cancer risk from radon exposure is related to both the radon level and the length of time one is exposed. Consequently, if the exposure time is short, even large radon concentrations may not contribute to a significant risk.

Fix any radon problem. If the testing determines that radon levels are elevated in your home, then fix the problem. Radon reduction systems can reduce radon levels in your home by as much as 99 percent. EPA recommends fixing your home if one long-term test, or two short-term tests, show radon concentration levels above 4 pCi/L (or 0.016 working levels, also used in the industry). However, no safe level of radon has been established. The EPA also recommends that you consider fixing your home if the radon level detected is above 2 pCi/L. If you have a radon problem and you decide to fix it, the EPA's *Consumer's Guide to Radon Reduction* has a good discussion of available technologies and how they work for different foundation types.[10]

Fix your water. If you have determined that elevated levels of radon are present in your drinking water, you can fix it before it enters your home with a point-of-entry system. A point-of-entry system will usually consist of granular activated carbon filters or aeration. Granular activated carbon may be less expensive to install, but the filters can collect radioactivity, thereby necessitating special handling upon disposal. An aeration system may cost more to install. A point-of-use system is also an option and will remove radon at the tap, from your drinking water. However, a point-of-use system will not eliminate exposure to radon escaping from other water uses in the home.

> **SMART MAMA WARNING**
> Sealing cracks and other openings to prevent radon from entering the home is an easy approach to radon reduction. However, the EPA does not recommend the use of sealing alone as a method to reduce indoor radon concentrations. Sealing has not been shown to lower radon levels significantly or consistently. Identifying and permanently sealing all the places where radon is entering is difficult. A home's normal settling will also open new ways for radon to enter.

Flame Retardants

Polybrominated diphenyl ethers (PBDEs) are flame retardants. They are added to consumer products to reduce the risk of injuries and damage from fires. Many of our consumer products are made from petroleum-based plastics, and these plastics ignite fairly easily and spread flames. Flame retardants prevent this from occurring. So if you drop a burning cigarette on your upholstered chair, it won't go up in flames as quickly. That's a good thing—flame retardants are credited with saving many lives.

But PBDEs are also persistent in our environment, and exposure to them may cause adverse health effects.

Three common mixtures of PBDEs exist: penta-BDE, octa-BDE, and deca-BDE. They are named for the number of bromine atoms attached, although it is a little more complicated than that because they are mixtures. Penta- and octa-BDE have been banned in Europe and some states, including California, after they were found to be bioaccumulative and toxic. The United States manufacturer of penta- and octa-BDE, Great Lakes Chemical, ceased manufacturing the compounds pursuant to voluntary agreement with the EPA. But millions of pounds remain in homes, offices, and the environment due to extensive use in consumer products. There is also no federal ban on products containing these chemicals, so they may still be found in imported products.

Originally, deca-BDE wasn't placed in the same category as penta- and octa-BDE because it was believed to be environmentally stable and not toxic. Yet recent evidence suggests that belief may have been wrong. In the U.S., deca-BDE has been found in peregrine falcons and other raptors and in their eggs—the ones that don't hatch—at levels ten to fifteen times higher than levels found in raptors in Sweden. The levels are also 100 times the levels found in aquatic species, traditionally used to measure a chemical's persistence and tendency to bioaccumulate. Looking soley at aquatic species may have been the wrong place to find deca-BDE, though, because peregrines in urban settings eat pigeons and sparrows, which in turn scavenge from the food we dispose of. It appears that deca-BDE is accumulating in the terrestrial food chain but not in the aquatic food chain.

Deca-BDE may also not be as safe as we thought. While industry maintains otherwise, some researchers say that deca-BDE may break down into more toxic compounds, such as octa-BDE, which, as noted, has been banned in some states.

It appears that PBDE-contaminated household dust is the primary source of our exposure.[11] Household dust is contaminated with PBDEs from releases to the environment during manufacturing and from PBDEs off-gassing and being released from wear and tear from consumer products in the home, such as computers, furniture, and other products. The air inside homes and offices has been found to have PBDE concentration levels as high as ten times outdoor air concentration levels.[12] Once PBDEs escape, they will settle and adhere to dust. This dust collects in our homes, schools, and day-care facilities. PBDEs have been found at levels in household dust as high as fifty times greater than levels in the outdoor environment.[13]

Once the PBDEs are released into our homes and adhere to dust, those newly flame-retardant dust bunnies multiply away. It is estimated that soil and household dust ingestion and skin contact may account for 80 to 90 percent of adult exposure to PBDEs.[14] And this contaminated dust is also picked up by our clothes and blankets. PBDEs have been found not only in household dust, but also in lint collected from clothes dryers.

PBDEs appear to disrupt the thyroid hormone system, which is critical for brain development. Laboratory animal studies have shown that low doses of PBDEs can disrupt brain growth and alter estrogen hormones, affecting male fertility and ovary development. In particular, laboratory animals exposed to PBDEs immediately after birth showed marked hyperactivity and learning and memory deficits. The brain continues development throughout infancy, so a baby may be particularly sensitive to exposure to PBDEs.

In the living room, the most likely sources of PBDEs include any upholstered furniture, both foam used for padding and the fabric, any polyurethane foam products, any draperies or fabric window coverings, and possibly flooring, depending on the type. For example, deca-BDE is used in the styrene rubbers used for carpet backing. Deca-BDE is also used in the housings for computers, televisions, DVD players, and other electronics.

Unless you recently won the Super Lotto or your state's equivalent, I'm not here to recommend you buy all new furniture to get rid of PBDEs, but if you are buying new, you may want to consider buying furniture that is free of PBDEs. You need to ask specifically whether flame retardants are used and what kind they are. Not only are PBDEs of concern, but as manufacturers switch out of PBDEs, they are starting to use other flame retardants that are toxic.

For example, some manufacturers are using decabromodiphenyl ethane (DBDPE) at an increasing rate in consumer electronics and wire and cable insulation. DBDPE can be used in place of deca-brominated diphenyl ether (deca-BDE, one of the PBDEs) in some products, such as televisions.

According to the industry, it is believed that DBDPE "is unlikely to have significant biological activity." But research published in *Environmental Science and Technology* shows that conclusion may be incorrect. Studies show that DBDPE is bioaccumulating in North American seagulls, certain Chinese waterbirds, and two kinds of pandas. And DBDPE is present in our environment. Studies published since 2004 have shown the compound to be present in wastewater, sewage sludge, indoor air, outside air, and household dust. In fact, DBDPE was found in the Environmental Working Group's study of flame retardants in U.S. homes. That study found that toddlers and preschoolers had flame retardants in their bodies at levels three times higher on average than their mothers.

Is there a risk? Well, DBDPE is similar in structure to deca-PBDE. Deca-PBDE is a neurodevelopmental toxicant. And DBDPE may also be toxic to development of the brain and nervous system. Heather Stapleton, an environmental chemist at Duke University's Nicholas School of the Environment, states, "We know that Deca-BDE has the potential to be a neurodevelopmental toxicant, and, given the similar structure of DBDPE, one has to ask if they are going to have similar toxicological endpoints."

We've also been using an old standby, chlorinated Tris. Tris is now being used as a flame retardant in foam products, more than thirty years after it was removed from use in children's pajamas. Since the voluntary phase-out of pentabrominated diphenyl ether (penta-BDE) in 2004 and the ban of penta-BDE in Europe, the use of chlorinated Tris as a flame retardant has increased.

In 1977, the CPSC banned brominated Tris, aka Tris (2,3-dibromopropyl) phosphate, for use in children's sleepwear when it was reported to be a mutagen (mutates DNA) and probable human carcinogen and it was found that children were exposed from treated sleepwear. When the same carcinogen and mutagenic effects were linked with chlorinated Tris, aka Tris (1,3-dichloro-2-propyl), it was removed too.

But it is back.

The CPSC is in the process of developing a flammability standard for upholstered furniture. Several states have banned or are in the process of banning or limiting deca-PBDE. So chlorinated Tris is becoming widely used in household products to meet flammability requirements.

The *Journal Sentinel* reported that chlorinated Tris is used as a flame retardant in foam for furniture, car upholstery, baby carriers, wall hangings, and mattresses, including crib mattresses and bassinet pads. Is chlorinated Tris a problem? It appears to be. Chlorinated Tris can be absorbed through the skin, or inhaled and ingested. According to the Centers for Disease Control and Prevention, infants and children are particularly prone to absorbing brominated flame retardants (BFRs) (such as the PBDEs) and chlorinated flame retardants (CFRs)—including chlorinated Tris—through direct physical or oral contact with these compounds in furniture, inhalation of furniture dust containing BFRs and CFRs, and also via ingestion of these substances from their mothers' milk and from their diets.

The most important step is to reduce your child's exposure to flame-retardant-contaminated dust. So any measures to reduce dust will reduce your baby's exposure. Also, keeping your baby's skin from contacting dust will reduce his exposure.

Flame Retardants in Household Dust: Smart Mama's Simple Steps to Reduce Exposure

Control those dust bunnies. Eliminating dust in and around your home will eliminate PBDE-contaminated dust too. Vacuum regularly and wet wipe. If you can't do the whole house—and who can with kids?—then concentrate on those rooms where your children spend the most time.

Ventilate. Get your air moving. Open windows, open doors, and use ceiling or portable fans. Do this daily to improve your indoor air quality.

Use a blanket. If you are placing your baby on the floor, put a blanket down first—preferably an organic cotton blanket, but any blanket will do. Preventing your baby from being exposed to surface dust on the floor will reduce your baby's exposure to PBDE-contaminated dust bunnies.

Buy PBDE-free products. If you are in the market to buy new furniture, window coverings, flooring, etc., then look for products made without PBDEs or products that don't need PBDEs. Some materials are naturally flame retarding, such as wool, cotton, jute, and hemp. Other materials that don't need chemical flame retardants are metal, leather, and glass.

Buy PBDE-free electronics. Not all electronics use PBDEs. Just ask before you buy. It is my understanding that Toshiba has replaced its casings with polyphenylene sulfide, which is inherently flame resistant and doesn't need PBDEs.

Mold

Mold isn't a toxic chemical, so to speak, but mold growth does concern most of us and can negatively impact indoor air quality. News reports have linked mold exposure to a range of adverse health effects, from minor allergic reactions to brain damage.

Molds are microscopic fungi found throughout our environment. They can grow on virtually any organic substance, as long as food, moisture, and oxygen are present. They play an essential role in nature, breaking down dead organic matter, such as fallen leaves. Molds are also useful to us. Penicillin, for example, is obtained from a specific type of mold.

Molds reproduce by releasing tiny spores. These spores are invisible to the naked eye. The spores float through the air, both indoors and outdoors. They can also be transported by water and insects. If the spores land on a surface with the right conditions, they can start growing and forming mold colonies. Many building materials, including wood and Sheetrock, provide enough food to support mold growth. In fact, even the dust settling on building materials or furniture can be a sufficient food source for molds, if moisture is also present.

Mold will always be present in your home. We are exposed to it all the time. You cannot eradicate all mold, nor should you even try. The presence of mold in your home's air is normal, but mold *growth* should not be permitted.

You can limit mold growth by preventing the germination and growth of mold. The key to mold growth is water. Moisture makes mold happy. Without water, mold growth cannot start. Water damage, excessive humidity, water leaks, condensation, flooding, and water intrusion are all conditions that can foster mold growth.

SMART MAMA SCARY FACT

Almost 50 percent of U.S. homes have dampness or mold problems.

Molds can colonize quickly. Some molds germinate in four to twelve hours. Left undisturbed, a mold colony can start forming within twenty-four to forty-eight hours after a water leak or water-intrusion problem. A quick response to water intrusion, including fixing the source of the water, can stop mold from growing.

So what are the typical problem areas? Generally, basements, bathrooms, crawl spaces, sinks, windowsills, air conditioners, and other areas where standing water can accumulate. Water in the home can come from any of the following sources:

- Water leaks into the structure, such as through the roof, walls, or floors;
- Flooding from the outside sources, such as storm water, overflowing streams, storm surge, etc.;
- Flooding from indoor sources, such as overflowing sinks, tubs, or toilets; air conditioner drain pans; or sewer systems;
- Condensation caused by indoor humidity that is too high or surfaces that are too cold;
- Indoor plumbing leaks or broken water pipes;

- Outdoor sprinkler spray hitting the walls or improper landscaping drainage that allows collection of moisture against the building;
- Inadequate ventilation;
- Humidifier use;
- House plants, especially if overwatered; and
- Moisture from our bodies, including sweat, wet hair on pillows, and respiration.

What should you look for? Discoloration, musty odors, and visible mold growth. For example, discoloration around baseboards or on walls may indicate mold growth. But it may not be mold. It could also be from outdoor pollution or even sooting from burning candles or wood. Or it can be the artistic expression of a creative child who has applied your best charcoal eye shadow (for making sultry eyes) to create the petroglyphs in *Ice Age*.

A musty or earthy smell may indicate hidden mold growth. (Of course, it could also just be that forgotten plastic bag with wet swimsuits.) But if you have a noticeable musty, moldy, or earthy odor, you should check around for signs of water intrusion, water damage, or discoloration. You can also try using a moisture meter to check the moisture content of building materials. For example, if you smell a noticeable musty odor in one corner of a room but don't see any signs of discoloration or water damage, a moisture meter can test the moisture content of the Sheetrock or other building material. An elevated reading may signal a water problem behind the walls, and possibly a mold problem.

Visible mold growth pretty clearly indicates mold. Visible mold growth may look fuzzy, cottony, velvety, powdery, or sooty, and may be green, white, black, red, orange, yellow, blue, or brown. If you have visible mold growth, it is important to address it properly. However, most regulatory agencies do not recommend testing to determine what type of mold it is. All molds should be treated in the same manner in terms of health risks and removal. The old adage applies: Be safe, not sorry. Of course, there may be specific reasons to determine what type of mold you have. If you can't tell whether it is mold, place a small drop of household bleach on the suspected spot. (Borrow some from a neighbor if you are a green mama who doesn't use bleach.) If the stain loses its color or disappears, it may be mold. If it doesn't, it probably isn't mold. Of course, try this only if it is safe to do so and wear appropriate personal protective equipment.

Mold growth can damage materials, especially fabrics and paper. I think all of us have thrown out books or papers that were damaged from mold growth. However, of greatest concern are the potential adverse health effects from exposure to molds. We are exposed to molds by inhalation of mold or mold spores, ingestion, and dermal exposure. Although no standardized method has been developed to measure the magnitude of mold exposure, a greater likelihood of illness exists with higher concentrations of molds or mold fragments.

The Institute of Medicine's comprehensive review of available studies found sufficient evidence of an association between the presence of mold or other agents in damp indoor environments and asthma symptoms in sensitized persons; cough, hypersensitivity pneumonitis in susceptible persons; and upper respiratory tract (nasal and throat) symptoms and wheeze.[15] A review of available studies found a 30 to 50 percent increase in a variety of respiratory and asthma-related outcomes associated with building dampness and the presence of mold growth.[16]

Infants and children may be affected more severely and sooner than others by exposure to elevated concentrations of mold.[18] A study found significant increased risk between lower respiratory illnesses in the first year, including croup, pneumonia, bronchitis, and bronchiolitis, and high indoor air levels of certain molds. The study concluded that the risk of lower respiratory illnesses in infancy was increased by exposure to high fungal levels.[19] The Institute of Medicine's review also found the evidence suggestive of a link between mold or other agents in damp environments and lower respiratory illness in otherwise healthy children. Exposure to molds in infants may increase the risk of developing asthma.[20] In fact, one study found that exposure to mold and dampness in homes doubles the risk of asthma development in children.[21]

SMART MAMA SCARY FACT

It is estimated that 21 percent, or one out of five, of current U.S. asthma cases are attributable to dampness and mold exposure.[17]

Allergic reactions to mold are relatively common, occurring in about 10 percent of the population. Allergic reactions to mold include sneezing, runny nose, red eyes, runny eyes, throat irritation, coughing, and skin rash. More severe allergic reactions include allergic bronchopulmonary aspergillosis, allergic fungal sinusitis, and hypersensitivity pneumonitis. Molds can also trigger asthma attacks in asthmatics with mold allergies.

Molds can also irritate the eyes, skin, nose, throat, and lungs. Most molds emit microbial volatile organic compounds (mVOCs). These mVOCs are the cause of the musty or earthy odors encountered with some molds. The mVOCs may cause irritant responses in some individuals. Exposed persons have reported headaches, fatigue, and nausea resulting from exposure to mVOCs. Also, beta-1,3-glucan is a major structural component of almost all fungal cell wells. Exposure to beta-1,3-glucan is associated with headaches, although researchers are investigating the contribution of beta-1,3-glucan to irritant responses to mold.

Molds can cause infection, especially in susceptible people. Although this is an uncommon adverse health effect of mold exposure, the U.S. Centers for Disease Control and Prevention (CDC) has found that 9 percent of hospital-acquired infections are caused by molds.[22] It is important to keep immunocompromised or otherwise sensitive individuals out of environments with elevated mold concentrations.

Some molds release small molecular toxins, called mycotoxins, under certain conditions. These conditions may include competition from other organisms or changes in the supply of moisture or nutrients.

Exposure to mycotoxins can occur through inhalation, dermal exposure, or ingestion. Mycotoxins may cause toxic effects in people. In news stories, the molds that are capable of producing mycotoxins are often referred to as "toxic molds." Despite media hype, considerable debate exists in the scientific and medical communities about claimed toxic effects resulting from mold exposure by inhalation. Though toxic effects resulting from ingesting mycotoxin-contaminated foods are well known, toxic effects resulting from inhalation of molds and mycotoxins are unresolved despite several high-profile lawsuits and news reports. Claimed toxic effects include wheezing, difficulty breathing, nasal and sinus congestion, light sensitivity, blurry vision, watery or runny eyes, sore throat, cough, skin irritation, chronic fatigue, immune suppression, aches and pains, loss of memory, constant headaches, mood changes, diarrhea, and brain damage. The health effects associated with long-term exposure to mycotoxins are unknown.

Molds produce mycotoxins only under specific environmental conditions, so just because you have a mold known to produce mycotoxins does not mean that the mold is in fact releasing them. Molds known to release mycotoxins under certain circumstances include *Stachybotrys chartarum, Aspergillus versicolor,* and several toxigenic species of *Penicillium.* When mycotoxins are present, they occur in both living and dead mold spores, and may be present in materials that have become contaminated with molds. The infamous "toxic black mold" discussed in news stories is *Stachybotrys chartarum.* "Stachy" is a greenish-black mold that can grow on materials that contain cellulose, such as drywall or Sheetrock, ceiling tiles, and wood. Not all greenish-black molds are *Stachybotrys chartarum.* It does not grow on glass or ceramic tiles or cement, so the mold in your shower is most likely not Stachy.

In infants, Stachy exposure has been linked to acute idiopathic pulmonary hemorrhage (AIPH), better known as bleeding lungs. The first widely publicized report of this link came in 1994 when the CDC investigated whether Stachy exposure was related to an incidence of bleeding lungs in infants in Cleveland, Ohio. Though the CDC initially concluded that there was a possible link, a subsequent review determined that the link was not proven. The Institute of

Medicine's comprehensive review found insufficient evidence to determine whether Stachy exposure was associated with bleeding lungs. However, the American Academy of Pediatrics has stated that "although the causal association between AIPH in infants has not been firmly established, the Cleveland study, additional case series, case reports from independent sources, and basic scientific studies in animal models have provided some evidence of plausibility."[23]

You will never eliminate all mold and mold spores from your home. But you can control indoor mold growth.

Mold: Smart Mama's Simple Steps to Reduce Exposure

Respond quickly to water problems. Mold cannot grow without moisture, so don't make the mold happy. If you fix plumbing leaks and other sources of water intrusion as soon as possible, you will eliminate the environment that molds need in order to thrive. If you have water damage, take action within twenty-four to forty-eight hours to prevent mold growth. Porous and semi-porous materials such as ceiling tiles, fiberglass insulation, and non-valuable books and papers should be discarded and replaced. For upholstered furniture and carpeting, remove water with water extraction and accelerate drying with dehumidifiers, fans, and heat, as appropriate. Always check underflooring and allow it to dry as well. For wood surfaces, remove moisture and accelerate drying.

Control humidity. In your home, keep humidity levels below 60 percent or even below 50 percent if you can.

Use your eyes and nose. Your eyes and nose can tell you a lot. That musty odor? A good indication that mold is present. Signs of water damage? A water problem that might lead to mold. If you see or smell mold, fix the moisture source and then remediate the mold (see below).

Ventilate. Make sure you have and maintain adequate ventilation in "wet" rooms, such as the bathroom, the kitchen, the laundry room, the basement, and the mud room. Again, controlling moisture and humidity is the key to preventing mold growth. And an ounce of prevention is better than a pound of cure.

Be safe, not sorry. All molds should be treated in the same manner in terms of health risks and removal.

Dry completely. After fixing a water problem and remediating the mold, make sure you dry out water-damaged areas completely. Porous and semi-porous materials may need to be disposed of if they get moldy or wet.

Change filters. If you use an air conditioner or dehumidifier, make sure you change the filter regularly in accordance with the manufacturer's instructions.

Discard moldy items. Don't be a packrat! If you have moldy books, magazines, newspapers, clothing or other items, discard them appropriately.

Limit houseplants. Houseplants, especially if overwatered, can contribute to dampness. Mold can grow in the soil and on the bark and leaves.

Remediate. The appropriate method to use to clean up mold will depend on the area covered by mold growth and the material(s) involved. According to the EPA, if the impacted area is less than 10 square feet, most regulatory agencies indicate that you can clean it up yourself. If the impacted area is more than 100 square feet, you should use a professional. If the total affected surface area is between 10 and 100 square feet, you may want to consult a professional. If impacted area is less than 10 square feet, the following cleanup methods are recommended. To protect yourself, you should wear a N-95 respirator, gloves, and goggles.

Material	Cleanup Method
Books and papers	Discard non-valuables. If possible, copy and dispose of originals. Thoroughly dry and then HEPA vacuum. Dispose of contents of HEPA vacuum in well-sealed bags.
Carpet and backing	Remove water-damaged materials and discard in sealed bags. HEPA vacuum area. If removal is not possible, wet vacuum or steam clean. HEPA vacuum after thoroughly drying.
Concrete and cinder block	Wet vacuum. HEPA vacuum after thoroughly dried.
Drapes	Discard water-damaged materials in sealed plastic bags. Wet vacuum or steam clean and HEPA vacuum after thoroughly dried.
Hard, porous or semi-porous flooring (linoleum, ceramic tile and vinyl)	Discard water-damaged materials in sealed plastic bags. Wet vacuum, steam clean, or damp-wipe as appropriate. HEPA vacuum after thoroughly dried. Make sure underflooring is dried.
Hard, non-porous surfaces (metals, glass and plastic)	Wet vacuum or damp-wipe surfaces with water and detergent or wood cleaner if wood. HEPA vacuum after thoroughly dried.
Upholstered furniture	Discard water-damaged materials in sealed plastic bags. Wet vacuum or steam clean and HEPA vacuum after thoroughly dried. Spot clean with water and detergent and scrub as needed. HEPA vacuum after thoroughly drying.
Wallboard (drywall and gypsum board)	Discard water-damaged materials in sealed plastic bags. HEPA vacuum after thoroughly dried.
Wood surfaces	Discard water-damaged materials in sealed plastic bags. Wet vacuum, steam clean, or damp-wipe as appropriate. HEPA vacuum after thoroughly dried. For wood floors, make sure underflooring is dried.

Environmental Tobacco Smoke

Most of us know that environmental tobacco smoke (secondhand smoke) is harmful, but perhaps we aren't aware of just how harmful it can be. Secondhand smoke is produced from the burning end of a cigarette, pipe, or cigar, or is exhaled from the lungs of smokers. Secondhand smoke is a mixture of over 4,000 scary-sounding chemicals, including toluene, polyaromatic hydrocarbons, propylene glycol, benzene, lead, formaldehyde, cyanide, and nicotine.[24] In fact, some of the toxic chemicals found in secondhand smoke are present at higher concentrations than in inhaled cigarette smoke!

Secondhand smoke contains over sixty chemicals that are known or suspected to cause cancer. It is classified as a carcinogen by the U.S. Environmental Protection Agency, the National Toxicology Program, and the International Agency for Research on Cancer. The United States Surgeon General concludes, "The scientific evidence indicates that there is no risk-free level of exposure to secondhand smoke."[25]

SMART MAMA SCARY FACT

If a parent smokes around her children, her children may inhale the equivalent of 102 packs of cigarettes by age five.

More than one in ten children under the age of six years is regularly exposed to secondhand smoke in their homes, "regularly" meaning four or more days per week, and 25 percent[26] of children have at least one parent who smokes. Parents are responsible for 90 percent of children's exposure to secondhand smoke.[27] Caregivers play a role as well. Almost 60 percent of children between the ages of three and eleven are exposed to secondhand smoke.[28]

The health consequences of that exposure are significant. Secondhand smoke is particularly harmful to infants because infants are still developing and their breathing rates are higher than adults. Exposure to secondhand smoke increases the risk of SIDS in babies exposed in utero and after birth.[29] In 2005, an estimated 430 newborns died from SIDS as a result of exposure to secondhand smoke.[30]

Exposure to secondhand smoke also increases the risk of developing asthma and can increase the seriousness of asthma in asthmatic children.[31] In 2005, an estimated 202,300 episodes of asthma in children were related to exposure to secondhand smoke.[32] The U.S. Surgeon General has found the evidence sufficient to link parental smoking and cough, phlegm, wheeze, breathlessness, and even suffering an asthma episode among school-age children and the onset of wheeze illnesses in early childhood. Children who grow up with smokers in the family are more likely to have asthma by the age of six than children living in non-smoking households.

The rate of bronchitis, pneumonia, colds, and other respiratory infections is four times higher in children exposed to secondhand smoke than in those living in smoke-free environments. Exposure to secondhand smoke is responsible for between 150,000 and 300,000 lower respiratory tract infections in children under eighteen months of age across the United States each year.[33]

Exposure to secondhand smoke also causes an estimated 789,700 cases of middle ear infections in children each year.

Environmental Tobacco Smoke: Smart Mama's Simple Steps to Reduce Exposure

Quit smoking. Okay, I readily admit that quitting smoking is no simple step. And having never been a smoker, it is easy for me to tell you to quit smoking. But quitting truly is the most effective way to reduce your children's exposure to secondhand smoke. If you stopped smoking while you were pregnant, it might be easier to quit now or just not start again.

Encourage all household members to quit smoking. Easy to recommend, hard to implement. But you never know.

Take it outside. Don't smoke in your home or car. Until you can quit, smoke outside. Simply moving to another room or smoking near an open window is not sufficient to protect your children. Secondhand smoke can be distributed throughout homes and buildings by heating, ventilation, and air-conditioning systems. The smaller particles and gases found in secondhand smoke cannot be removed by conventional air-cleaning systems. Our house motto is "If you are smoking in this house, you had better be on fire."

Make others smoke outside, too. Don't allow others, including child-care providers, to smoke in your home or your car.

Ask child-care providers about smoking. It may seem intrusive, but you have the right to ask. If you are looking for a child-care provider, make sure the person will conform to any restrictions you have about smoking. If you are seeking care out of your home, inquire about rules about smoking. Most day-care centers have fairly strict rules, but home-based day cares may not be as strict about smoking outside of day-care hours.

Asbestos

Asbestos can be found in many building materials, including those in our homes, offices, and day-care centers. The sprayed-on ceiling in your living room? The floor tile in your kitchen? You probably don't even think about it, but those building materials and many others can contain asbestos.

Many people assume that asbestos products are banned, but they aren't, even though at least thirty other countries have banned asbestos. The EPA's ban of most asbestos-containing products was thrown out by a court. The court's decision was one of the more spectacular failures of the Toxic Substances Control Act (TSCA). As a result, except for certain applications, asbestos continues to be used. In 2001, approximately 29 million pounds of asbestos was used to manufacture products in the United States.[34] However, although asbestos has not been banned per se, individual product uses have been controlled.[35]

Asbestos kills an estimated 10,000 people in the U.S. each year. The three major health effects associated with exposure to asbestos fibers are asbestosis, lung cancer, and mesothelioma. Children are potentially more at risk of suffering adverse health effects of asbestos exposure.

The term "asbestos" actually refers to a number of naturally occurring, fibrous silicate materials, including chrysotile, crocidolite, amosite, tremolite, actinolite, and anthophyllite. These fibers provide a number of desirable properties, including heat insulation, fire resistance, and strength. But asbestos poses a health problem because of its physical characteristics, as opposed to its chemical properties. Asbestos fibers are long and microscopically thin—so thin you can't see them. They are also light, so once released, they can remain suspended in the air and float from room to room.

The regulations regarding asbestos-containing products are a little confusing, and depend on the federal agency with authority over the product. Certain asbestos-containing industrial and commercial building and construction products are under the EPA's jurisdiction, including piping wrap, asbestos cement corrugated sheet, asbestos cement shingles, and roof coatings. These products are not always labeled as asbestos-containing products. Sometimes the label identifies asbestos as "Canadian Mineral Fiber" or "Chrysotile." But other asbestos-containing consumer products are subject to the CPSC's jurisdiction, as opposed to the EPA. Products subject to the CPSC's jurisdiction are required to be labeled if, under reasonably foreseeable conditions of handling and use, they are likely to release asbestos fiber.[36]

The real risk of exposure for most of us comes from building products, insulation materials, and consumer products that may have been used or found in our homes. Asbestos building products and insulation materials were widely used up until the late 1970s, when many common and significant uses were banned. If your home was built before 1978, you're most at risk as it is likely that you have some asbestos-containing materials present.

But before you panic about asbestos in your home, keep in mind that a risk exists only if the asbestos is friable, or if you are cutting into or removing such materials. What is friable? Friable means the asbestos-containing product can be crumbled with hand pressure. Friable asbestos-containing materials are a health risk because they can release asbestos fibers into the air, where they can be inhaled by occupants.

Another potential risk of exposure is if a household member works in an industry that may use asbestos-containing products, such as brake shoes and the auto and auto-repair industries. A household member working in the industry can bring home asbestos fibers on his or her clothing. Other occupations that may result in exposure to asbestos are the construction industry, particularly demolition, and the maintenance of buildings and equipment.

Asbestos has been used in over 3,000 different products, though, as noted earlier, products used in your home may not be labeled or easily identified as containing asbestos. To give you an idea of the types of products in which asbestos could be present, consider these building products commonly found to contain asbestos:

- resilient floor tiles, the backing on vinyl sheet flooring, and adhesives used to install floor tile;
- paper tape and blankets used to insulate steam pipes, boilers, and furnace ducts;
- cement sheet, millboard, and paper used as insulation around furnaces and wood-burning stoves;
- door gaskets used in furnaces, wood stoves, and coal stoves;
- soundproofing or decorative material sprayed on ceilings and walls;
- compounds used for patching and joints;
- textured paints; and
- cement roofing, shingles, and siding.

In 2001, asbestos was used in the United States to manufacture asphaltic roofing compounds, gaskets, friction products—including brake linings and clutch facings, and coatings and compounds. Products imported into the United States may also contain asbestos. Other consumer products that have historically been found to contain asbestos are electric blankets, heat guns, molding clay, disc brake pads, crayons (!), automatic transmission components, artificial ashes and embers used in gas-fired fireplaces and fireproof gloves, stovetop pads, ironing board covers, and even hair dryers. A more comprehensive list can be found at the CPSC's Web site.[37] Even if the manufacturer voluntarily stopped using asbestos in the product, as was the case with hair dryers, you may still be using the asbestos-containing version in your home.

Contaminated vermiculite can be another source of asbestos. Vermiculite has been used in construction and consumer materials, including loose-fill insulation, acoustic finishes, spray-on insulation, concrete mixes for swimming pools, and agricultural and horticultural products (e.g., potting mixes and soil conditioners). A former substantial source of vermiculite ore, a mine near Libby, Montana, was contaminated with asbestos and asbestos-like fibers.

The mine supplied more than half the worldwide production of vermiculite from 1925 until the mine stopped production in 1990. There is a potential risk of exposure to asbestos from contaminated vermiculite from the Libby mine. Much of the vermiculite from the mine near Libby was used in the manufacture of Zonolite Attic Insulation, although not all Zonolite product was made with vermiculite from that same mine.

I can't emphasize it enough: Even if you think you have asbestos-containing materials in your home, don't panic. Asbestos does not present a problem unless it is friable or disturbed. Asbestos is generally combined with other materials. As long as the materials remain bonded, the asbestos fibers are not released. If you have asbestos-containing building materials in your home and they are in good condition, just leave them be. Asbestos fibers will generally not be released from material that is in good condition.

The EPA acknowledges that slightly damaged material may be best dealt with by not touching or disturbing the material and limiting access.[38] But if the material is more than slightly damaged, meaning that it is deteriorating, torn or worn, or cannot be dealt with by limiting access and not touching, then you need to repair or remove it.

If you are going to be remodeling or making changes to your home that could disturb asbestos-containing materials, you may need professional help. Unless it is labeled, you won't be able to tell whether a material contains asbestos. You can't sample the material yourself, since sampling can release asbestos fibers.

The risk is increased with the amount of asbestos to which you are exposed and the length of exposure. Asbestos fibers inhaled into the lungs can remain in the lungs for a long time, increasing the risk of disease. The risk of lung cancer and mesothelioma increases with the number of fibers inhaled.

Children are potentially more at risk of adverse health effects resulting from exposure to asbestos. The latency period for the onset of asbestos-related disease is between ten to fifty years after first exposure. Therefore, because infants are exposed early in life, they are more at risk than people exposed later in life because of the long latency period. Also, infants are more likely to disturb asbestos-containing materials, fiber-laden soils, or indoor dust containing asbestos while playing than adults. Infants are generally closer to the ground and thus more likely to breathe contaminated soils or dust.

Asbestos: Smart Mama's Simple Steps to Reduce Exposure

Inspect your home. If you have an older home, you may want to inspect it to indentify suspect materials. If you still have your home inspection report from when you purchased the home (if you had one), it may identify suspect materials.

Let it be. If the material is in good condition, let it be.

Don't disturb it. Make sure you don't cut, saw, sand, drill holes in, or otherwise disturb asbestos-containing building materials.

Repair it. If the material is not in good condition, you probably need to repair it or remove it. Repairing it usually involves either sealing or enclosing the asbestos material. Sealing the asbestos material involves using a sealant that binds the asbestos fibers together or coats the fibers so that they cannot be released. Covering the asbestos material usually involves preventing the release of asbestos fibers by putting something over it, like a protective wrap over insulated piping or new flooring over asbestos-containing floor tiles. Of course, repairing it means that that asbestos fiber remains in place. If you ever remodel or replace the material containing asbestos, you will need to take further action. A professional trained in handling asbestos should be used even for minor repairs because a risk of exposure exists and improper handling can result in a hazard where none existed before.

Remove it. Removal of the asbestos-containing material will eliminate the risk if the removal is done properly. Make sure you use a professional trained in asbestos handling. Removal can be expensive and hazardous.

Don't bring it home. If you work in an industry where asbestos exposure is a possibility, don't bring asbestos dust home. Change you clothes and shoes before you get in your car or enter your home.

Are Portable Air Cleaners or Air Purifiers Effective?

That depends. Removing sources of indoor air pollution is better than trying to clean the air after the fact. Your mom was right: An ounce of prevention is worth a pound of cure. A portable air-cleaning device cannot effectively remove all indoor air pollutants from the home. Most devices will adequately remove particles from the air but will not effectively remove pollutants such as carbon monoxide, radon, lead dust, and allergens.

Ventilation is also a better solution than air cleaning. Open windows when possible and use the fans in the kitchen and bathroom. If you have a central forced-air system, maintain your filter. You can even upgrade the filter to one with a higher rating for removing contaminants.

However, air-cleaning devices may be helpful, especially when used with prevention and ventilation. The best type appears to be those equipped with a high-efficiency particulate air (HEPA) filter combined with a carbon filter. A HEPA filter can remove dust, pollen, and smoke without generating ozone. A carbon filter can remove some volatile organic compounds (VOCs).

Electrostatic precipitators can also remove dust, pollen, and smoke, but some generate ozone as a by-product, and ozone can cause respiratory problems. A recent report by the California Air Resources Board (CARB) found that none of the tested ionizers and electrostatic precipitators produced indoor ozone levels that exceeded the California health-based outdoor air standard for ozone, but noted that other research had.[39] Whether you purchase a filter-based cleaner or an electrostatic precipitator, make sure it is adequately sized for your room. Undersized systems will not be effective.

Skip air-cleaning devices that intentionally produce ozone. Ozone is a prime component of smog, and has been linked to several health problems. Ozone can damage the linings of the respiratory tract and cause respiratory tract infection and breathing difficulty. Ozone exposure is associated with coughing, chest tightness, shortness of breath, and worsening of asthma symptoms. Ozone-generating air purifiers are sometimes advertised as providing energized, super oxygenated, or activated oxygen. Ozone-generating air purifiers have been found to produce indoor ozone levels well above California's one- and eight-hour outdoor standards. The CARB investigated ozone-generating air purifiers and found that they could generate enough ozone to have an indoor air concentration of ozone three times the health standard for outdoor levels (maximum setting). CARB adopted a 0.050 ppm ozone emission standard for such devices, which will most likely be in effect in 2010.

Another problem with ozone-generating air purifiers: they may react with terpenes (fragrance compounds such as limonene and pinene) and other chemicals, resulting in an increase in formaldehyde, ultrafine particles, and other pollutants.[40] On its Web site CARB maintains a list of air cleaners that intentionally emit ozone.

Keep in mind that little definitive medical evidence establishes that air purifiers help relieve respiratory symptoms. However, my husband, who has allergies, always claimed his symptoms improved when he used a portable air cleaner.

Arsenic

Arsenic is a naturally occurring carcinogen. It is an odorless, tasteless, colorless poison that can be readily dissolved in any drink. You may be familiar with it because it is used in fictional murder mysteries for slow poisoning, such as lacing a powdered-sugar doughnut with arsenic. It usually isn't used for a quick death because a heavy dose of arsenic shows up on a toxicology screen.

Arsenic is found in groundwater, so we are exposed to it in our drinking water. The water consumed by 13 million Americans has arsenic present in excess of the drinking-water standard, primarily in rural areas.

Our children can also be exposed to arsenic via arsenic-treated wood in decks and playgrounds. Outdoor wood was treated with chromated copper arsenate or CCA to preserve it for years. CCA has been used to treat wood since the mid-1930s to preserve it against wood-attacking insects and decay. CCA-treated wood is also call pressure-treated wood, although not all pressure-treated wood is CCA-treated since other preservatives have been used.

The arsenic present in CCA-treated wood can leach out. The EPA banned the manufacture and sale of arsenic-treated wood for most uses in 2004. Wood decks and kids' play sets built before 2004 usually contain arsenic. Seventy percent of the homes in the U.S. are estimated to have arsenic-treated structures, and 14 percent of public children's playgrounds are estimated to contain arsenic-treated wood.

If you have a wood deck or any outdoor wood structures, or if your school or day care has any such structure, there is a risk that your kids might be exposed. CCA-treated wood can be identified by the greenish tint it gives to wood, although this tint can be covered up.

Kids may ingest arsenic after they touch treated wood or nearby soils. Arsenic exposure is by ingestion, not simply skin exposure. Kids can become exposed if they place their hands in their mouths after touching arsenic-treated wood. They may also be exposed from arsenic leached into nearby soils. Acidic soils, or soils with a lower pH, may increase the leaching of arsenic and can be more of a source of arsenic exposure than alkaline soils (clay soils with a high pH).

If you want to test your wood, or have your school or day care test its wood, you can order a test kit from the Environmental Working Group. I have found arsenic in most of the wood decks I have tested.

If you do have a wood deck from 2004 or before, or an older wooden kids' play set, you can take precautions to reduce the potential exposure and protect your kids.

Arsenic: Smart Mama's Simple Steps to Reduce Exposure

Wash hands! It seems like washing hands is always recommended to reduce chemical exposures, from arsenic to lead. Washing with soap and water removes arsenic from the hands and reduces risk.[41] Wash water from children washing their hands after playing on arsenic treated wood had arsenic levels 400 percent greater than the arsenic levels in wash water from children playing on other structures. To wash, use a liquid or bar castile soap and wash for twenty seconds.

Seal regularly. Seal the wood regularly using a non-toxic, water-based paint or sealer.

Replace high-traffic areas. Replacing the entire structure or play yard may be too expensive or impractical, but perhaps you can replace the frequently handled areas, such as handrails.

Skip pressure washing. As much as your husband may love his pressure washer, don't use it on arsenic-treated wood as this may result in the release of arsenic from the wood. If you need to clean, do it gently with liquid castile soap and water, not harsh detergents. And don't sand arsenic-treated wood—you'll release arsenic-contaminated dust.

Watch the dirt. Nearby soils may become contaminated, particularly if they are located where water runoff drains. Consider making this area inaccessible to children with some bushes, and don't use the area for planting edibles.

Chapter 4

Getting the Lead Out

Most of us have a vague understanding that lead was phased out of gasoline and paint years ago, and we believe that these bans have successfully all but eliminated the risk of lead poisoning. As a result, we are pretty confident that our children are not exposed to lead as long as they aren't playing with lead-contaminated toys. But don't be too quick to dismiss the risk—children are still exposed to lead.

I find that it is a fairly common misconception that only children living in low-income housing are exposed to lead-based paint. Many moms have told me that they don't have to worry about lead because they live in a "nice house" and their children don't "lick the walls." But lead exposure isn't about living in a nice house or not eating paint chips.

Lead remains, even today, the number-one preventable childhood environmental poison. The best way to limit exposure to lead is to eliminate sources of lead in your child's environment.

Lead is a naturally occurring, abundant metal that is easily worked. It has been used for

---

SMART MAMA SCARY FACT

One out of every ten American children has a blood lead level in excess of 5 ug/dl, putting them at risk for IQ deficits and other adverse health effects from lead.

---

thousand of years in a variety of products. Lead is widespread in our environment because of its wide and varied uses.

Children are particularly sensitive to lead exposure because of their smaller size, greater rate of absorption of lead (around 50 percent of the lead that reaches their stomach, as opposed to 11 percent in adults), and ongoing neurological and physical development. John Rosen, M.D., director of the lead program at Children's Hospital, Montefiore Medical Center, emphasizes that "lead can be extremely dangerous for young children and can affect their lives forever. It is better to be conservative and safe and not ever sorry about excessive lead exposure."

Lead is a potent neurotoxin. Lead poisoning can only be detected by a blood test. The current screening level or "level of concern" established by the Centers for Disease Control and Prevention (CDC) for pediatric blood lead levels is 10 ug/dl. That isn't much—a microgram is about one-millionth of the contents of a packet of sugar, and a deciliter is approximately 3 fluid ounces, or one-fourth of a canned soda. But recent research indicates that negative health effects occur at blood lead levels of 2.5 ug/dL, well below the current level of concern of 10 ug/dL.

There is no "safe" level of lead exposure. In fact, more than ten years ago, the National Academy of Sciences wrote that "there is growing evidence that even very small exposures to lead can produce subtle effects in humans [and] that future guidelines may drop below 10 ug/dl as the mechanisms of lead toxicity become better understood."[1] Indeed, at least seven peer-reviewed recent studies have found that lead levels believed to be safe in children actually produce a severe impact on intellectual development. According to a study reported in April 2003 in the *New England Journal of Medicine* and funded by the National Institute of Environmental Health Sciences, infant blood lead levels below 10 ug/dL produced a large drop in IQ, up to a decline of 7.4 points. The researchers also discovered that the amount of impairment was more pronounced at lower levels of blood lead levels. That is, IQ scores of children with blood lead levels of 10 ug/dl were 7.4 points lower than the children with blood lead levels of 1 ug/dl, but an increase in lead blood levels from 10 to 30 ug/dl was only associated with a small additional decline in IQ.

John Rosen, M.D., states "A threshold of 10 is no longer protective of children. I would very strongly suggest lowering the threshold to 5, based on abundant data in the last five years."

Lead exposure can result in developmental disabilities and cognitive impairment or lowered IQ. Lead exposure can also cause slowed growth, damage to the central nervous system, hypertension, impaired hearing acuity, impaired hemoglobin synthesis, and male reproductive impairment. Lead exposure has been linked with aggression and attention problems, hyperactivity, and impulsivity. In a child, lead exposure resulting in moderately elevated blood levels impacts the way the nerves communicate. This can lead to adverse effects on hearing, balance, attention, and the ability to learn new material.

Lead has been linked with attention deficit hyperactivity disorder (ADHD). A survey of just over 4,700 children found that children with blood lead levels of greater than 2.0 ug/dL were at a four times greater risk of having ADHD than children with blood lead levels less than 2.0 ug/dL.[2]

Lead exposure can also affect the immune system. Children with lead exposure demonstrate an increased production of immunoglobulin E antibody, and elevated levels of immunoglobulin E antibody can result in stronger asthmatic and allergic reactions.[3] Research has also shown that if lead exposure occurs while certain signalling cells are forming, the cells change in form and how they respond, ultimately resulting in hypersensitivity to allergens.[4]

Unfortunately, lead poisoning may have no major symptoms. A child may only exhibit tiredness or nonspecific complaints that are similar to those associated with the flu. In some cases, a toddler may have delayed speech. A school-age child may seem more aggressive, or may have trouble paying attention. Symptoms can include headaches, appetite loss, impaired hearing, hyperactivity, irritability, and learning disabilities.

The lack of major symptoms is really the problem with lead. Adverse health effects can occur with unnoticed exposure over time, with behavior occurring at the age of six or seven years that might be related to early childhood exposure to lead. Once the child enters school, the child might be unable to sit still and listen, may be unable to focus, or may be hyperactive. School-age children exposed to lead at a younger age may be disruptive in the classroom and described as fidgety.[5]

Acute lead poisoning is rare, but it can cause vomiting, abdominal pain, diarrhea, weakness in the limbs, seizures, coma, and death. The well-published tragic death of a little boy occurred in 2006 after he swallowed a heart-shaped charm.

It was believed the impacts of lead disappeared or declined if the child's exposure to lead was stopped or reduced. Unfortunately, recent studies suggest that the effects are largely irreversible.[6] In fact, the effects of lead on a child's health do not stop even after the child's blood lead levels fall or the brain and central nervous system mature. IQ may continue to fall even after blood lead levels are reduced, as demonstrated by a study of seven-year-old children who were exposed to lead before the age of three.[7]

The irreversible health effects that occur as a result of exposure to low levels of lead, coupled with the lack of specific symptoms, highlight the importance of preventing children's exposure to lead.

Lead Exposure During Pregnancy

Exposure to lead during pregnancy and lead accumulated in a mother's body throughout her lifetime put the fetus at risk. Lead is passed across the placenta. Lead and lead compounds are highly toxic and target the central nervous system.

Average blood lead levels (BLLs) for women of childbearing age are below the 10 ug/dL "level of concern," but it is estimated that between 0.5 and 2 percent of women giving birth in the United States have BLLs at or above 10 ug/dL.[8] Pregnant women with elevated blood lead levels are at risk for spontaneous abortion, premature birth, and pregnancy-induced hypertension. Fetal blood lead levels are about 90 percent of maternal blood lead levels. The risk of lead exposure to a fetus remains disproportionately high for pregnant women who live in housing built before 1978 (even if the paint is in good condition), the poor, African Americans, and Hispanics.

Moreover, blood lead levels don't tell the whole story. Lead accumulates in our bones and can be released months or years later. Lead primarily enters the body through the gastrointestinal tract, and then circulates in the bloodstream and gets deposited in tissues, including the brain, kidney, and bone. As much as 90 percent of an adult's total lead burden is stored in the skeleton, where it can remain for years, until it is mobilized. When you're pregnant, your body needs more calcium, which is drawn from your bones, but this causes lead stored in the bones to be released.

Pregnancy can result in a *doubling* of blood lead levels as lead stored in the bones is mobilized, even if the lead exposure happened early in a woman's life.[9] Accordingly, a blood lead level test prior to pregnancy may not accurately reflect fetal exposure. Nursing is another time when lead can become mobilized, as discussed in Chapter 6. You may be at particular risk if you were exposed to lead as a child, perhaps from deteriorating paint in your home, or if you grew up outside the United States in a country that still uses leaded gasoline. That lead will have been stored in your bones, and when you get pregnant it can be released and expose your baby. While dietary lead, lead in the food and drink a mother consumes, constitutes approximately two-thirds of fetal exposure, skeletal lead constitutes one-third.[10]

Lead has been detected in the fetal brain as early as the end of the first trimester. The adverse effects of lead exposure may be more pronounced as a result of first-trimester exposure. Specifically, maternal lead levels during the first-trimester are linked to poorer Mental Developmental Index scores.[11] Exposure to lead in utero can affect neurodevelopment and can result in lowered intelligence, shortened attention span, impaired motion development, learning disabilities, and attention deficient disorders.

Children's Exposure to Lead

Children are exposed to lead from ingestion and inhalation as a result of our use of lead in so many different ways and in so many different products. As discussed in this chapter, children are exposed to lead in drinking water, lead-based paint chips, lead-contaminated dust, lead-contaminated soils, lead in herbal remedies, lead in children's toys, PVC stabilized with lead, and more.

Children are more at risk for lead poisoning because they are more likely to engage in mouthing activity, thumb-sucking, and hand-to-mouth behavior, which exposes them to lead-contaminated dust. Video studies of young children demonstrate that they put objects into their mouths more than twenty times per hour. Thumb-sucking and other hand-to-mouth behaviors may account for as much as 80 percent of all children's lead-related exposures.

Infants ingest an average of 0.02 to 10 grams of dust per day. By the time a child is six, he or she may have eaten more than half a cup or more of "fine dust"—dust minus the big stuff like dog hair, sand, crumbs, etc.

Children also ingest soil. Children between the ages of two and six years (data are not available for children less than two years of age) typically ingest between 0.04 and 0.27 grams per day of soil, with a maximum soil ingestion rate of 1.4 grams per day.[12] The EPA's *Exposure Factor Handbook* uses a dust/soil ingestion rate for children of 100 micrograms per day (or 0.1 grams per day) for children under the age of six years, with an upper percentile of 400 mg/day.

According to the National Safety Council, on average, children under six absorb 30 to 75 percent of the lead that reaches their digestive tract. In comparison, adults absorb only about 11 percent of the lead they ingest. Children absorb about 50 percent of lead from the lead dust they inhale.[13]

Data suggests that the source of exposure for 70 percent of children with elevated blood lead levels is lead paint and contaminated dust and soil. But 30 percent of children with elevated blood lead levels do not have an immediate lead paint hazard.[14] Let's talk about these sources and how to reduce exposure to lead from them.

The primary sources of lead for children are deteriorating lead-based paint and lead-contaminated dust in the home. Lead exposure also occurs from the air, bare soil, herbal remedies, drinking water, children's toys and jewelry, and PVC household products stabilized with lead. Since lead exposure is additive, meaning that each exposure adds to the cumulative effect, it is important to eliminate or reduce all sources of lead in your child's environment.

Reduction of lead in the environment is already an environmental success story. The ban against lead in paint used for housing and consumer products; the elimination of lead as a gasoline additive; and the limitation of lead solder in public water systems, plumbing components, and food and drink cans have all been extremely successful. Children's average blood lead levels in the United States have declined significantly, almost 80 percent since the 1970s.

But children are still exposed to lead. Lead enters the environment through releases from burning coal, oil, or waste; mining lead and other materials; factories that make or use lead, lead alloys, or lead compounds; weathering of structures painted with lead-based paint; and vehicle exhaust before lead was banned for use as a gasoline additive in the U.S. An estimated 400,000 to 600,000 tons of lead are released to the environment every year. Once released, lead is removed from the air by rain and falling particles, and is ultimately deposited in our soils, where it sticks strongly and usually remains in the upper layer of soil. Lead does not biodegrade or dissipate, so once it contaminates dust or soil, it stays until it is properly cleaned up. An estimated 4 to 5 million metric tons of lead are present in soils and dust from being used as a gasoline additive.[15]

We track lead-contaminated dust and soils into our homes on our shoes. Wind blows lead into our homes. Lead-contaminated dust is created in our homes from lead-based paint. Lead-contaminated dust is also present in our homes from many consumer products. It is present in the air we breathe, the food we eat, and the water we drink.

Lead in Drinking Water

Your child gets exposed to lead from drinking water. If your baby ingests formula made from drinking water, he consumes lead. The EPA estimates that non-nursing infants can receive 40 to 60 percent of their exposure to lead from drinking water in the first six months of life. For young children, the EPA estimates that lead in drinking water contributes 10 to 20 percent of total lead exposure.

To determine how much lead is in your household tap water, you have to test the water. Community water suppliers are required to provide you with a short report, called a Consumer Confidence Report, which is an annual water-quality report. It will give you information on some of the contaminants present in your tap water, including lead. If your water supplier is a non-community system, you should contact it for water-quality information.

However, these reports and water-quality information are based upon water samples that may not reflect lead concentrations at your tap because the plumbing of your home, and your home's fixtures and faucets, may contribute to lead in the tap water.

The lead content of household tap water varies. Though lead is generally not found in the source water, lead enters the water through contact with pipes, solder, fittings and fixtures, and faucets as it makes its way to your house.

Lead leaches into the water as a result of corrosion, that is, the dissolving or wearing away of metal caused by a chemical reaction between water and the lead used to construct parts of the water delivery system. Lead can also enter the water as a result of the galvanic reaction between copper in pipes and lead in solder. This reaction is vigorous in new piping. After about five years, lead levels are governed largely by the water's corrosiveness.

To figure out your plumbing, consider when your house was built and take a look at the pipes:

- Lead pipes were used before the 1930s. Lead pipes are dull gray in color and are soft. They may be easily scratched by a metal object such as a knife or key. Scratched lead will be shiny underneath.
- In the 1930s, galvanized metal pipes or copper pipes replaced lead pipes in most residential plumbing. Galvanized metal pipes are gray or silver-gray, and were used between the 1920s and the 1950s. Galvanized pipes are usually fitted together with threaded joints, like the end of a lightbulb that screws into the socket. However, compounds containing lead may have been used to seal the threads joining the pipes. Copper pipes are red brown and were used after the 1930s. Copper pipe joints were typically sealed together with lead-based solders until about 1988. Lead can leach from the lead-based solder into the drinking water supply.
- Plastic pipes, especially those manufactured abroad, may also contain lead. If your home has plastic pipes, make sure that they meet the NSF International standards. Plastic plumbing designed for potable water should be designated as "NSF-PW" or "NSF-61" and is often identified on the piping.

You are not safe even if your home is new. Very new homes may be at risk because, unfortunately, piping and pipes in new homes aren't really lead free. Almost all household faucets, plumbing fixtures, check valves, and well pumps are manufactured with brass parts. Lead is added to brass to make casting and machining easier.

You thought all drinking water components were now required to be lead free? Unfortunately, lead free doesn't really mean "lead free" under federal law. Federal law allows pipes to contain up to 8 percent lead by weight, and allows lead-free solder and fluxes used for drinking water applications to contain up to 0.2 percent lead by weight.[16] So you may have some lead leaching from your pipes even if they are new. Any plumbing device or fixture that contains lead (even if it is "lead free") and is in contact with water is a potential source of lead contamination.

If lead is leaching from the pipes and solder by corrosion and the water is not too corrosive (naturally soft water is usually more corrosive than hard water), lead levels generally decrease as a building ages. As time passes, mineral deposits form a coating on the inside of the pipes (if the water is not too corrosive). This coating insulates the water, and protects against lead contamination. It takes about five years for an effective mineral scale to form. So during the first five years, water is in direct contact with the lead in any brass faucets, valves, and fittings containing lead. As a result, water in buildings less than five years old may have high levels of lead contamination.

Also keep in mind many day-care and school-facilities are older so always ask about their policies to reduce exposure.

Lead in Drinking Water: Smart Mama's Simple Steps to Reduce Exposure

Test your water. If you are concerned, you may want to have your water tested. You cannot see, taste, or smell lead dissolved in water, so testing is the only sure way to find out whether there are harmful quantities of lead in your tap water. Testing usually costs between $20 and $100. Most states have a list of laboratories certified to test lead in tap water. You can also contact the National Lead Information Center (1-800-424-LEAD). It can provide a list of EPA-certified laboratories in your area.

Inspect your pipes and plumbing. Find out what you have. If your home was built before 1930, you may have lead pipes unless your home was re-piped. If your home was built before 1988, you probably have lead solder joining your pipes. Experts regard this lead solder as the major cause of lead contamination of household water in the United States today.

Know your faucet. Brass materials are used in most residential, commercial, and municipal water distribution systems. Brass fittings, faucets, and valves are golden yellow, although they may be plated with chrome. Brass generally contains lead in the range of 2 to 8 percent. Although lead content is restricted by law to 8 percent, lead can still be leached from new brass faucets and fittings. The amount of leaching depends on the water's corrosiveness (soft water is more corrosive) and the manufacturing process used. Fabricated faucets tend to leach less lead than faucets manufactured by a permanent mold press. Brass faucets installed before 1986 (the date federal law limited the amount of lead in faucets to 8 percent, although some states restricted lead in faucets earlier) may leach high levels of lead. If you are buying new faucets, pipes, etc., make sure they have the NSF/ANSI 61 certification.

Know your water. If the water in your community is especially acidic, or "soft" (soap lathers easily), it can be very corrosive. The more corrosive the water is, the more lead it can dissolve as it stands in pipes. Also find out whether your community's water-distribution lines still have lead service connections. Just call your water service provider.

Let it run! Your inner environmentalist may cringe, but run your water at least fifteen to thirty seconds before using it. If the water has been sitting in your home's plumbing for more than six hours, let it run until you feel the temperature change before using the water. This may take as long as two minutes, depending on your system. This flushes out the water that has been standing in your pipes. Water standing unused for as little as six hours in pipes joined with lead solder can contain harmful levels of lead. It is important to do this for each tap—brushing your teeth using your bathroom faucet will not flush your kitchen faucet. Flushing may not work if you live in a large apartment building with large-diameter pipes.

> **SMART MAMA TIP**
>
> Watch the water softener. While a water softener can reduce lead in the water entering your home, it can also contribute to the corrosiveness of the water and, thus, to the potential for lead contamination. Treating hard water can remove or prevent the protective mineral coating, and thereby increase the potential for lead contamination from your pipes.

Use it cold. Always use cold tap water for drinking, cooking, and preparing baby formula. Hot water dissolves metals faster, including lead. If you need hot water, heat it on the stove or in the microwave.

Consider a filter. When buying a filter, don't be fooled by pitches. Generally, carbon filters, sand filters, and cartridge filters do not remove lead, although they do filter out other water contaminants. Specially designed carbon filters can effectively remove lead, but not all carbon filters can. If you are investing in a filtration system to reduce lead, make sure it is certified for lead removal by NSF International. Also, make sure you maintain and service it as required by the manufacturer to keep it effective.

> **SMART MAMA TIP**
>
> To soothe your inner environmentalist, conserve water by filling a couple of bottles for drinking water after flushing the tap and store them in your refrigerator. During flushing, collect the water and use it to water indoor plants or for other purposes that do not involve cooking or drinking.

Lead-Based Paint

Along with lead-contaminated dust, lead-based paint continues to be one of the primary sources of lead exposure for children. In 2000, a two-year-old died from exposure to lead paint,[17] and numerous other incidents of lead poisoning from lead-based paint are reported each year.

Residential use of lead-based paint was banned in 1978. That same year, lead-based paints and coatings were also banned for use on children's toys and household furniture. However, much of the U.S.'s housing stock was constructed prior to the ban on lead-based paint. Lead may also be found in varnish or wood surfaces in older homes. Although lead has been banned in paints and varnishes, the toxic legacy of lead persists in our homes, day-care centers, churches, and schools. Both lead from paint chips, which you can see, and lead dust, which you can't always see, can be serious hazards.

Lead-Paint Risk in Homes

A house built before 1940 has an 87 percent chance of containing lead-based paint.

A house built between 1940 and 1959 has a 68 percent chance of containing lead-based paint.

A house built between 1960 and 1977 has a 24 percent chance of containing lead-based paint.

Lead-based pigments were used in almost all paints up until the 1930s. In the 1930s, other paint formulations, including zinc- and titanium-based pigments, began increasing their share of the market, but lead-based pigments continued to be used. The lead-paint industry was extremely successful in stopping attempts to require warnings on paints or limits on lead content. Finally, in 1971, the Lead Based Paint Poisoning Prevention Act was enacted. In 1977, the Consumer Products Safety Commission banned any paint or coating containing more than 0.06 percent lead (or 600 ppm) for consumer use. This will be reduced to 0.009 percent lead (90 ppm) in August 2009.

A Toxic Legacy: The Dirty History of Lead Paint in America

Despite the hazards of lead paint being known in the very early part of the twentieth century, the United States didn't ban lead in residential paint and on consumer products until 1978. Medical and scientific journals published numerous articles between 1904 and 1955 detailing the hazards associated with exposure to lead and lead-based paints. In fact, Australian physician J. Lockhart Gibson published an article in 1904 on lead-contaminated dust coming off of lead-painted walls being the source of childhood lead poisoning among his patients. In 1905, he wrote, "The use of lead paint within the reach of children should be prohibited by law." In 1914, Americans Kenneth Blackfan and Henry

Thomas published a report on a boy who died of lead poisoning after ingesting leaded paint on his crib railing. His death was not an isolated case. Eighty-nine cases of childhood lead poisoning were reported by the Boston Infants' and Children's Hospital between 1924 and 1933.

The paint industry was aware of the link between childhood lead poisoning and lead-based paint. In fact, in 1904, just before getting into the lead-paint business itself, the Sherwin Williams Company published an article stating that "white lead is poisonous to a large degree, both for the workmen and for the inhabitants of a house painted with white lead colors."[18] This was in 1904—seventy-four years before lead paint was banned in the United States. The evidence documenting that the lead-paint industry was well aware of the significant hazards associated with lead-based paint is well detailed in the thought-provoking book, *Deceit and Denial,* by Gerald Markowitz and David Rosner.

Although other countries banned lead paint early in the twentieth century (e.g., France and Austria in 1909), the United States didn't act, even in the face of mounting evidence, because of the strength of lobbying by the lead-paint industry. For example, the Massachusetts Department of Labor attempted to regulate lead-based paint in 1933, but the industry lobbied officials and obtained what it described as a "satisfactory adjustment." That adjustment? A recommendation, not a regulation, added to the Massachusetts Department of Labor's paint regulations stating: "Many serious and even fatal cases of lead poisoning among infants have been traced to the sucking or chewing of lead-painted surfaces. Toys, cribs, furniture, and other objects with which infants may come in contact should not be painted with lead colors."[19]

At the same time, the lead-paint industry's advertising in the first half of the twentieth century aggressively promoted lead paint for interior use, and targeted children. In retrospect, some of the advertising is truly frightening.[20]

The lead-paint industry aggressively challenged the scientific reports, and dismissed the scientific evidence. In 1945, the industry's organization complained in response to questions regarding the safety of lead paint, "If anything, the problem has become even more serious in the last five years than ever before, owing primarily to the spread of considerable anti-lead propaganda and also to occasional faulty medical research which has penetrated deep into medical annals and caused many physicians and hospitals to assume erroneous positions on the question of lead poisoning."

It wasn't until the 1950s that the paint industry implemented a voluntary restriction to 50 percent lead in residential paint products. Finally, in 1978, the standard limiting lead to 600 parts per million (ppm), or 0.06 percent, was adopted. And in the face of the impending lead-based paint ban, Executive Vice President Bernhard Mautz of Mautz Paint (later acquired by Sherwin Williams) issued the following memo to the Mautz sales force:

> I want you to begin the continual program with each of your dealers of making sure their stock is rotated with the older material being sold first.
>
> This is a very important project due to the lead regulations. At the very present time we are cleaning up our material of heavy metals and putting this into our stock items.
>
> When the lead regulation is finally put into effect those dealers who have old material will not be able to sell it. The only alternative they will have is to dump it.
>
> Let's do our dealers a favor now by rotating their new stock.[21]

And what are we left with? A legacy of lead-contaminated homes, schools, and day cares.

But lead-based paint hazards persist. One in four homes has significant lead-based paint hazards. One in four! I think that number is staggering when you consider the health risks associated with lead exposure.

SMART MAMA SCARY FACT

HUD estimates that about 38 million homes in the United States still contain some lead paint. HUD also estimates that a whopping 25 percent of the nation's housing stock contains *significant* lead-based paint hazards.

It doesn't take much to elevate an infant's blood lead level. A toddler's blood lead level can be raised above the 10 ug/dl "level of concern" by ingesting a paint chip the size of a staple.[22] Although peeling or flaking paint poses the biggest hazard, surfaces with lead-based paint can be hazardous for children who are prone to chewing. In Fresno, a five-year-old boy suffered lead poisoning after chewing on a window ledge coated with lead paint in the home his family rented. The home was built in 1916. His blood was tested after it was found that he had swallowed wood and paint chips. His blood test detected lead present at 54.4 ug/dl, well above the "level of concern" of 10 ug/dl. Nearly five years later, his blood lead level had dropped to 13.4 ug/dl, which is great progress but still above the level of concern, which itself may be too high.[23]

Ingrained Hazards

Lisa A. Taggart

The wand turned pink. It wasn't the color I was hoping for. And so began a domestic frenzy.

My husband and I were long past drugstore pregnancy tests—our four-month-old baby boy was sleeping in a crib at my side. I'd been meaning to test our home for lead at some point during my pregnancy. It was part of the plan for those two weeks I was going to take off of work before my due date. Then Will arrived six weeks early, my work ended dramatically and untidily, the crib parts we'd left stacked in the backyard urgently needed assembling, and I entered a months-long, dreamlike, difficult-to-recall, sleepy emotional state that seems now like those moments when your airplane passes through clouds.

The lead in our home brought me back to earth. I'd expected that under the layers of paint on the walls of our 1912 California bungalow, constructed long before regulations banned lead in paint, there was lead. Though I knew that every room had been painted and repainted many times since those days, I figured I'd need to just liberally cover any nicks or scratches. I'd tested in Will's room, and found one spot on the doorway near the baseboard where a gouge (probably from me moving furniture) exposed an awful lime green fleck; here the Home Depot–purchased disposable wand turned up pink, meaning lead was present—rather than the desired white, for all's safe for gumming.

But now I'd moved on to the living and dining rooms, where our house showed its charms. The rooms had built-ins, paneling, elephant-leg column dividers—all classic Craftsman details, done in faux-painted Philippine gumwood by the home's builder. My husband and I had swooned over this stuff when we were looking to buy four years earlier. We'd invested all the money we had, and promised all future earnings-plus, to buy the small place with a tiny yard, and we'd been thrilled about it. Friends (who could afford it) had purchased larger, fancier homes, ones in hipper neighborhoods and with larger yards. But we'd been content, smug, even—we wouldn't want one of those new, generic homes. Sure, our place was small. But it had character.

Then I swiped some of that historic wood with my lead-testing wand, and it turned fuchsia faster than you can say "lead encapsulation." I swiped the bookcase: pink. The built-in desk with the old-fashioned mail slots: pink. The columns, the trim, the drawers: pink, pink, pink. Even the built-in china cabinet—significantly, the place where I kept *the dishes we eat off of.* PINK.

"Oh, that's bad," my engineer/lawyer/environmental health advocate sister said.

Thanks.

We were surrounded by lead. Reveling in lead. Storing our napkins in a lead cabinet; writing our bills at a lead desk. How the lead had gotten into the wood, I didn't know. Maybe through the faux paint. Maybe through a fungicide treatment in the lumber yard. My sister did some research, and found that lead had been added to wood varnish. Maybe that was the source. We had a problem. Lead is just the stuff that stymies all that important neurological development in babies. You know, the really really important development.

My sweet-faced son was dozing in his crib, unaware. How much lead had he already ingested? How much lead dust was on our floors, on my hands, in our curtains? How could I stop him from ingesting *any* particle of dust from our home?

If we had a lot of money, my sister pointed out, we could hire a hazmat team, tear out all of those beautiful, toxin-laden historic pieces, bring in a super-suction house-sized lead vacuum, send it all to toxin-heaven, and then spend a small fortune replacing the huge holes in our house. Fun as it sounded, we didn't have the money for this. So we went for encapsulation: covering all of the wood.

But how to do this was a big question. I ordered some Childguard lead-encapsulation paint for Will's bedroom walls. But I didn't want to paint over the woodwork; that was a big Craftsman no-no. Though I now saw the wood as the enemy, I was cautious about cutting the resale value of our house in half. I spent days researching lead encapsulation in historic homes (not finding a lot of useful stuff), comparing clear polyurethane to TSP lead wipes to an insulating clear nanotechnology coating. I spent $250 for two gallons of something that promised to encapsulate without obscuring the wood. I ordered the TSP wipes, then discovered research that said that phosphate wipes in the home are damaging. I ordered a groovy, non-toxic lead abatement cleaner, then wondered if I'd just spent $35 for a four-ounce bottle of dish soap. I washed everything. Then I wondered what to do with the contaminated rags. I washed my hands sixty times a day.

The $75 gallon of clear coating had the consistency of Elmer's glue. I spent a day covering everything with it, then swiped the wood and the wand came up pink. I covered everything in polyurethane. I painted and painted; I got high from the fumes. I worried about the fumes Will was inhaling. I needed some kind of toxic-chemical-exposure calculator—is the hazard of fumes from some little-understood nanotechnology clear coating *greater* or *less than* the known damage from lead dust on our fancy dishes? It was beyond me. I had my husband keep our son in the backyard. I applied more coatings of polyurethane. I coated everything three times. I worried I'd missed spots. It's hard to tell with clear stuff. I painted some more. I painted again, for insurance. As I stood on a ladder, wobbling, dizzy from fumes, my hand cramped, my husband wondered aloud if it was really necessary for me to coat the picture railing in our dining room for the fourth time.

"Will isn't likely to crawl up there, is he?" my husband asked. He had a point; the railing was eight feet off the ground.

"But if the curtains hit the railing and there's dust on it and it rubs off on the curtains, and the dust drops down the curtains onto the floor, and Will crawls underneath and then puts his hand in his mouth . . ."

I was right. But also, crazy. I finished the final coat and stopped there. All of the wood in our house is very shiny now. You can't have a perfectly toxic chemical–free house. But I'm trying.

Lisa A. Taggart is the mom of my most wonderful nephew. She is the co-editor of Tied in Knots: Funny Stories from the Wedding Day *and* The Bigger the Better, the Tighter the Sweater: 21 Funny Women on Beauty, Body Image and Other Hazards of Being Female.

Lead-based paint in good condition is usually not a hazard. If the paint is in good condition, most experts recommend that you do not touch it. But even if the paint is in good condition, it can still be a problem if it is present on surfaces that children chew on, such as railings, or surfaces that get a lot of wear and tear.

If lead-based paint is blistering, cracking, or peeling, or is otherwise is poor condition, it must be addressed. Peeling paint may be consumed by children. Peeling paint also results in lead dust that contaminates the home and soil surrounding the home.

Lead-Based Paint: Smart Mama's Simple Steps to Reduce Exposure

Maintain your paint. If your home was built before 1978, keep your paint well maintained.

Remediate the lead. Four options exist. The only permanent option is permanent removal of the lead-based paint, called lead abatement. *Abatement must be done by a certified lead-abatement contractor.* Call your state agency for help. If you have an older home, do not renovate or remodel without addressing lead-based-paint hazards and the generation of lead dust. Temporary options are replacement, enclosure, and encapsulation, discussed below.

Replace lead-painted items. If a lead-painted item is easily removable, such as an interior door, you may want to replace it. However, this should be considered only if you can remove the item in a manner that doesn't disturb the lead-based paint.

Cover the lead-based paint. You may be able to enclose lead-based-paint surfaces with wallboard or encapsulate them with a specially formulated sealant.

Avoid activities that disturb or damage lead-based paint. Lead-contaminated dust can be distributed throughout the home if you scrape, sand, chip, grind, cut into, or otherwise disturb or damage lead-based paint. Work done by someone unfamiliar with lead-based-paint dangers can create significant hazards. Many horror stories exist of homeowners or contractors contaminating homes by improper handling of lead-based paint during home renovation activities.

Lead-Contaminated Household Dust

Lead-contaminated dust comes from deteriorating lead-based paint flakes and chips that have broken down, wearing of lead-based paint at friction surfaces, lead dirt tracked into the home, and from consumer products in the home.

A home's construction date is the best predictor of lead-contaminated dust. Houses built before 1978, especially those constructed before 1949, are much more likely to have lead-contaminated dust. Household floor dust lead levels strongly correlate to blood lead levels.[24]

Even in older homes with paint in good condition, the wearing at friction points where lead-based painted surfaces rub—such as the opening and closing of painted windows, doors, and cabinet doors and drawers—creates dust contaminated with lead. This fine dust settles on surfaces and in cracks and crevices.

Lead-contaminated dust is also blown into our homes, day-care centers, schools, and work environments. Wind-blown lead-contaminated dust may be a significant source of lead poisoning of children living in cities.[25]

In addition to exposure resulting from coming into contact with lead-contaminated soils, we pick up lead-contaminated dirt from all of these sources on our shoes and carry it into our homes, day-care centers, workspaces, etc. One study found that 85 percent of the dirt in our homes comes from outside. That contaminated dirt then falls off our shoes and onto our floor coverings, where it can be picked up by our children.

Once created in or transported into the home, lead-contaminated dust settles and accumulates on the floor and floor coverings—even in homes as clean as Bree's in *Desperate Housewives*. Children's normal mouthing activities, or handling food without washing hands, can lead to ingestion of lead-contaminated household dust. As explained by John Rosen, M.D., pediatrics professor at the Children's Hospital at Montefiore Medical Center, "Very small particles of paint get into household dust you cannot see, that gets on hair, fingers, toys, and skin. Through normal hand-mouth activity, that paint is absorbed."[26] Dr. Rosen warns that "if the amount of hand-to-mouth activity is robust, and the concentrations of lead in that housing unit are substantial, it does not take long."

> **SMART MAMA TIP**
>
> I would use baby wipes to wipe down critical surfaces in the nursery after changing a diaper. I'd just fold as I went to make sure I had a clean surface.

Some dust that settles on a carpet is at the surface, available for pickup by a child. But some dust becomes deeply lodged. Normal vacuuming will not remove deep dust—in fact, a quick vacuuming may just bring some of it to the surface without removing it.

John Roberts, who has been studying dust for twenty years, found that the median amount of dust in a ten-year-old carpet is *almost two pounds*. This dust can contain lead and other chemicals, including pesticides. Mr. Roberts found the median concentration of lead in dust from twenty-five houses to be 164 parts per million (ppm) lead, with a maximum concentration of 1,200 ppm. For reference, the maximum contaminant level for lead in water is 0.015 ppm, and California's Proposition 65 maximum allowable daily dose of lead (reproductive toxicant) is 0.00005 ppm/day.

Lead in Outside Soils

Lead in outside soils comes from its former use in gasoline and from weathering or chipping of structures coated with lead paint. Although lead in gasoline was phased out many years ago, lead remains deposited in our communities, especially in dirt along roadways, as a result of its use as a gasoline additive. Lead may also be present in soils near industrial sources such as lead smelters, hazardous waste sites, battery manufacturing plants, garages working with car batteries, welding areas, and near and around construction sites. In urban areas, lead in soil can average between 800 and 1,200 micrograms lead per gram of soil. In rural and suburban areas, lead in soils may also be present due to its historical use as a pesticide, particularly in fruit orchards until the late 1950s. Eight decades of lead use in paint, gasoline, manufacturing, and pesticides have resulted in lead-contaminated soils.

Outside, children playing in lead-contaminated soil can be exposed to lead. Soil in play areas has the most significant impact on children's blood lead levels. Blood lead levels can run 1 to 5 ug/dL for every 1,000 ppm increase in soil lead concentrations. The risk, of course, depends on the amount of dust and soil ingested and the concentration of lead present in the soil and dust. As discussed in this chapter, children ingest quite a bit of dirt.

Lead in Dust and Soils: Smart Mama's Simple Steps to Reduce Exposure

Take off your shoes. You track lead contaminated dust and dirt into your home on the bottom of your shoes. If you take off your shoes, that dust will not make it into your home. One study found that simply taking off your shoes can reduce the amount of lead-contaminated dirt in your home by 60 percent.

Invest in good-quality doormats. If you don't want to take off your shoes, or you don't want to force your guests to take off their shoes, invest in good-quality doormats. Look for one that will remove dirt from your shoes. Look for heavy-duty, coarse threads or fibers, with a high nap. A good-quality doormat used to wipe shoes can go a long way toward reducing the amount of lead-contaminated dirt and dust tracked into the home.

Use walkways to prevent soil tracking. If you can, make sure all walkways to the house are cement, gravel, stepping-stones, or something similar, and not soil. This will prevent contaminated soil from being tracked into the house.

Plant bushes in the "drip zone." The "drip zone" is the area where old paint chips and dust have fallen around buildings painted on the exterior with lead-based paints. This area is usually relatively close to the building. The "drip zone" can contain lead levels as high as an industrial site, particularly if paint has been scraped off the building at some point. To keep children out of this area and from playing in the dirt, plant dense bushes, particularly under any friction points such as windows.

Import clean topsoil. If you garden and your home was built before 1978, bring in clean topsoil for your garden.

Buy a good-quality vacuum with a HEPA filter, a dirt finder or sensor, and a power head. A high-efficiency particulate air (HEPA) filter is a special filter that can trap very fine dust particles. Vacuuming with a regular household vacuum will not remove the very small dust particles in the home that can poison children. With a regular vacuum, much of the dust that is picked up is blown back out the vacuum's exhaust, which then resettles on toys, furniture, and floors, where small children become exposed. Make sure you get a good vacuum—you don't want to redistribute the dust. You may want to consider a vacuum with a dirt finder (a light that tells you where the dirt is). Also, a vacuum with a power brush or head is six times more effective than a vacuum without one.

Vacuum properly. If the whole house is being HEPA vacuumed for the first time, start in the room farthest from the main entrance or exit door so that dirt is not tracked into areas that have already been HEPA cleaned. Vacuum from room to room, working toward the main entrance or exit door and finish there. If only one room is being HEPA vacuumed, work from the farthest area from the door and finish at the doorway.

Wash your hands and wash your baby's hands. Wash your hands, and wash your baby's hands, regularly, especially after playing outside and after playing with any pets. Dust and soil can collect on a pet's coat, and can be transferred to hands upon contact. Always wash hands before eating. Bonus: You'll reduce some of the pesky germs that can make you and your baby sick.

Wet wipe regularly. Lead dust is sticky, and requires wet wiping to remove. Keep the areas where your baby spends time dust free. Wet wipe or mop those areas your baby is likely to touch—floors, windowsills, tables, crib rails, etc.—to remove lead dust. Just make sure you don't re-contaminate the surface as you are cleaning—make sure you use a clean surface each time you wipe. Many guidelines recommend using a cleaner with a high phosphate content or trisodium phosphate (TSP). However, recent evaluations have determined that TSP or phosphate-based cleaners aren't any more effective, so skip them, especially since TSP can burn skin, damage furniture and paint, and leaves a film, and TSP and phosphate-based cleaners are bad for the environment. Instead, use an all-purpose cleaner or a cleaner designed specially for lead-dust cleanup such as Ledizolv. These perform as well as TSP for cleanup, and are better than water alone.

Wet wipe or wash toys. Regularly wet wipe or wash those toys your baby plays with to remove lead-contaminated dust.

Check the diet. Maintaining a diet that is sufficient in iron, vitamin C, and calcium may inhibit the absorption of lead. This is more important as your baby moves from nursing or formula to solid foods.

First-Time Cleaning for Lead

If you are doing a cleaning specifically to remove lead dust and small paint chips to make areas lead-safe for children, follow this procedure recommended by the Michigan Department of Environmental Health: First, use the HEPA vacuum on all surfaces. Follow the HEPA vacuum with a wet wash of all hard surfaces with a soapy detergent and rinse with fresh water. After the hard surfaces have dried, use the HEPA vacuum a final time. To wet wash or mop, make a soapy solution using a small amount of soap or use a general-purpose cleaner. Wipe each surface clean without re-contaminating any surface. The Michigan Department of Environmental Health recommends using disposable paper towels, even though that isn't particularly "green." Dip the paper towel in the soapy solution or use the general-purpose cleaner, and then wipe the surface clean. Throw away the towel and start again with a new one until the whole area is clean. Follow up this cleaning with new paper towels wet with fresh water and wipe the surface again to get the soap residue and any remaining dust off of the surface. Use this three-step process to clean one room in the house at a time before moving on to the next room.

Workplace and Hobby Sources of Lead

You or your partner may bring lead-contaminated dust into the home from your work. Eighty percent of elevated blood lead levels in adults come from workplace exposures to lead, even though the Occupational Safety and Health Administration (OSHA) published standards for lead in general industry in 1978. Below is a list of industries and activities where lead exposure may occur:

Occupations That May Cause Lead Exposure

Ammunition and explosives production
Automotive repair shops
Battery manufacturing and recycling
Brass, bronze, copper, and lead foundries
Bridge, tunnel, and highway or subway construction
Cable or wire stripping, splicing, or production
Ceramic manufacturing
Chemical preparations—production and use
Firing-range work

Glass production and recycling
Home renovation and restoration
Industrial machinery and equipment—manufacturing
Lead abatement
Lead production
Lead smelting
Machining or grinding lead alloys
Motor vehicle parts and accessories—manufacturing
Occupations using firearms
Plastics manufacturing
Plumbing components—manufacturing and installation
Pottery making
Recycling operations
Rubber manufacturing
Sandblasting, sanding, scraping, burning, or disturbing lead paint
Scrap yards
Stained-glass manufacturing
Use of lead paints (lead paints are still permitted for certain applications)
Welding or torch-cutting painted metal

And keep in mind that you don't have to be directly involved in the activity to be exposed to lead. Employees such as clerical or housekeeping staff have been shown to be at risk for lead exposure.[27] Also, if a family member is involved in any of the potentially at-risk occupations, that family member can bring home lead dust on his clothes, hands, or hair.

You may also be exposed to lead as a result of hobbies or other activities done outside or in the home:

Hobbies and Activities That May Cause Lead Exposure

Bronze casting
Casting ammunition
Copper enameling
Electronics with lead solder
Fishing with lead weights
Glassblowing with leaded glass
Hunting and target shooting
Jewelry making with lead solder
Liquor distillation
Pottery and ceramic ware with lead glazes and paints
Printmaking and other fine arts
Stained-glass making or painting on stained glass

Workplace and Hobby Lead: Smart Mama's Simple Steps to Reduce Exposure

Change your clothes. If you are employed in an occupation or hobby that may result in exposure to lead or lead dust, change your clothes before you come into the house.

Take off your shoes. Don't track in that lead-contaminated dirt from the construction site or the shooting range. Just take off your shoes before entering your home, or change your shoes.

> **SMART MAMA TIP**
>
> Keep a pair of indoor shoes or slippers for each member of the family by each entrance to your home.

Wash your hands. Wash your hands before coming into the house to remove any lead-contaminated dust.

Folk and Traditional Remedies and Cosmetics Containing Lead

Several commonly used traditional and folk remedies have been found to contain lead. Some are contaminated with lead from the manufacturing process or soils. Some are made of lead or lead salts. For example, *greta* is a traditional Mexican folk remedy commonly used to treat children's stomach ailments. But *greta* is almost 99 percent lead oxide, and can poison children instead of making them better. One young mother expressed grief and guilt over poisoning her two children and a niece with *greta*. She gave it to them to help with stomach problems. Luckily, the high levels of lead were detected a week later during a routine checkup. The children have reportedly suffered no ill effects.[28]

The CDC estimates that traditional or folk remedies may account for as much as 30 percent of all childhood lead-poisoning cases in the United States, making them the second most common source of lead poisoning in the United States.[29] But many cases may go undetected because many doctors don't ask about alternative medicines, most people don't volunteer the information, and only about 14 percent of children are tested for lead.

Most of these remedies are manufactured outside the United States and are purchased in ethnic grocery stores and neighborhood shops, or are brought into the United States by travelers. These remedies are often cultural traditions handed down through generations. For example, Ayurvedic remedies have been used in India for at least the last 2,000 years. But one survey of Ayurvedic remedies sold in the Boston area found that 20 percent of them contained potentially harmful levels of lead, mercury, and arsenic.

Many people think *My grandmother used it, so it must be okay.* Unfortunately, that doesn't make it safe. The traditional or home remedies can cause serious cases of lead poisoning because the lead concentration is often very high and the medicine is intentionally swallowed.

Alternative or Folk Remedies and Cosmetics Found to Have Lead Present

Name	Used to Treat	Origin	Notes
Al murrah	Colic, stomachache, diarrhea	Saudi Arabia	
Albayalde or albayaidle	Vomiting, colic, apathy, lethargy	Mexico, Central America	
Alkohl (aka kohl, surma, or saoott)	Umbilical stump remedy (also used as a cosmetic)	Middle East, Africa, Asia	Can contain up to 83% lead
An kung niu huan wan		China	
Anzroot	Gastroenteritis	Middle East	
Ayurvedic remedies (listed separately below)[30]		India	
Azarcon (aka rueda, liga, coral, alarcon and Maria Luisa)	Empacho, vomiting, diarrhea	Mexico	95% lead
Ba bow sen (aka ba baw san or ba baw sen)	Colic, hyperactivity, nightmares and to detoxify "fetus poisoning"	China	
Bal chamcha	Liver problems, digestion, teething, milk intolerance, irregular stools, bloating, colic, poor sleep, poor dentition, myalgia	India	
Bal jivan	Baby tonic	India	
Bala goli (aka fita)	Stomachache	Asia, India	Often dissolved in gripe water
Bala guta	Children's tonic	India	
Bala sogathi	Improve growth, teething, cough, cold, fever, diarrhea	India	
Balguti kesaria	For children and infants	India	
Bao ning dan	Acne, pain, removing toxins	China	
Bezoar sedative pills		China	

Bint al zahab (aka bint or bent)	Diarrhea, colic, constipation, and general neonatal uses	Saudi Arabia, Oman, and India	
Bint dahab		Saudi Arabia	
Bokhoor (and noqd)	Calming	Kuwait	
Cebagin	Teething powder	Middle East	
Chuifong tokuwan		Hong Kong	
Cordyceps	Hypertension, diabetes, bleeding	China	
Deshi dewa	Fertility	Asia, India	
Emperor's tea pill	Maintain body's natural balance	China	
Farouk	Teething powder	Saudi Arabia	
Ghazard (aka ghasard or qhasard)	Digestion, relieve constipa-tion in babies	Asia, India	
Guglu (Ayurvedic remedy)		India	Reports of 14,000 ppm lead
Greta	Digestive problems	Mexico	97% lead
Hai ge fen		China	Powder added to tea
Hepatico extract	Healthy liver and promote regularity	China	
Jambrulin (reports of 44,000 ppm lead)[31]			
Jeu wo dan	Cast dressing	China	
Jim bu huan	Pain	China	
Kandu	Stomachache	Asian, India	Red powder
Koo sar (or koo soo) pills	Menstrual cramps	China	Lead believed to be present in red dye
Kohl (aka alkohl)	Cosmetic, skin infections		
Kushta	Diseases of the heart, brain, liver, and stomach, aphrodisiac	India, Pakistan	
Litargirio	Deodorant, foot fungicide, burns, wound healing	Dominican Republic	Approx. 80% lead
Lu shen wan		China	
Mahayogaraj gugullu	High blood pressure	India	
Mahalakshmi vilas ras with gold	Cold-related symptoms, blood deficiency, wound healing, asthma	India	

Navratna rasa	General debility, rickets, calcium deficiency	India	
Ng chung brand tik dak win		China	
Pay-loo-ah	Rash, fever	Southeast Asia	
Po ying tan	Minor ailments	China	
Qing fen	Cast dressing, pain	China	
Santrinj	Teething remedy	Saudi Arabia	98% lead
Sundari kalp (Ayurvedic remedy)	Menstrual health	India	Reports of up to 96,000 ppm lead
Surma	Teething powder	India	
Swarna mahayograj guggulu with gold	Rheumatism, gas, menstrual cycles, progesterone deficiency, mental disorders, fertility, menopause	India	
Tibetan herbal vitamin	Strengthen brain (remedy for mental retardation)	India	
White peony scar repairing pills	Scar	Hong Kong	
Zhui feng tou gu wan	Bone ailments, joint pain, numbness	China	

Lead in Folk Remedies: Smart Mama's Simple Steps to Reduce Exposure

Skip the remedy. I understand that many of these remedies have been used for generations, but they can contain high levels of lead. If you don't know whether they are safe or not, then skip them.

Discuss with caregivers. Discuss all medications and remedies with all caregivers. Make sure your caregivers, including your relatives, do not provide any medical care, including home remedies, without checking with you.

Consumer Products Containing Lead

Enamel bathtubs: Older enamel bathtubs can be a source of lead. The enamel glaze can contain as much as 88 percent lead. It is reported that lead was used in glaze for bathtubs up until at least 1995. A study conducted by Unique Refinishers of Atlanta found that 64 percent of 600 tubs tested had leachable lead on the surface. The president of American Lead Consultants, a national franchise company that specializes in the inspection of homes for lead, has stated that "we find lead in the tubs 50% of the time, when we inspect an older home, and we almost always test the tub for lead. In many cases, the enamel is cracking and it is clear that the lead is leaching into the water when a bath is drawn. . . . In other situations, due to the hardness of the water, or the use of harsh detergents, the enamel finish is worn down, and even though no perceptible cracks are there, the lead can still get into the water in which the child is bathed, or can be picked up by the child simply playing in the tub, touching the tub surface, and placing his hand into his mouth."

Enamel doorknobs: Just like enamel tubs, enamel doorknobs can have lead in the glaze. You may want to replace enamel doorknobs, since kids will invariably touch them.

Painted or decorated glassware: See Chapter 5.

Lead crystal: See Chapter 5.

Pewter: See Chapter 5.

Folk or handmade pottery: See Chapter 5.

Toys: See Chapter 8.

Decorated tiles: Some Mexican or folk-style tiles have been found to have lead in the glaze. Decorated tiles in good condition probably do not pose much of a risk. However, tiles that are cracked or broken can generate dust-containing lead and should be replaced or at least taped or sealed to prevent lead-dust generation.

Fishing lures and weights: Fishing lures and weights can be made of lead. Lead fishing weights and lures are harmful to wildlife, and have been phased out in many states. They can also expose people who use them to lead. Children can be exposed, particularly if they play with the lures and weights and then transfer lead from their hands to their mouths. Exposure can also occur if lead fishing weights are made at home. Choose some of the lead-free fishing lures and weights available on the market to reduce exposure and protect the environment.

Vinyl mini-blinds: Vinyl (or polyvinyl chloride plastic) is often stabilized with lead. In 1996, the CPSC found that imported vinyl mini-blinds could result in a significant exposure to children.[32] The CPSC found that in some blinds, the levels of lead in the dust around vinyl mini-blinds was so high that a child ingesting dust from less than one square inch of the blind a day for about fifteen to thirty days could result in blood levels at or above the 10-microgram-per-deciliter blood lead "level of concern." The CPSC found that the vinyl deteriorated with time from exposure to sunlight and heat, resulting in lead dust on the surface of the blind and on the windowsill. The CPSC recommended that all imported vinyl mini-blinds be removed from houses with children under the age of six. The CPSC requested that mini-blinds be manufactured without lead as a stabilizer. If you purchased blinds after 1996, they should be free of lead. If you have older blinds, consider replacing them, particularly in those rooms used most frequently by your children.

Vitamins: The FDA's analysis of lead in vitamins found that only 4 of the 324 tested did not contain lead.[33] The FDA found lead in children's vitamins and vitamins intended for pregnant and lactating women. For children, the maximum concentration of lead detected would result in an exposure of 2.88 micrograms (ug) lead per day. The FDA found that maximum exposure for pregnant or lactating women was 8.97 (ug/day) and the median exposure for pregnant or lactating women was 0.845 micrograms per day, based upon the concentrations of lead detected in the vitamins. The FDA concluded that there is nothing to worry about since both the maximum and median exposures were less than the FDA's provisional tolerable total daily intake, which is 6 ug/day for children and 25 ug/day for pregnant and lactating women. But California's Proposition 65 standard for lead is 0.5 ug/day. So the lead-concentration levels deemed safe by the FDA are higher than California's Proposition 65 standard.

Brass keys: As part of a lawsuit brought under California's Proposition 65, a study was conducted to evaluate the claim that there is enough lead in brass keys to present a lead-exposure concern for children. It was determined that lead can come off the keys onto the hands and can end up in the body through key-to-mouth and hand-to-mouth activity. You can't tell by looking at a key because some brass keys are covered by nickel-plating. To reduce exposure, do not give your keys to your children to play with. Also, plated keys have less lead available on the surface, so choose plated keys over brass keys without plating. (For more information on lead in keys, see Chapter 8.)

Lead Testing

If you are concerned, you may want to get your home tested. You can either get an inspection, where the lead content of all painted surfaces is analyzed, or a risk assessment, which will tell you the sources of lead exposure and outline recommended actions. Testing an entire home can be expensive, so you might want to try the home test kits yourself. Home-based test swabs are not recommended by the EPA because they cannot distinguish between high and low levels of lead. They just tell you if lead is present. They generally work by rubbing a swab on the surface, and the tip will change color if lead is present. One limitation: they cannot detect paint below the surface. The CPSC doesn't recommend them because they can give both false positives and false negatives. However, they are a quick, inexpensive initial screen to detect problems. I have found them a useful tool; you can screen and then have positive results confirmed by laboratory analysis. Also, you can use lead dust wipes to test your home. With a lead dust wipe, you collect a wipe sample pursuant to a specified procedure and send it to a certified laboratory. These can tell you more accurately the levels of lead present in surface dust. The National Safety Council offers a lead-dust test kit that includes everything needed to determine the presence of lead in the home.

Lead Test Kits: Testing for Lead at Home

Several relatively inexpensive home lead test kits exist. They basically look like pens. You rub the tip of the test kit on a surface, and the tip changes color if lead is present, usually pink. The CPSC issued a statement finding the home test kits unreliable. However, *Consumer Reports* conducted its own testing of the home lead test kits, and found that three of the five home lead test kits were "useful though limited screening tools if you are worried about specific items in your home." *Consumer Reports* concluded that the Homax Lead Check and the Lead Check Household Kit (made by the same company) were the easiest to use and identified accessible lead, although low concentrations could take up to two hours to turn the test stick pink to indicate the presence of lead.

I think that the kits are a great tool if you understand their limitations. They only detect lead on the surface, so you have to scratch away the top coats if you want to test beneath the surface. The test kits are also subject to interference. For example, a red-painted item may result in red paint turning the test kit's tip pink, as opposed to the presence of lead. And it is important to follow surface-preparation instructions.

A portable XRF analyzer is also available to test for lead and other elements. At $30,000 plus, though, they are not a practical option for most parents, but several companies offer services that test toys and other household goods using these portable analyzers.

Testing Your Child

If you are concerned, you can get your child tested for exposure to lead. Many pediatricians are now recommending that all children get tested. Testing is the only way to determine your child's blood lead level decisively. Before you get your child tested, ask your pediatrician whether your child has been or will be tested. Many states and some insurance and government programs require it. Current recommendations are that children get tested between the age of six months and one year (six months is recommended if you live in a home that may have lead-based paint), and again at the age of two. However, other factors might suggest earlier testing, or testing at a later age (if not previously tested). The FDA has approved a rapid screening device that can give an answer within three minutes.

Here is a checklist for determining risk of lead exposure:

- Was your home built before 1978? Have there been any renovations in the last year?
- What about other structures in which the child spends time? Have there been any renovations in the last year? (Consider homes of relatives, babysitters, day-care centers, schools, and churches.)
- What are the occupations and hobbies of household members? Other persons with whom the child spends time?
- What is the condition of the area(s) where the child plays? Is the ground bare dirt?
- Does the child engage in mouthing activities? How frequently?
- Does the child have a brother or sister (or playmate) with lead poisoning?
- Does your family use any folk or homemade potteries for cooking, serving, or storing food and drink?
- Does your family use any home remedies that may contain lead?
- Are there imported vinyl mini-blinds purchased before 1997 present in the home?

Chapter 5

Pat-a-Cake, Pat-a-Cake: The Kitchen

Because food is such an integral part of all of our lives, the kitchen is a great place to reduce toxic chemical exposures. The old adage "We are what we eat" is true—and that includes any pesky toxic chemicals along for the ride in our food and drinks. At issue in the kitchen are items we use to prepare, cook, serve, and store our foods and beverages, and the foods and beverages themselves.

Plastics: What Those Numbers Mean

Contrary to popular wisdom, the numbers on the bottom of plastic items don't tell you how to use a particular plastic. They also don't tell you that the plastic is recyclable. Those numbers are resin identification codes. They indicate the type of plastic polymer. The plastic may be recyclable, and the numbers help in sorting the plastic. But not all numbers are recyclable by all municipalities.

So what does each number mean?

- #1 is PETE or PET (polyethylene terephthalate). Used for most clear beverage bottles.
- #2 is HDPE (high-density polyethylene). Used frequently for cloudy milk and water jugs and opaque food bottles.

- #3 is PVC or V (polyvinyl chloride). Used in some fencing, soft toys, baby bibs, raingear, lunch-box linings, shower curtains, and flooring.
- #4 is LDPE (low-density polyethylene). Used to make food storage bags and some soft bottles.
- #5 is PP (polypropylene). Used in rigid containers, including some baby bottles, and also in some cups and bowls.
- #6 is PS (polystyrene). Used in foam "clam shell"–type containers and packaged meat and bakery trays. In its rigid form, used in clear takeout containers.
- #7 is Other. This means that the item is made from a resin other than the six listed above, or is made of more than one plastic resin and used in a multi-layer combination. Often, the number 7 signals that the plastic is polycarbonate plastic (see section on BPA below), but not always.

BPA: Baby Bottles, Sippy or Toddler Cups, Other Food Storage Containers, and Canned Foods

Your child's very first food storage container item is usually a baby bottle. Whether you breast-feed or use formula, you will use a baby bottle at some point. Then your child will graduate to a sippy or toddler cup. But if you use polycarbonate plastic baby bottles and sippy or toddler cups, as most of us do, along with the breast milk, formula, juice, or milk, you may be giving your baby bisphenol A (BPA), an endocrine disruptor.

Who would ever have guessed that baby bottles could pose a risk? The baby bottle is a universal symbol of infancy. (Okay, I realize that many debate the appropriateness of an artificial feeding symbol to designate, for example, nursing rooms. And yes, I support the international breast-feeding symbol. Nevertheless, so far, the baby bottle persists as a modern symbol of infancy.) Unfortunately, at least until recently, most plastic baby bottles have been made from polycarbonate plastic. Lots of toddler and sippy cups are also made of polycarbonate plastic. BPA is the key monomer that makes up polycarbonate plastic (think of BPA as a railroad car and polycarbonate as the train with all the cars linked). BPA is also found in the epoxy resins used to line virtually all cans that contain foods and drinks. And polycarbonate plastic and epoxy resins can leach BPA.

Why are baby bottles and sippy cups made of polycarbonate plastic? Polycarbonate plastic is used because it is clear, hard, shatterproof, and lightweight—all great characteristics for a plastic used to store food items. And polycarbonate plastic has been used for food contact storage items for more than fifty years, a fact routinely cited by the plastics industry when touting its safety.

Historically, it was believed that BPA did not leach out of polycarbonate plastic. Testing seemed to confirm this assumption. However, the test equipment available could not detect the low levels we can now find in current studies, a fact conveniently ignored when the plastic industries point to older studies that support the safety of BPA. Today, it is fairly well accepted that BPA does leach from polycarbonate plastic into foodstuffs. In fact, the "Opinion of the Scientific Panel on Food Additives, Flavourings, Processing Aids and Materials in Contact with Food" *assumes* migration of BPA, and uses this assumption to derive estimates of BPA daily intake.[1] For three-month-old infants fed formula with a polycarbonate plastic bottle, the estimated daily exposure is 11 micrograms per kilogram body weight per day.[2] Compare this with the animal studies that show an adverse health effect at exposures of only 0.025 micrograms per kilogram body weight per day.

In a study of BPA exposure in the United States population, of over 2,500 samples, 93 percent of the people had BPA in their urine.[3] This means that we are continuously exposed, since BPA spends only about 10 hours in the adult body. The results were troubling, however, because they showed that children had "significantly higher" levels of BPA than adolescents, who in turn had higher levels than adults. Unfortunately, none of the samples came from children under the age of six years, so the results do not provide any answers regarding the amount of exposure to BPA for infants and toddlers using polycarbonate baby bottles. Their exposure may be even higher. Frederick vom Saal, Ph.D., professor at University of Missouri–Columbia and a leading BPA researcher, commented that the results are "disturbing in that it confirms without a doubt that the youngest are most at risk."[4] The study concluded that many Americans are exposed to BPA levels above the current safety threshold set by the EPA, a threshold level that is believed to be too high, as discussed below.[5] Smaller studies have confirmed that fetuses and babies are exposed to BPA.[6]

You can't look at a polycarbonate plastic container and tell that it is leaching BPA. The precise conditions that lead to leaching of BPA are not fully understood. It appears that leaching can occur in common, everyday situations. Heat appears to be the most important factor. A recent study looked at leaching from new and old plastic bottles commonly used by hikers (not baby bottles). The study found that new and old bottles released BPA at the same rate when exposed to room temperature. The study also found that new and old bottles released BPA at the same rate when exposed to boiling water. But the study found that the bottles exposed to boiling water released BPA at a rate fifty-five times greater than the bottles exposed to room-temperature water, regardless of whether the bottles were used or not.

Studies with plastic baby bottles have also demonstrated leaching of BPA, and that leaching is increased with exposure to heat. A study with various brands of new polycarbonate plastic baby bottles found that the bottles did not show notable levels of leaching when exposed to room-temperature water, but all bottles showed leaching when exposed to water at 176 degrees Fahrenheit (80 degrees Celsius) in the range of 5 to 8 parts per billion (ppb).[7, 8] Leaching may also be higher when polycarbonate plastic is scratched or worn.[9]

For adults, canned foods and sodas seem to be the primary source of BPA exposure, although BPA is found in many items, including toilet paper made from recycled content. With extremely limited exceptions, virtually all canned foods and beverages sold in the United States are protected with a lining containing BPA. The Environmental Working Group (EWG) conducted a study involving the analysis of BPA in 97 canned-food items. BPA was detected in just over half of the samples. Of the canned goods tested, the EWG found that chicken soup and ravioli had BPA levels of highest concern. In fact, the EWG's report points out that just one serving of some of the foods concentrations could expose a pregnant woman to BPA levels that caused serious adverse effects in laboratory animals.[10] The EWG also found that the resulting chronic exposure levels to BPA for women of childbearing age who routinely ate canned food could result in BPA exposure levels during pregnancy in excess of those levels believed to be safe based upon laboratory animal testing.

Recently, a lot of media attention has been focused on BPA exposure from certain plastic sports bottles. But our exposure to BPA from canned foods is probably higher than any exposure from sport bottles because of the high temperature used in the canning process. Of course, leaching from sports bottles does occur—as much as 2 micrograms BPA per liter at room temperature, and it is higher if you put hot beverages in a sports bottle.

Health Risks of BPA Exposure

Why do we care about exposure to BPA? BPA mimics the hormone estrogen. Estrogen is part of the body's endocrine system. The endocrine system regulates all biological processes in the body, including the brain and nervous system's development, the reproductive system's growth and function, and metabolism and blood sugar levels. So BPA is an endocrine disruptor, or a synthetic chemical that when absorbed into the body either mimics or blocks and disrupts the body's normal functions.

Contrary to popular belief, estrogen is not just the female sex hormone. It is an important chemical messenger found in both men and women. Hormones, including estrogen, stimulate and regulate growth, digestion, reproduction, and sexual function. Estrogen is especially critical during fetal development. Disrupt the messenger and you can irreversibly alter a developmental process.

Based upon animal studies, BPA exposure is linked to early onset of puberty, increased diabetes risk, hyperactivity, and certain cancers, including breast cancer. A Yale University School of Medicine study found that BPA exposure can impair brain function, leading to learning disabilities and age-related neurodegenerative diseases. Similarly, another study found that BPA exposure disrupted the developing brains of rodents.[11] The study showed "that environmental estrogens like BPA appear to alter, in a very complicated fashion, the normal way estrogen communicates with immature nerve cells," said lead researcher Scott Belcher in a statement. "The developmental effects that we studied are known to be important for brain development and also for normal function of the adult brain."

Other studies have shown that low doses of BPA (lower than the EPA oral reference dose) in female rats inhibited estrogen-induction of synaptic connections in the hippocampus, an area of the brain involved with the expression of sexually differentiated behaviors. One study found that BPA exposures to pregnant mice caused chromosomally abnormal grandchildren.

Whether the low-level exposures to BPA shown to be harmful to research animals are also harmful to humans has not been conclusively established. It is complex to link the laboratory and animal evidence with health effects in humans.

But that BPA mimics estrogen is not a startling new revelation. BPA's estrogenic effects were discovered in 1936. BPA, along with diethylstilbestrol (DES) and other chemicals, was investigated for use as synthetic estrogen in the 1930s. BPA wasn't used, but DES was. DES was prescribed in 1938 to women who experienced miscarriages or premature deliveries. It was considered safe and effective for a pregnant woman and her developing baby. But we were wrong about the safety of DES. DES tragically illustrates the risks of exposing a fetus to a synthetic chemical that mimics estrogen. It was only after DES was given to millions of women that it was found that DES causes reproductive defects and increased the risk for rare cancers in the daughters of the women who had taken DES during their pregnancies.[12]

BPA and Pregnancy

Fetal exposure to BPA may be particularly significant. BPA produces adverse effects in "phenomenally small amounts," according to Frederick vom Saal, professor of biology at University of Missouri–Columbia.[13] In fact, Patricia Hunt, molecular biologist at Case Western Reserve University, says, "The fetus is exquisitely sensitive to bisphenol A. One hit during a brief window of time can influence further development."[14]

In animal studies, BPA, once ingested, rapidly enters fetal blood, reaching higher peak concentrations in the fetus than in the mother.[15] The real question is whether women pass along BPA to their fetuses. Adults appear to metabolize BPA relatively quickly, in about ten hours. And certain data suggests that as a result, pregnant women may not pass along significant concentrations of BPA to their fetuses. While rodent studies suggest that BPA is passed to their fetuses, humans seem to process BPA differently. So it remains uncertain to what extent a pregnant woman passes BPA to her fetus. However, if she does, her fetus does not have the necessary enzyme to process BPA.

In animal studies, fetal exposure to BPA is linked to a number of adverse health effects, including the incorrect sorting of chromosomes. A study of laboratory animals found that exposure to BPA prevented chromosomes from correctly lining up, resulting in an error in cell division that can cause spontaneous miscarriages and birth defects, including Down syndrome.[16]

Fetal exposure to BPA may increase the risk of developing breast cancer later in life. Based upon their laboratory studies, researchers found that the results suggest "that alterations in mammary gland phenotypes observed at puberty and adulthood" have their origins in fetal development for mice exposed in utero. The researchers concluded that exposure to BPA may be an underlying cause of the increased incidence of breast cancer in the U.S. and Europe over the last fifty years.[17]

Fetal BPA exposure may also disrupt fetal programming. Healthy development depends on genes being turned on and off at the right time. This process is known as gene expression. Which genes are turned on and off for certain tissues allows the specialization of tissues, although the tissues all contain the same genes. In a study involving agouti mice, BPA exposure below the current level of human exposure and the EPA's supposed safe level interfered with this process.

Other health effects associated with fetal exposure to BPA include a predisposition to obesity. Fetal exposure to BPA may also result in reproductive and ovarian abnormalities later in life. A study of mice found that fetal exposure to environmentally relevant BPA doses resulted in the presence of paraovarian cysts, fibroids, and increased polyps in the mice in middle age.[18]

Exposure to BPA during fetal development can cause changes that do not manifest themselves until much later in life. For example, one study found that prenatal exposure can cause genetic changes resulting in a greater risk of prostate cancer later in life. BPA exposure can affect the mom by altering the uterus, the developing fetus, and, if the fetus is a girl, her children because fetal BPA exposure disrupts normal egg-cell growth in the developing baby.

With BPA, it appears that the timing of the exposure may be critical. According to Randy Jirtle, BPA exposure very early in the pregnancy—probably before you even know you are pregnant—is the most sensitive period for interfering with gene expression. It was at this time of early development that his study determined that exposure to BPA would change the coat color of agouti mice. Tellingly, Jirtle states that "if I was a woman who was pregnant—or thinking about becoming pregnant—I would try hard to avoid exposure to BPA."

Exposure Levels: What Is Safe?

BPA's safety at the levels to which we are exposed is being hotly debated right now.[19] The plastics industry maintains that BPA use in food contact items is safe. But these assurances seem to be based on outdated studies and research. The industry points to, among other things, the EPA's oral reference dose, currently 50 micrograms of BPA per kilogram of body weight per day, which is much higher than the levels to which most of us are exposed. This reference dose was established in 1988, before scientific technology was even sufficiently developed to detect low doses leaching from plastics and before the first study was published showing ill health effects from low doses of BPA in 1997 (and there have been well over 100 such studies published since 1997).

The plastics industry also points to research studies, many of which also predate the development of scientific technology capable of measuring low concentration levels. For whatever reason, it seems like the studies funded by the chemical industry don't find health effects. An investigation by the *Journal Sentinel* looked at 258 studies and determined that four out of five found health effects. Of the studies that did not find any health effects, most were paid for by the chemical industry or were partially written by scientists funded by the chemical industry. The plastics and chemical industries have been accused of paying to manufacture doubt.

One of the problems is that BPA seems to be harmful at low doses, but not harmful at higher doses. This is contrary to conventional toxicology thought. We discussed previously the dose–response relationship and basic principles of toxicology. One of the more fundamental principles is "The dose makes the poison."[20] The typical example used to illustrate this is water. Water is necessary for us to live, but too much water can kill you. In fact, the principle "the dose makes the poison" is the basic premise behind our public health standards. The dose–response relationship is usually plotted as a rising straight line. We use this premise to specify maximum allowable concentrations of contaminants in our drinking water, food, environment, etc. But with BPA and other synthetic hormones, this might not be the case. An endocrinologist will explain that hormones usually stimulate their receptors at low doses, and at higher doses, the receptors can become saturated and "ignore" the messengers. So the dose may make the poison, but for an endocrine disruptor, it isn't necessarily true that the higher the dose, the greater the impact.

To attempt to resolve the debate, the National Institute of Environmental Health Sciences' National Toxicology Program recruited two expert panels to review the available research on BPA's reproductive and developmental effects. In 2007, these panels issued reports that offered somewhat contradictory opinions. The NTP reviewed the information from the two panels, as well as other information, and issued its final report in September 2008. The NTP uses a five-point scale of concern: negligible, minimal, some, concern, and serious. The final report on BPA found:

- The NTP has some concern for effects on the brain, behavior, and prostate gland in fetuses, infants, and children at current human exposures to BPA.
- The NTP has minimal concern for effects on the mammary gland and an earlier age for puberty for females in fetuses, infants, and children at current human exposures to BPA.
- The NTP has negligible concern that exposure of pregnant women to BPA will result in fetal or neonatal mortality, birth defects, or reduced birth weight and growth in their offspring.
- The NTP has negligible concern that exposure to BPA will cause reproductive effects in non-occupationally exposed adults and minimal concern for workers exposed to higher levels in occupational settings.

In connection with the report, NTP associate director John Bucher, Ph.D., stated, "There remains considerable uncertainty whether the changes seen in the animal studies are directly applicable to humans, and whether they would result in clear adverse health effects. But we have concluded that the possibility that BPA may affect human development cannot be dismissed."

The FDA has continued to maintain that BPA is safe. In August 2008, the FDA published a draft safety assessment finding that BPA as then in use for food contact items was safe. The safety assessment was widely criticized for relying on only two industry-funded studies and disregarding over 100 peer-reviewed animal studies involving low-dose exposure. So the FDA asked a subcommittee to review the draft BPA safety assessment.

The subcommittee issued a report denouncing the FDA's draft BPA safety assessment, finding that the FDA should not have excluded the scientific studies that it had excluded. The subcommittee stated that the FDA's approach "creates a false sense of security about the information that is used in the assessment . . . as it overlooks a wide range of potentially serious findings." In other words, the FDA created a false sense of security in the American public about BPA's safety.

The subcommitee's report criticizes the FDA's draft BPA safety assessment for, among other things:

- failing to consider the cumulative effects of being exposed to BPA from dozens of products, severely limiting the usefulness of the FDA's safety estimate (remember our discussion in Chapter 2 about risk assessments not reflecting all of our exposures?);

- failing to consider that parents heat baby bottles in the microwave and sterilize them with boiling water, thereby potentially increasing the rate of BPA leaching;
- relying on industry-funded studies that were not designed to study newborns;
- failing to include significant new reports; and
- excluding studies that should have been included.

The FDA's Science Advisory Board then unanimously endorsed the subcommittee's report. Now the FDA is requesting more research before it will take any steps.

And the industry? The American Chemistry Council responded to the NTP's report with the statement that "there is no direct evidence that exposure to bisphenol A adversely affects human reproduction or development."

So what can a parent do if the experts can't decide? Michael Shelby, Ph.D., director of the Center for the Evaluation of Risks to Human Reproduction stated, "If parents are concerned, they can make the personal choice to reduce exposures of their infants and children to BPA." My advice: With alternatives readily available, be safe rather than sorry. As Scott M. Belcher, Ph.D., associate professor at University of Cincinnati and lead researcher in BPA, says, "You have to estimate the relative benefit and understand the possible risks, or the fact that the risk is unclear because the science is lacking. There are many 'maybes' in the equation. But what is known is that BPA has estrogen-like activity." His conclusion? "Based on my knowledge of the scientific data, there is a reason for caution. I have made a decision for myself not to use polycarbonate plastic water bottles."[21]

Particularly troubling is that infant exposure to BPA may be more significant than adult exposure. Newborns do not metabolize BPA quickly because they express at low levels the liver enzyme needed to deactivate BPA.[22] The necessary liver enzyme is not expressed until after birth, with the full complement at three months, but at about 25 percent of the adult level.[23] Thus, fetal and infant exposure at critical development stages may cause significant health effects.

Personally, I didn't want to take a chance with my baby's health while the debate continued. I tried to stay away from BPA when I was trying to get pregnant, and chose BPA-free baby bottles. My son preferred Medela's bottles, which are made of polypropylene plastic. My daughter, on the other hand, liked the Playtex drop-in nurser (while the bottle is polycarbonate, the liner to which the breastmilk or formula is exposed is polyethylene). Many children's environmental health advocates and scientists are recommending that parents skip polycarbonate plastic bottles. If you don't want to wait for the conclusion of the debate and don't want to expose your baby to a potentially harmful chemical, there are options.

Bisphenol A: Smart Mama's Simple Steps to Reduce Exposure

Skip polycarbonate plastic. If you can, skip the polycarbonate plastic baby bottles. A number of baby bottles on the market are BPA-free, and more are becoming available. For the most part, these bottles are now clearly labeled as BPA free. Similarly, choose sippy cups and re-usable cups that are not made of polycarbonate plastic. Stainless steel is a great option for children and adults. Be careful of aluminum bottles because aluminum is lined, and that lining can contain BPA.

Recycle or replace scratched or worn bottles. If you can't get your baby to switch from his current bottle, make sure you replace any scratched or worn bottles. BPA leaching may be increased with worn or scratched bottles.

Don't heat. Never add boiling water to polycarbonate baby bottles. Adding boiling water and letting it cool will increase the leaching.

Skip polycarbonate packaging. Choose soups, milk, and soy milk packaged in cardboard "brick" cartons.

Can the cans. Choose fresh, frozen, dried, or glass-jarred over canned foods.

Breast Milk Storage Bags

With all of the concern over baby bottles, you might wonder about the safety of plastic breast milk storage bags. Most breast milk storage bags are made of polyethylene plastic. Polyethylene is considered a safer plastic than polycarbonate plastic and others. Polyethylene has a simple polymer structure and its monomer is not BPA like polycarbonate. Also, it does not require plasticizers like polyvinyl chloride plastic does. Studies have shown no leaching of chemicals from polyethylene plastic.

Even with this assurance of safety, you may still want to stop using plastic altogether. Polyethylene does use some additives, such as UV and heat stabilizers, and antioxidants. Polyethylene is also a petroleum product, and production of polyethylene bags contributes to air pollution and energy consumption. If you want a "greener" solution, you can use glass jars to store breast milk. Glass jars can withstand both cold and heat, so you can take them from the freezer and place them in hot water to thaw. Just be sure to leave room for expansion if you are freezing breast milk in glass jars.

Baby Bottle Nipples

Nipples for baby bottles are usually made of silicone or rubber, although I have heard reports of other plastics being used.

Choose bottle nipples made from silicone. They are the most durable and inert of the options. An added benefit, and a very helpful one for a sleep-deprived parent, is that silicone nipples can be thrown in the dishwasher to clean. If a silicone nipple gets torn or cracked, however, it should be thrown out. Cracks and tears provide surfaces on which bacteria can grow.

When purchasing silicone nipples, choose nipples made with medical-grade silicone. Although very rare, I have seen reports of contamination during manufacturing of lower grades of silicone. These contaminants are then present in the final product.

Latex rubber nipples tend to break down faster than silicone nipples, and this can provide cracks and fissures that allow bacteria to grow. Also, some infants who are allergic to latex may react to latex rubber nipples, although reaction to a latex rubber nipple is relatively rare.

Another potential problem with latex rubber nipples is the presence of volatile N-nitrosamines, a class of carcinogenic chemicals. After scientists found that rubber nipples leached nitrosamines into milk and infant formula, the FDA set standards for rubber nipples. The current standard is that the level of any individual volatile N-nitrosamine cannot exceed 10 pbb.[24]

There have been reports of nipples made from polyvinyl chloride (PVC) plastic. I haven't seen any on the market. But avoid PVC nipples. Not only can PVC be stabilized with lead or cadmium, PVC is softened with hormone-disrupting phthalates (see below).

Baby Bottle Nipples: Smart Mama's Simple Steps

Choose medical-grade silicone nipples. Medical-grade silicone nipples are the preferred choice to eliminate the potential exposure to volatile N-nitrosamines.

Discard cracked, torn, or worn nipples. Don't let bacteria grow.

Phthalates and PVC Plastic

Phthalates are added to polyvinyl chloride (PVC) plastic to make it soft and flexible. They can also be found in other products, such as synthetic fragrance and cosmetics (as discussed in Chapter 9). Phthalates may cause adverse health effects in children.

Phthalates are known developmental and reproductive toxicants in laboratory animals. Some of them are also endocrine disruptors. Baby boys seem to be particularly sensitive to the hormone-disrupting effects of phthalates, and phthalate exposure has been linked with the "feminization" of boys. Exposure to phthalates has been linked to lower sperm concentrations, reduced sperm motility, sperm-morphology changes, DNA breakage in sperm, and changes in levels of reproductive hormones in men and male infants. A recent comprehensive analysis of over 300 laboratory animal studies found that fetal exposure to hormone disruptors such as phthalates was also associated with females developing reproductive disease later in life. Exposure to phthalates may also cause thyroid problems in both men and women. Research has associated exposure to phthalates with asthma and other respiratory problems, rhinitis and eczema in children, and premature breast development in girls.

We are all exposed to phthalates. The Centers for Disease Control and Prevention (CDC) detected phthalates in urine samples from all but 12 of 2,790 people tested. And we are exposed to many different phthalates. Six or more phthalates were found in 84 percent of people tested. The Consumer Product Safety Improvement Act of 2008 banned six phthalates in children's toys and child-care articles (defined as products intended for children under the age of three that facilitate sleeping and eating) as of February 2009, but it will take awhile to see existing inventory replaced with phthalate-free products.

Baby Bibs

Although not a food storage item, baby bibs are used in the kitchen. What potential harm could result from a baby bib? Well, baby bibs made of or having a facing or backing made of PVC plastic can expose your baby to lead and phthalates.

PVC plastic must be stabilized to maintain its integrity. It is often stabilized with lead, although cadmium, organotin, and other compounds can be used. Lead compounds may also be added as pigment. Lead isn't bound up in the polymer, so it tends to migrate to the surface, especially when exposed to heat and friction. Once present on the surface, it can be picked up. As discussed in Chapter 4, exposure to lead can be harmful, especially for infants. Lead exposure is cumulative, so even though the amount of lead from a baby bib may be small, it is another exposure.

Several advocacy groups have published reports on testing of baby bibs, reporting elevated levels of lead. The Center for Environmental Health found that baby bibs with vinyl fronts purchased at Wal-Mart in 2006 and Toys R Us, Babies R Us, and Lisa Kline in 2007 had lead levels above 600 ppm.

The CPSC maintains that there is no risk of exposure from mouthing bibs in good condition. The CPSC only recommends that parents and caregivers discard bibs that are worn or have deteriorated. The CPSC warns that the amounts of lead could approach the level of concern if a baby swallows a piece of vinyl containing lead.[25] The recently enacted Consumer Product Safety Improvement Act of 2008 (CPSIA) should stop lead in vinyl bibs since it establishes a lead content limit for all children's products.

Another problem with vinyl baby bibs is that vinyl may contain phthalates that may cause adverse health effects in children. The CPSIA also banned certain phthalates in children's products effective February 2009. So after that date vinyl baby bibs should no longer include the banned phthalates. However, it is unclear what will be used in place of phthalates and how complete compliance with the law will be, especially as the retroactivity of this provision was only decided after litigation five days before the February 10, 2009, compliance date.

Baby Bibs: Smart Mama's Simple Steps

Skip PVC bibs. It is easy to find baby bibs that aren't made of or contain a facing of PVC plastic. If a bib says it is vinyl, then it has PVC plastic. Just skip it.

Melamine Dishes

Melamine has been in the news because of fears stemming from contaminated pet foods and contaminated milk products, including infant formula. In milk products, melamine powder is added to fool inspectors about the protein content of food items. These scares may cause you to question the safety of melamine dishes—those hard, lightweight, virtually unbreakable plastic plates and cups with cute pictures and bright patterns used for kids' tableware.

Yes, melamine dishes are made from the same melamine that has sickened thousands and killed a few babies in China who consumed infant formula contaminated with melamine, but it is a resin when used for tableware. Formaldehyde has been added to make melamine resin. The general consensus is that melamine dishes are safe. However, studies have shown low-level leaching of melamine and formaldehyde into foods, particularly when dishes are in visibly poor condition or weren't made properly.[26, 27]

Ceramics

Ceramics and other tableware can have glazes containing lead, which may leach into food. Lead-containing glazes may be found on earthenware, terracotta, porcelain, and ceramic wares. Lead may also be found in certain paints and decal-type decorations used on all tableware, including glass.

Lead can leach into food or drink, and then be ingested. Recently, a one-year-old had an elevated blood lead level that was traced to ceramic dinnerware without visible signs of wear.[28]

The U.S. Food and Drug Administration (FDA) has established limits on lead (and cadmium) in ceramic ware products in contact with food. The current standard has been in place since 1991. Ceramic ware products that do not meet this standard must be labeled that they are not intended for food use. Typically, the label will read "WARNING: NOT FOOD SAFE. Not intended for food contact. For decorative use only."

You can't determine the potential leaching of any particular piece without testing. However, certain pieces are more likely to leach lead:

- Pieces handed down from previous generations are more likely to leach lead. However, you may be able to get information on compliance with the lead standards, from the manufacturer.
- Homemade or handcrafted pieces are more likely to leach lead. If you are buying pieces from an artist, ask about the glaze used. Make sure a lead-free glaze and high-temperature, commercial firing practices were used.
- Latin American folk terra-cotta pottery has been found to have high lead content, and has been documented as a source of lead poisoning, primarily in Hispanic children. In fact, according to the California Childhood Lead Poisoning Prevention Branch, almost all terra-cotta folk pieces from Latin American contain heavily leaded glazes. The most common pieces are ollas, deep pots used for cooking beans; cazuelas, shallow, open pots used for cooking moles, stews, meat dishes, and rice; jarros, pitchers used to store and serve juices and other drinks; and cantaros (if glazed), used for water. But be careful of all pieces. A San Joaquin girl was poisoned from using small terra-cotta cups for her tea parties.[29]
- Certain highly decorated traditional dishes used in Asian communities have been found to have high lead content. The most common dishes found to leach high levels of lead are those with the Long Life/Four Seasons pattern and decoration on top of the glaze, or a rough, chalky feel to the piece.
- Pieces purchased in other countries and brought to the United States by private citizens in luggage are more likely to leach lead.
- Highly decorated, multi-colored inside surfaces are more likely to leach lead than white china that is not decorated. Of course, this is a generality. Many highly decorated patterns meet the federal and even the stricter California standards.

> **SMART MAMA WARNING**
>
> If you have a piece with corroded glaze, or a dusty- or chalky-looking residue on the glaze after the piece is washed, stop using it—these signs indicate lead. China in this condition could be very dangerous.

Lead in China: Smart Mama's Simple Steps to Reduce Exposure

Focus on your daily ceramic pieces. Make sure the ceramic pieces you use every day—your coffee mug, your baby's cereal bowl, and your everyday plates—are safe. Don't worry too much about Grandma's platter if you only use it once or twice a year, especially if you don't serve highly acidic food on it (see below).

Check your china. For pieces that you use regularly, if the dishes have been handed down, or if you are unsure about their origin, see if you can find out whether they meet the federal lead standard. Most should have a permanent identifiable mark for this very purpose. If you can't determine the manufacturer, consider the china "questionable" until you can get more information.

Choose glass, stoneware, or lead-free china. Glass (not leaded crystal) that is free of painted or decal-type decorations is almost always lead free. Stoneware that is not painted or does not have a decal-type decoration is also usually lead free. Lead-free china is also available.

Don't use questionable items regularly. Questionable ceramic ware pieces aren't for daily use.

Don't store food or drink in questionable items. If you don't know whether a piece is glazed with a lead-containing glaze, do not store food in the piece. The longer food remains in contact with a china surface containing lead, the more lead can be drawn into the food.

Don't heat questionable items in the microwave. Heat can also increase the rate of leaching.

Don't serve highly acidic food or drink in questionable ceramic pieces, especially to children. The rate of leaching is increased if the food or drink is acidic. To avoid exposure, never serve highly acidic food or drink in questionable items, especially to children. Acidic foods and drinks include cola-type soft drinks, orange and grapefruit juice, applesauce and apple juice, tomatoes and tomato-based products like ketchup and spaghetti sauce, salad dressings with vinegar, and tea and coffee.

Don't store acidic beverages in lead-glazed pitchers. The FDA advises consumers to avoid storing acidic beverages, such as fruit juices and iced tea, in lead-glazed pitchers because acidic beverages, even cold, have a greater tendency than other foods to cause leaching of lead.

Follow labels. This seems pretty simple. If an item has a label indicating that it is not intended for food use, don't use it for food. These labels mean that the item does not meet the FDA's limits for lead for food contact ceramic items.

Crystal and Glass

Ordinary glass does not contain lead, but some paint or decal-type decorations on glass contain lead. The federal standards for lead in food contact items don't apply to paint or decal-type decorations on glass items.

Lead crystal also may contain lead, just as the name implies. Lead crystal for ornaments and decorations is quite safe. The lead is bound into the glass. However, the lead can leach out when liquids are put into lead crystal. The leaching happens over time, so the real concern stems from storing food in lead glass containers, such as liquor in lead crystal decanters. Leaching is also accelerated by acidic solutions, so fruit juices, wines, and similar drinks should not be stored in lead crystal containers.

Lead Crystal and Decorated Glass: Smart Mama's Simple Steps to Reduce Exposure

Skip lead crystal decanters and pitchers. Don't store liquids in lead crystal bottles, decanters, or pitchers.

Don't drink daily from lead crystal. If you are pregnant or nursing, you should skip using lead crystal glasses as your daily glassware.

Don't feed infants from lead crystal. Although they may be beautiful or heirlooms, don't use lead crystal baby bottles, cups, or bowls to feed an infant.

Pewter

Pewter, especially antique pewter, can contain lead. Pewter is an alloy, usually consisting of mostly tin with the remainder being copper. Sometimes lead can be added, and is reported to give a bluish tint.

Libby McDonald writes in her book *The Toxic Sandbox* about her personal experience with lead. Her son had a lead blood count of 10 ug/dL, and she learned that the antique pewter bowl she used to feed her youngest was possibly the source of the lead.

But even new pewter may have lead. I tested some pewter items for a client and found lead. The items were wineglasses and cups purchased at a Renaissance fair. She had been assured that the items were lead free, but it turned out that wasn't quite accurate.

Pewter: Smart Mama's Simple Steps to Reduce Exposure

Don't store food or drink in antique pewter. Your antique pewter may be a family heirloom or recent find, but don't use it to store food or drink.

Don't feed your infant from pewter. Avoid using pewter to feed your infant—simple as that.

Pots and Pans

Stainless steel is a good choice for pots and pans. Some people have expressed concerns about the possible presence of chromium and/or nickel in stainless steel. Hexavalent chromium is linked to reproductive system effects and is a carcinogen. Nickel can cause respiratory problems and cancer when inhaled, although the most common effect is allergic reactions. Ten to twenty percent of the population is sensitive to nickel. It is believed that if the stainless steel is in good condition and of good quality, little risk of exposure of significant levels of nickel or chromium exists. People sensitive to nickel usually experience a reaction only with dermal exposure, and they'd have to eat very large amounts to suffer any reaction. If you do use stainless steel, make sure you do not use an abrasive cleaning pad and don't use it if it is in poor condition.

Cast iron is a good choice—it leaches small amounts of iron into food, which can actually help those with iron deficiencies. Cast iron enamelware is another option, although it is subject to chipping and scratching.

Aluminum pots and pans are very light and often inexpensive, but some can be reactive. Acidic or salty foods may discolor the aluminum and storing salty or acidic food in an aluminum pot will pit the metal surface and result in the food being contaminated. Some have expressed concerns about aluminum and its link to adverse health effects, including Alzehimer's disease, but anodized aluminum has been shown not to leach into food.

Non-Stick Cookware, Convenience Food Packaging, and Microwave Popcorn

Are you worried about toxic Teflon? Well, you may want to be more concerned with convenience food packaging and microwave popcorn when it comes to perfluorinated compounds.

Teflon uses a perfluorinated compound in its manufacture—namely, perfluorooctanoic acid (PFOA). Although PFOA is used as a processing aid in the manufacture of non-stick cookware, it does not appear to be present in cookware under ordinary cooking conditions. The Food and Drug Administration and industry claim that testing has shown PFOA present only when non-stick cookware has been ground up, a process unlikely to occur in most kitchens. However, studies have shown that fumes from overheated non-stick cookware have been known to kill household pet birds. Industry representatives contend that non-stick cookware will only release chemicals at temperatures above at least 500 degrees, but some environmental groups have demonstrated that that heated pans off-gas toxic chemicals at lower temperatures, as low as 325 degrees. Non-stick cookware used in the home may reach 325 degrees.

PFOA and related compounds have been shown to be unexpectedly toxic and bioaccumulative. In animal studies, PFOA has been shown to be toxic to the liver, development, and the immune system. It also disrupts the hormone system. Occupational data with highly exposed individuals has found increased risks of dying from prostate cancer and stroke.

Studies have found PFOA present in the blood of 95 percent of all Americans, although at low levels. Of more concern is that one study found that 96 percent of 598 children tested had PFOA in their blood. PFOA is also very persistent in the environment.

Researchers are currently investigating the source of PFOA and related compounds. Our primary source does not seem to be non-stick cookware, but grease- and stain-repellent coatings used on food packaging, clothing, upholstery fabrics, carpets, and other similar products. One animal study found that chemicals used to make oil- and water-repellent food packaging—polyfluoroalkyl phosphate surfactants—appear to break down to PFOA in the body. The study found that exposure to polyfluoroalkyl phosphate surfactants injected into animal digestive tracts resulted in elevated PFOA in the blood. Fluorinated telomer products are routinely used to coat fast-food packaging, such as McDonald's french-fry boxes, Chinese food takeout containers, pizza boxes, and microwave popcorn bags. Research into the migration of perfluoro coatings into foods is currently underway. Initial research suggests that microwave popcorn bags may offer one of the higher exposures. Microwave popcorn bags get very hot in a short time and the amount of fluorotelomers in the coatings is high. PFOA and related compounds cross the placenta, so you may want to reduce your exposure while pregnant.

PFOA: Smart Mama's Simple Steps for Reducing Exposure

Don't overheat. Don't overheat your non-stick cookware by letting it heat up without adding food. You don't want it to reach 325 degrees.

Don't use non-stick cookware that is in poor condition. If your non-stick cookware is scratched and worn, get rid of it.

Take food out of fast-food packaging. The longer food is in contact with coated packaging, the greater any leaching. So take food out of coated packaging. Take pizza out of pizza boxes quickly and serve on plates. If you have leftovers, store the pizza in a different container. Same with fast food, Chinese food, and any other products in containers with stain- and grease-repellent coatings.

Pop naturally. Skip the microwave popcorn and pop with air. Very retro.

Use alternate cookware. Ceramic and glass cookware are good choices for baking. And some really good perfluorinated chemical-free non-stick cookware is available on the market. For example, I really like Cuisinart's Green Gourmet non-stick. The technology involves a baked-on ceramic, and the packaging is very green—post-consumer recycled cardboard and soy ink.

Chapter 6

You Are What You Eat: Food and Beverages

In addition to the containers in which we store and serve our food, our food and drink, including water and breast milk, can contain harmful contaminants. Some chemicals reach our food and water supplies through pollution in the environment, while others are applied directly (such as pesticides). Some toxic chemicals, such as mercury, bioaccumulate, meaning that animals at the top of the food chain will have much higher concentrations because the chemical accumulates in fat and is passed up the food chain. Those larger animals farther up the food chain may, in turn, be a food source for us. We'll look at more specific examples of this as they apply in the text below. What is also alarming is that even chemicals that were banned decades ago still show up in the food chain and ultimately end up on our dining tables.

Pesticides in Food

Generally, at around six months, most parents begin to introduce solid foods to their babies. But introducing baby foods to your baby can also introduce your baby to pesticide residues on those foods. And these exposures may be more significant for children as opposed to adults. As noted earlier, on a body-weight basis, children are exposed to greater amounts of toxic chemicals because they eat, breathe, and drink more. It is estimated that a two-year-old drinking non-organic apple juice can be exposed to as many as eighty different pesticides, and her exposure to these pesticides is twenty times what her mother's is on a body-weight basis.[1]

Pesticides have been linked to numerous adverse health effects, including increased risk of cancer and neurological and reproductive disorders. The U.S. Environmental Protection Agency estimates that 80 percent of our pesticide exposure comes from our diet, and the remaining 20 percent comes from pesticides in our drinking water and used in and around our homes.

A study of school-age children found that eating conventional foods resulted in exposure to organophosphates. Low-dose exposure to organophosphate pesticides has been associated with adverse effects on brain development and behavior in animal studies. Switching these children to an organic diet resulted in no pesticide markers being detected in the children's urine and saliva eight to thirty-six hours after the switch to organic was made. The study's principal author, Chensheng Lu, notes that "the transformation is extremely rapid. Once you switch from conventional food to organic, the pesticides (malathion and chlorpyrifos) that we can measure in the urine disappears. The level returns immediately when you go back to the conventional diets."[2]

The EPA maintains that dietary exposure to pesticides is safe for the U.S. population, including infants. However, many health advocates disagree, contending that the EPA's pesticide tolerance limits aren't sufficient to fully protect our children.

Buying organic can be expensive. Because there are some fruits and vegetables that tend to have higher pesticide residues, the Environmental Working Group (EWG) and *Consumer Reports* have issued recommendations for what products to buy organic. The combined lists are:

Strawberries
Raspberries
Apples
Grapes (and raisins) (if imported)
Peaches
Nectarines
Apricots
Pears
Cherries
Lemons (if zesting)
Potatoes
Corn
Cucumbers
Spinach
Lettuce
Green and red bell peppers
Green beans
Limes (if zesting)
Bananas
Kiwis
Pineapples (depends on source)
Cantaloupe (from Mexico)

Other products that you should buy organic are rice, milk and dairy products, and eggs. Most children's health advocates recommend that you always buy organic jarred baby food.

What Is "Organic"?

The USDA National Organic Program defines the term "organic" as follows:

> Organic food is produced by farmers who emphasize the use of renewable resources and the conservation of soil and water to enhance environmental quality for future generations. Organic meat, poultry, eggs, and dairy products come from animals that are given no antibiotics or growth hormones. Organic food is produced without using most conventional pesticides; fertilizers made with synthetic ingredients or sewage sludge; bioengineering; or ionizing radiation. Before a product can be labeled "organic," a Government-approved certifier inspects the farm where the food is grown to make sure the farmer is following all the rules necessary to meet USDA organic standards. Companies that handle or process organic food before it gets to your local supermarket or restaurant must be certified, too.

Pesticides in Foods: Smart Mama's Simple Steps to Reduce Exposure

Got organic? Switch to organic foods certified organic by the USDA. Organic means that the food is grown without the use of pesticides, synthetic fertilizers, sewage sludge, genetically modified organisms, or ionizing radiation. Because pesticides are so ubiquitous in our environment, even organic foods may have some pesticide residues, but you can lower your pesticide exposure from your foods by going organic.

Wash your food. Washing your food with water and a brush or washcloth can reduce pesticide residue on the food's surface. This can remove surface residues, but not those residues absorbed in the food.

Eat a varied diet. Introduce your baby to a wide variety of foods, following the recommendations of your pediatrician. By eating a wide variety of foods you eliminate the risk of overexposure to a pesticide residue found in any one food.

Mercury

Tuna fish sandwiches are relatively easy to prepare and can be a great part of a healthy diet. But along with the tuna in that sandwich, your toddler might get a potentially harmful dose of mercury. Mercury can also harm fetal development because it passes across the placenta and can be passed through breast milk (see later in this chapter).

Mercury is a trace element that occurs naturally in the environment, but it is now a widespread pollutant. Human activities have increased the amount of mercury present in our environment by as much as a factor of five.[3] Sources in the United States include coal-fired power plants (mercury occurs naturally in coal), waste incinerators that burn products containing mercury such as batteries and fluorescent bulbs, and chlor-alkali plants. Coal-fired power plants and municipal and medical waste incinerators burning mercury-containing trash account for 85 percent of the mercury pollution released in the United States each year.[4] These sources release over 150 tons of mercury per year into the atmosphere.[5] Historically, mercury was added to paints to control mildew, used to kill weeds, and used to prepare felt for hats (yes, that may be the source of the phrase "mad as a hatter"). In the home, schools, and day-care facilities, mercury can be found in fluorescent lights, thermostats, and thermometers.

Most of the mercury in our atmosphere is elemental mercury vapor. Wind can carry mercury for thousands of miles from its original emission source. Even though it is far removed from any mercury emission source, the Arctic has high mercury concentrations. Mercury is generally removed from the atmosphere by rain or snow (although dry deposition does occur), and is deposited onto land and into rivers, lakes, and oceans.

In the water, microorganisms convert mercury to methylmercury (or organic mercury). Fish absorb methylmercury as the water passes over their gills and when they eat smaller aquatic organisms. Methylmercury accumulates in fatty tissues and is excreted slowly so that it tends to concentrate in an organism, meaning it bioaccumulates. Methylmercury also biomagnifies in the food chain so that fish species at the top of the food chain, the longer-lived predatory fish species, have the highest concentrations of mercury. In fact, methylmercury is so efficiently bioaccumulated and biomagnified that fish at the top of the food chain can have levels of mercury in their muscle tissue one million times higher than the mercury concentration in the water in which they swim.

Although mercury exists in many forms, including the elemental mercury discussed in the sidebar, methylmercury is the most toxic form to which most

Magical Mercury

Elemental mercury is used in the United States in ceremonial and religious rituals in certain Afro-Caribbean, Latin American, and New Age practices, including Santeria, Palo, voodoo, and Espiritismo. *Botanicas,* stores specializing in herbal remedies and religious items, have been found to sell mercury. A 1995 survey of New York *botanicas* found that thirty-eight of forty-one reported selling mercury, at a rate of one to four capsules per day. Other surveys have similarly reported high percentages of *botanicas* selling mercury.

Mercury is the only metal that is liquid at room temperature. It slowly vaporizes at room temperature, and more quickly when heated. Elemental mercury vapors are toxic when breathed. Also, elemental mercury can enter the body through skin pores when handled, such as when a broken thermometer is improperly cleaned up.

In *botanicas,* mercury is typically sold in a small capsule, often without any warning labeling. Mercury is reported to bring luck in love, wealth, or health; attract luck; and ward against evil. It can be carried on a person as an amulet. It may also be sprinkled in the home. Other reported uses of mercury are burning it in a candle, mixing it with perfume, adding it to face cream, or sprinkling it in a car.

But mercury's use in ceremonial or religious practices, often in an enclosed space or carried on a person, combined with the fact that small amounts of mercury can remain for long periods of time, create the potential for very high direct exposures to individuals. Mercury's use in ceremonial or religious practices can also result in the home becoming contaminated with mercury. This can impact not only the current residents, but also future residents. And those living nearby may also be affected, particularly in multi-unit buildings with common areas.

of us are exposed. Even at low doses, methylmercury is toxic. When methylmercury is ingested, it is absorbed into the bloodstream.

Adults and children are primarily exposed to methylmercury through diet. The body absorbs approximately 90 to 100 percent of the methylmercury ingested. Methylmercury contamination is pervasive in fish and shellfish, and fish species matters. As noted, long-lived predatory fish, such as swordfish, shark, tilefish, and king mackerel, tend to have high concentrations of mercury. And so does tuna, particularly albacore canned tuna.

The EPA and the United States Food and Drug Administration (FDA) have recommended guidelines for fish consumption for pregnant women, nursing mothers, and young children (see below) because of mercury contamination. Even so, some environmental health advocates challenge these guidelines, contending that EPA's reference dose is too high and should be lowered to be more protective of children's health. One reported study found that children exposed to methylmercury from fish at doses below the current EPA reference dose nevertheless showed some adverse effects on brain function.[6]

Mercury and Pregnancy

If a pregnant woman ingests mercury, she passes it to her developing fetus because it easily crosses the placenta. Fetal exposure to high doses of mercury can cause mental retardation and problems with gait and vision. You are unlikely to be exposed to high levels of mercury, barring unusual circumstances. But low levels of mercury exposure may also cause harm. Fetal exposure to low levels of mercury can cause impairment of language, attention, and memory. Mercury is a developmental neurotoxicant, meaning that it may directly interfere with the processes required for normal brain development.

SMART MAMA SCARY FACT

At least 240,000 babies born each year are at risk of learning disabilities resulting from fetal exposure to mercury.

The developing fetal nervous system is highly sensitive to methylmercury.[7] The National Academy of Sciences (NAS) concluded that the population with the highest risk to mercury exposure is the offspring of women of childbearing age who consume large amounts of fish and seafood during pregnancy. The NAS states that "the risk to that population is likely to be sufficient to result in an increase in the number of children who have to struggle to keep up in school and who might require remedial classes or special education."[8]

Methylmercury enters the fetal brain and causes abnormal DNA and RNA synthesis.[9] At low fetal doses, methylmercury interferes with brain development and can lead to neurological diseases and developmental problems, including delayed language development, impaired memory and vision, impaired IQ and learning disabilities, impaired motor skills, and attention deficit disorders.[10] The NAS reports that chronic, low-dose prenatal methylmercury exposure from maternal consumption is associated with poor performance on neurobehavioral tests, particularly on tests of attention, fine-motor function, language, visual-spatial abilities, and verbal memory.[11]

Elevated levels of mercury in pregnant women may also put them at risk of delivering their babies preterm.[12]

It is well established that we are exposed to methylmercury. The United States Centers for Disease Control and Prevention's National Health and Nutrition Examination Survey (NHANES) analysis of blood samples from women of childbearing age (women between the ages of sixteen and forty-nine) found that approximately 6 percent had blood mercury concentrations above 5.8 micrograms per liter whole blood (or 5.8 parts per billion [ppb]).[13,14] A mercury blood level above 5.8 ppb exceeds the EPA's reference dose, the dose at which it is assumed that no appreciable harm occurs. But this isn't a safe level (although it was established with a safety factor of 10). With this mercury exposure level, approximately 240,000 babies per year are at an increased risk of learning disabilities due to fetal exposure to methylmercury. This risk is based upon maternal blood mercury levels, not umbilical cord blood mercury concentrations. Fetal blood actually contains *more* mercury than maternal blood, approximately 1.7 times more than the maternal mercury level.

The EPA contends that it takes the difference into account in the uncertainty factor of 10 applied to derive the reference dose. However, the EPA's senior researcher on mercury hazards until August 2008, Dr. Kathyrn Mahaffey, has asserted that the maternal mercury blood level should be adjusted to reflect this difference between maternal blood mercury levels and cord blood mercury levels. She argues that since fetal blood contains 1.7 times more mercury than maternal blood, the maternal mercury blood level at which no appreciable harm occurs should instead be 3.5 ppb (5.8 ppb divided by 1.7).[15] According to Dr. Mahaffey, this would mean that approximately 410,000 babies are born every year at risk for learning disabilities as a result of maternal mercury exposure. Dr. Mahaffey has been criticized by the fish industry for overstating the potential risk. And, I must tell you, it is controversial to link maternal exposure to low levels of mercury to fetal harm from mercury.

Another factor to consider is that mercury and polychlorinated biphenyls (PCBs) exposure may interact to magnify adverse effects on fetal neurological development.[16] If the combination of exposure to PCBs and mercury does magnify the adverse health effects, the consumption advisories based solely on mercury exposure are flawed. It also highlights the fallacy of relying on risk assessment that considers only a single chemical to determine safety. (PCBs are discussed later in this chapter.)

A study found even more women—approximately 23 percent of women of childbearing age—potentially at risk for exposing their babies to levels of mercury above the EPA's reference dose using hair samples as opposed to blood samples.

> **SMART MAMA TIP**
>
> Test your hair for mercury. If you are interested in testing you hair to determine your mercury body burden, you can order test kits from the Sierra Club. Each test kit costs $25.

All of this may be a little confusing. Blood levels, hair levels—how do you know what is safe? Ultimately, my own conclusion from this information was that I didn't want to take the risk. If I could reduce my body burden of mercury before I got pregnant and thereby reduce the amount of mercury to which my baby would be exposed, why not do it?

With all of this information, you may elect to forgo eating fish at all to avoid mercury exposure. That seems like a pretty easy solution, and I actually did it in connection with one of my pregnancies. But there are benefits to eating fish as well, ones you need to consider before forgoing fish altogether. And some scientists maintain that the benefits from eating fish outweigh the potentially speculative risks from mercury exposure.

What are the benefits? Fish are a source of beneficial omega-3 fatty acids. Certain of these omega-3 fatty acids may reduce the risk of coronary heart disease, but there is a more important benefit to pregnant women. The omega-3 fatty acids, especially docosahexaenoic acid (DHA), appear to be particularly important during fetal development. They support the developing brain. DHA and another fatty acid, linoleic acid, make up more than a third of the fatty acids in the brain and the retina. During pregnancy, especially in the last trimester, fatty acids accumulate in the fetal brain and eyes. Babies born to mothers with DHA-deficient diets have exhibited behavioral problems and abnormal visual acuity, so getting enough omega-3 fatty acids is critical during pregnancy. The NAS, after extensively reviewing the data, concluded that Americans should eat more fish, but should vary their choices and avoid certain fish species because of mercury contamination (see box).

Balancing the benefits and the risks, the key Smart Mama's Simple Step to reduce mercury exposure is to be selective about the fish you eat.

FDA and EPA Advisory for Fish Consumption

The Food and Drug Administration (FDA) and the Environmental Protection Agency (EPA) advise women who may become pregnant, pregnant women, nursing mothers, and young children to avoid some types of fish and eat fish and shellfish that are lower in mercury:

- Do not eat shark, swordfish, king mackerel, or tilefish because they contain high levels of mercury.

- Eat up to twelve ounces (two average meals) a week of a variety of fish and shellfish that are lower in mercury.
  - Five of the most commonly eaten fish that are low in mercury are shrimp, canned light tuna, salmon, pollock, and catfish.
  - Another commonly eaten fish, albacore (white) tuna has more mercury than canned light tuna. So, when choosing your two meals of fish and shellfish, you may eat up to 6 ounces (one average meal) of albacore tuna per week.
- Check local advisories about the safety of fish caught by family and friends in your local lakes, rivers, and coastal areas. If no advice is available, eat up to six ounces (one average meal) per week of fish you catch from local waters, but don't consume any other fish during that week.

Mercury in Tuna

Although tuna isn't the most heavily mercury contaminated fish, it is the most widely consumed in the United States. Tuna is big business. It is the nation's second most popular seafood. So warnings, advisories, and regulations about mercury in tuna are a big issue. Canned albacore tuna typically has higher concentrations of mercury than canned light because canned light tuna is usually made from skipjack. The FDA/EPA recommendation for consumption of canned light tuna over canned albacore (or white) tuna is based upon the average concentration of mercury found in canned tuna. But some environmental health groups contend that following the recommendations for consumption of canned tuna could result in consumption of mercury above the recommended reference dose because of the variability in mercury concentrations.

Consumer Reports reported in July 2006 that its review of the FDA's test results for canned tuna found that some samples of canned light tuna had more mercury than the average for canned albacore tuna, some as high as twice as much. *Consumer Reports* reported that the source may be yellowfin tuna, which generally has more mercury than skipjack. Approximately 15 percent of canned light tuna is made from yellowfin.[17]

Consumer Reports recommends that pregnant women skip canned tuna entirely because of the uncertainty about the amount of mercury. *Consumer Reports* also recommended that pregnant women also skip Chilean bass, American lobster, halibut, and Spanish mackerel.

And is the FDA's recommendation even safe? It was reported that an FDA official stated at a public meeting that the FDA classified canned light tuna as low in mercury to "keep market share at a reasonable level."[18]

Mercury in Folk Remedies

In addition to diet, your children can be exposed to mercury by using or ingesting some traditional or folk remedies. In Chinese folk medicine, the coating of traditional pills called "dan" is most often made with cinnabar, which contains mercury. The following traditional or folk remedies have been found to contain elevated levels of mercury:[19]

Traditional or Folk Remedies That May Have Mercury

Product Name	Uses	Origin Country
An gong niu huang wan	Spasms, stroke, seizure	China
An kung niu huan wan	High fever	China
An shen bu nao pian (or Ansenpunaw tablets)	Neurasthenia, Ménière's syndrome, hyperthyroidism	China
Azoque	Stomach ailments	Mexico
Bai zi yang xin wan (or Pai tze yang hsin wan)	Neurasthenia with chills, palpitations	China
Bao ying dan	High-grade fever, acute pneumonia, bronchitis	China
Bezoar sedative pills	Sleeping aid	China
Ci zhu wan	Kidney/heart disharmony, epileptic seizures	China
Emperor's tea pill (or Tian huang bu xin wan)	Maintain body's natural balance, "promote concentration and relaxation," insomnia, restlessness, anxiety, palpitations, vivid dreaming	China
Fufang luhui jiaonang	Constipation	China
Hepatico extract (Shu gan wan)	Healthy liver and regularity	China
Hu po bao long wan (or Po lung yuen medical pills)	Acute bronchitis, pneumonia, epidemic encephalitis, high-grade fever associated with measles	Hong Kong
Jeu wo dan	Cast dressing	China
Jian nao wan (or healthy brain pills)	Ménière's syndrome	China

Kweiling chi super tonic	Impotency, nocturnal emissions, anemia, lassitude, poor appetite, weakness after childbirth	
Lu shen wan	Sore throat	China
Mahalakshmi vilas ras with gold	Cold symptoms, blood deficiency, wound healing, asthma	India
Maha yograj guggul	Musculo-skeletal disorders	India
Mahayograj guggulu with silver and Makardhwaj	Rheumatic pain, bile, pigmentation disorders, blood purification, eye problems, weakness	India
Maja sudarshan	Flu, body aches	India
Nardiya or Lakshmivilash ras	Chronic fever, cold, cough	India
Navratna rasa	General debility, rickets, calcium deficiency	India
Niu huang xiao yan Wan/bezoar antiphlogistic pills	High fever	China
Qi li san	Skin infections	China
Qing fen	Cast dressing	China
Sha hee pills	Good health	China
She dan chen pi san	Pneumonia, bronchitis, whooping cough	China
Swarna mahaograj guggulu with gold	Rheumatism, gas, menstrual cycles, progesterone deficiency, fertility	India
Tse koo choy	Respiratory problems	China
Xi gua shuang (or water melon frost)	Mouth diseases, burns	China
Zhui fen tou gu wan/zhiufeng tongu wan	Bone ailments, joint paint, numbness	China
Zhu sha an shen wan (or Cinnabar sedative pill)	Depression, hysteria	China
Zi jin ding	Pediatric pneumonia and bronchitis, heat stroke, skin infection	China

Mercury: Smart Mama's Simple Steps to Reduce Exposure

Reduce your mercury body burden. Before you get pregnant, you may want to lower your mercury level. Methylmercury has a half-life of approximately forty-five to seventy days in the body,[20] the half-life being the amount of time required to eliminate one-half of a quantity of chemical from the body. So, assuming no additional exposure to mercury occurs, you can eliminate the bulk of mercury in your body in about four to five months. Although, if the body converts methylmercury to inorganic mercury in the brain, then the mercury can remain for a much longer period of time.

One fish, two fish, do fish, don't fish. The concentration of mercury varies significantly across seafood species. Generally speaking, the longer-lived, predatory fish species have higher concentrations of mercury. To determine your mercury dosage from any particular fish, you need to consider your body weight, the fish species, the amount of mercury present in the fish, and the amount of fish you consume. Low-mercury species include wild salmon (Alaska) or canned salmon, shrimp (U.S. farmed or pink Oregon), clams, tilapia (U.S.), oysters, hake, sardines, crawfish, pollock, herring, flounder, sole (Pacific), mullet, scallops (farmed), crab, farmed striped bass, and Atlantic mackerel. Fish with high levels include king mackerel, marlin, orange roughy, shark, swordfish, tilefish, bigeye, tuna, and ahi tuna.

If you eat canned tuna, choose canned light tuna. If you are going to eat canned tuna, choose canned light over albacore tuna. Canned light has lower amounts of mercury because it is usually skipjack. Make sure your canned light doesn't have yellowfin tuna in it, which has mercury levels similar to albacore. "Gourmet" or "tonno" on the canned light tuna may signal that yellowfin tuna is used. Another option is to buy canned tuna from some of the canneries that are using a mercury screening concentration lower than the FDA's level of 1 ppm.

Better choice: use canned salmon. Canned salmon is usually sockeye or pink from Alaska—low in contaminants, high in omega-3 fatty acids, and sustainably caught.

Seek out other sources of omega-3 fatty acids. Alternate sources of omega-3 fatty acids include flax seed, canola oil, kiwifruit, lingonberry, walnuts, grass-fed beef, milk and cheese from grass-fed cows, and certain boutique eggs. You may also want to consider a fish oil supplement. Just make sure that it is screened for mercury. The Environmental Defense Fund has an evaluation of various suppliers of fish oil.

Skip folk remedies that may contain mercury. The list in this section identifies folk remedies that have been found to have elevated levels of mercury.

Avoid using elemental mercury. Skip the elemental mercury if possible in ceremonies and rituals.

Skip dental amalgam. If you are pregnant, or for your children, you may want to skip using silver if a cavity needs to be filled. A silver filling is usually 50 percent mercury. Elemental mercury is released from the filling as a vapor. Mercury released from dental fillings and drilling results in exposure, including the fetus's exposure if you are pregnant. The FDA finally admitted in 2007 that mercury in dental fillings may be harmful to pregnant women, children, fetuses, and people sensitive to mercury exposure. The FDA states that "dental amalgams contain mercury, which may have neurotoxic effects on the nervous system of developing children and fetuses." One option is to opt for a resin filling, but make sure it doesn't contain bisphenol A. If this isn't an option, have the dentist take precautions to reduce mercury exposure, including using lots of cold water irrigation to minimize heat and a rubber dam to isolate the rest of the mouth.[21]

Polychlorinated Biphneyls

Polychlorinated biphenyls (PCBs) are a group of chlorinated compounds that have been banned in the United States since 1977. However, PCBs are still present in some electrical transformers and are present in landfills and hazardous waste sites. PCBs don't burn easily and are good insulators, so they were widely used as coolants and lubricants in transformers, capacitors, and other electrical equipment, and as insulating materials in electrical transformers, fluorescent lighting fixtures, and electrical appliances. PCBs were also used as stabilizers in polymers, paint, and adhesives, as flame retardants, in cutting oils, in hydraulic fluids, in sealants such as caulking, in wood floor finishes, and in carbonless copy paper.

Although PCBs have been banned in the United States, they may still be released to the environment from hazardous waste sites; illegal or improper disposal of industrial wastes and consumer products; leaks from old electrical transformers containing PCBs; and burning of some wastes in incinerators. Some environmental experts believe at least 75 percent of PCBs are yet to be released to the environment.

Unfortunately, PCBs do not readily break down in the environment. They are classified as persistent organic pollutants. PCBs can travel far from where they are released. In water, PCBs tend to stick to organic particles and bottom sediments. They bind strongly to soil. They are still the most abundant pollutants in wildlife and humans.

Persistent organic pollutants (POPs) are organic compounds that resist being broken down in the environment by photolytic, biological, or chemical means. They bioaccumulate in fatty tissues.

PCBs bioaccumulate in animals. They are taken up by small organisms and fish in water. They are also taken up by other animals that eat these aquatic animals as food. PCBs biomagnify up the food chain (like mercury in predatory fish, as we discussed earlier).

Children's main source of exposure to PCBs is eating contaminated food, particularly fish or wildlife caught from contaminated locations. In the Great Lakes area, consumption of PCB-contaminated fish has been associated with a higher PCB body burden in that area. The levels of PCBs in fish from the Great Lakes area are much higher than fish caught in most other areas. Children exposed to elevated PCB levels have lower IQ and exhibit more anti-social behavior, depression, and attention deficit hyperactivity–type disorders.

PCBs and Pregnancy

PCBs cross the placenta. PCBs and PCB metabolites are transferred at concentrations of 30 percent and 50 percent, respectively, of maternal levels.[22] Research indicates that fetal exposure to high levels of PCBs may result in low birth weight. But the more serious problem with fetal exposure to PCBs is that PCBs can affect the developing fetal brain. Although the mechanisms are not fully understood, PCBs' toxicity to the fetal brain may be because PCBs inhibit the maternal thyroid gland, proper function of which is essential for normal fetal brain development. By inhibiting the maternal thyroid gland, PCBs reduce the thyroid hormone available for the fetus. Fetal exposure to relatively low levels of PCBs may result in poor reading comprehension, lower IQ, shortened attention span, hyperactivity, impairment of higher cognitive functions and learning, neurodevelopmental delays, adverse effects on motor skills, and memory problems. Fetal exposure to PCBs may also adversely affect the immune system. PCBs are also suspected human carcinogens and some are endocrine disruptors, meaning that they mimic estrogen in the body.

The same Smart Mama's Simple Steps for reducing kids' exposure to PCBs work for pregnant women.

PCBs: Smart Mama's Simple Steps to Reduce Exposure

Do fish, don't fish. Certain fish are known to have high concentrations of PCBs. So, just as with mercury, seafood species matters. Skip alewife, striped wild bass, blue fish, white croaker, American and European eel, shad, imported wild sturgeon, bluefin tuna, and weakfish. You should limit your intake of Atlantic croaker, summer flounder, winter flounder, opah, and farmed salmon.

Follow fish and wildlife advisories. Certain states, Native American tribes, and U.S. territories have issued advisories to warn people about consuming PCB-contaminated fish and fish-eating wildlife caught in certain areas. These advisories should be followed to reduce exposure to PCBs.

Prepare fish to minimize exposure. PCBs are present in the fatty tissues, so you can reduce exposure by preparing fish to eliminate or reduce ingestion of fatty tissues. (This doesn't work for mercury, since mercury is present in fish muscle.) To prepare the fish, clean and gut the fish you catch before cooking it because some chemicals, including PCBs, tend to concentrate in the organs, particularly in the liver. Trim the fat, remove the skin, and fillet the fish before cooking. Fat is located along the back and the belly, and in the dark meat along the lateral line running along the side of the fish. Skinning fish will remove the thin layer of fat under the skin. Skin removal reduces exposure from PCBs in the fish by approximately 25 percent. Use a cooking method, such as baking or grilling, that allows the juices to drain away, and then discard the cooking juices.[23]

Eat lean. PCBs accumulate in fatty tissues. So eating a lean diet, including low-fat and non-fat dairy products, can reduce exposure to PCBs.

Go grass. Grass-fed, that is. Grass-fed beef has significantly lower amounts of PCBs.

Dioxins

Polychlorinated dibenzo-para-dioxins (dioxins) and the related polychlorinated dibenzofurans (furans) are some of the most toxic chemicals known. But they are not intentionally produced. Instead, they are by-products of various chemical, manufacturing, and combustion processes including: production of certain pesticides; paper pulp bleaching; production of certain dyes and pigments; municipal waste, sewage-sludge and hospital-waste incineration; polyvinyl chloride plastic (PVC) production and incineration; diesel-engine exhaust; accidental fires and explosions of chlorine-containing material; metal production; and combustion of wood.

Like PCBs, dioxins are persistent organic pollutants. They bioaccumulate and biomagnify up the food chain. Dioxins and furans are widely distributed in our environment. Although dioxins and furans can be found in areas with little to no industry, higher levels are most commonly found in and around industrial areas.

The health effects of dioxins became widely publicized due to the use of Agent Orange during the Vietnam War. The most toxic dioxin—2,3,7,8-tetrachlorodibenzo-p-dioxin (TCDD), a known carcinogen—is a by-product of one of the components of Agent Orange, and is present as a contaminant in any of the herbicides that contained it.

Dioxins have been found in the general population at or close to levels associated with adverse health effects. Exposure to dioxins even at very low concentrations may seriously disrupt reproduction in humans. Exposure to dioxins has been linked with lower fertility, reduced sperm counts, inability to maintain pregnancy, and increased risk of endometriosis.

Dioxins and Pregnancy

Dioxins can cross the placenta. Exposure to dioxins is more significant in early development than exposure as an adult. Laboratory animal studies demonstrate that fetal rodents are more susceptible to adverse effects of TCDD and other dioxins than adult rodents. Fetal exposure to dioxins increases prenatal mortality, lowers birth weight, alters immune function, and affects neurobehavioral function. Dioxins apparently interfere with the production and function of many different hormones, growth factors, and enzymes.

We are exposed to dioxins and furans in a number of ways. Our primary exposure is eating contaminated food, primarily meat, dairy products, and fish. Ingestion of contaminated food accounts for 90 percent of our exposures to dioxins. Fatty foods usually contain more significant levels of dioxins because the animals are higher on the food chain and thus have accumulated more dioxin. On average, the total daily intake of exposure to dioxins breaks down as follows: eating beef (38 percent), eating dairy products (24.1 percent), drinking milk (17.6 percent), eating chicken (12.9 percent), eating pork (12.2 percent), eating fish (7.8 percent), eating eggs (4.1 percent), inhalation (2.2 percent), and soil ingestion (0.8 percent).

Dioxins and Furans: Smart Mama's Simple Steps to Reduce Exposure

Eat lean. Dioxins accumulate in fatty tissues, so eating lean will reduce your exposure. Eat leaner meat and low-fat or non-fat dairy products. Skim milk has virtually no dioxins because it has virtually no fat. Poultry has a lower concentration than beef.

Skip farmed fish. Farmed fish tends to have higher concentrations of dioxins because of the diet given to them.

Go Green and Prevent Dioxin Releases

To reduce the amount of dioxins released to our environment, go green and buy products that don't use chlorine bleach. The process of chlorine bleaching—in everything from paper to tampons—releases dioxins. So look for products that aren't bleached with chlorine.

Breast Milk

Breast milk is best for babies. It is perfectly designed to provide for their needs, and then some. The American Academy of Pediatrics advocates breast-feeding as the optimal form of nutrition for infants. Babies who are breast-fed get a healthy head start over formula-fed babies. But toxic chemicals can be passed to your infant through your breast milk. So if you are breast-feeding, what you eat, drink, and put on your skin is critical.

I don't mean to inject fear into one of the most intimate acts between a mother and her baby. I always hesitate before I start talking about chemicals in breast milk because I don't want to scare any new mom so much that she elects not to breast-feed her child. You may not breast-feed for lots of reasons, but the reason shouldn't be because of toxic chemicals in your breast milk (unless, of course, a doctor has advised you not to breast-feed because of certain conditions). Yes, there are chemicals in your breast milk, but that doesn't mean you should stop breast-feeding. Simply put, babies who nurse do better than babies who don't. It has been postulated by scientists that breast milk may help protect babies against environmental chemical exposures.

So before talking about toxic chemicals that are likely passed to your baby through your breast milk, let me emphasize that breast milk is best suited to nourish infants and protect them from illnesses. "There are 4,000 species of mammals, and they all make a different milk. Human milk is made for human infants and it meets all their specific nutrient needs," says Ruth Lawrence, M.D., professor of pediatrics and obstetrics at the University of Rochester School of Medicine in Rochester, New York, and spokeswoman for the American Academy of Pediatrics.[24]

It is well established that breast-fed babies have lower rates of hospital admissions, ear infections, diarrhea, rashes, allergies, and other medical problems than bottle-fed babies. According to the American Academy of Pediatrics, strong evidence indicates that babies fed breast milk have a lower incidence of bacterial meningitis, respiratory tract infection, urinary tract infection, bacteremia, and otitis media.[25] Studies also suggest decreased rates of sudden infant death syndrome in the first year of life and reduction in Type 1 and Type 2 diabetes mellitus, lymphoma, leukemia, Hodgkin's disease, and asthma.[26]

Breast milk contains the necessary balance of proteins, fats, carbohydrates, vitamins, and minerals for a developing infant, geared specifically for a human infant.[27] Breast milk also helps by passing antibodies. Antibodies are made by your body's immune system specifically to help you fight each illness. Infants have immature immune systems and less ability to fight illness-causing germs, and breast milk allows a mom to pass her antibodies to her baby. Nursing also allows a baby to give her mom her germs so that her mom's immune system can respond and synthesize the necessary antibodies. Next time her baby nurses, her mom will give the baby the antibodies she needs to fight off those pesky germs.

Breast milk also contains essential fatty acids. These fatty acids help with cognitive function and vision. In other words, breast milk impacts the growth of the central nervous system and gives the brain a boost. Studies have found that premature infants who received human milk via a feeding tube were more advanced developmentally at eighteen months and at seven to eight years of age than those of comparable gestational age and birth weight who had received infant formula by tube. These benefits are believed to be attributed to the presence of certain fatty acids, docosahexaenoic acid (DHA), and arachidonic acid (ARA). Infant formulas have added these ingredients, but it is unknown whether their presence in infant formula will provide the same benefit (we'll cover DHA and ARA later).

Nursing does not come naturally. I assumed throughout my pregnancy that nursing my baby would be a breeze. I don't think I even thought about it much—I just assumed that I would know what to do instinctively, as would my baby. But then the nurse handed me my baby to nurse, and I remember looking at her and thinking, *What the hell am I supposed to do?* Nursing can be quite a struggle until you get it figured out, and you might need some help, a lot of help, to do it right.

Figuring out pumping is difficult too. I knew I had to go back to work relatively quickly, and started pumping right away to make a store of frozen breast milk. So I diligently pumped each breast after each feeding. The hospital lactation consultant had suggested that I nurse my baby on each breast, then pump each breast. Little did I know I was convincing my body I had triplets. A couple of weeks into this routine, my body was in full milk-production mode. I was a milking mama. By this time, I was going to a new moms' breast-feeding support group (highly recommended), and I was the star milk producer of the class, desperate to figure out how to make my body cut back since I was full all the time. I could pump two six-ounce milk bottles in about two minutes flat. The group and its moderator, a fabulous lactation consultant, helped me out, but I still ended up donating over 500 ounces to another mom. Five years later, I happened to run into another mom who attended the same breast-feeding support group and she said to me, "Hey, you're the 'got milk' mom, aren't you?" My claim to fame.

And why did I digress to tell you this? Because I agreed with the experts who conclude that despite the presence of environmental contaminants, breast milk is best for infants. Research suggests that breast-feeding helps reverse exposure to neuro-toxic substances such as lead and mercury.[28] Even knowing about the contaminants I'm about to cover, I personally chose to breast-feed my child because of the benefits.

So if human breast milk is perfect for human babies, why does it potentially contain chemicals? They come from what you have been exposed to in your life. Certain chemicals accumulate in fatty tissues, and are excreted in breast milk. In your breast milk is your existing toxic chemical body burden, plus what you eat, drink, put on your skin, and inhale while you are nursing. Contaminants detected in breast milk include PCBs, dichlorodiphenyltrichloroethane (DDT) and its metabolites, dioxins, furans, polybrominated diphenyl ethers, mercury, nicotine, perchlorate, and various volatile organic compounds.[29]

I think the list of chemicals that can be found in breast milk is one of the most frightening things about toxic chemical exposures. It clearly illustrates the persistence of certain chemicals. PCBs were banned in the U.S. in 1978, but are still detected in the breast milk of American women. Similarly, DDT, made infamous by the decline of the bald eagle and by American biologist Rachel Carson's *Silent Spring,* was banned in the U.S. in 1972, yet it is still detected in the breast milk of American women. All this suggests a certain futility in trying to limit your toxic chemical exposures.

But it also indicates our success at reducing our exposure. Bans on PCBs and DDT in the United States have resulted in a *significant* decline in these chemicals in our breast milk over the years. It indicates we can make a difference and we are in control.

What are the risks of exposure to contaminants in breast milk? That's hard to say. For the common contaminants found in breast milk, the source and potential risks are discussed below. Although there is uncertainty, what is important is that breast milk remains the superior source of nutrition for babies, and you can make your breast milk healthier with some simple steps.

Smart Mama Real-Life Story: Just Say No to Toxic Chemicals in Breast Milk

Mary Brune

It was the most difficult thing I had ever done. Okay, maybe third in line behind giving birth and hiking up from the bottom of the Grand Canyon. But still, I was amazed that what had always struck me as an effortless process—breast-feeding—would present one of the greatest challenges of my life.

The first two weeks were torture: raw, bloody nipples, a sense of dread preceding every feeding. It had been my plan to nurse my daughter for at least a year, but when at three weeks I was still having trouble, I wondered if I'd even make it a month.

From everything I had read about breast-feeding, I did know that it was by far the most superior food source I could provide. I also knew that my discomfort during breast-feeding was only temporary, and insignificant compared with the lifelong health and developmental benefits my daughter would enjoy as a result of being breast-fed. So we kept at it.

And things were humming along quite nicely at six months when I happened to sit down to nurse after returning home from work one day. My daughter and I had just sat down on the sofa and latched on when I turned on the television. What I saw horrified me.

The local news reported that a university in Texas had tested the breast milk of women in nineteen states across the country. The results? A chemical called perchlorate, found in rocket fuel, was present in every single sample. As my daughter suckled away, a feeling of panic washed over me. Could perchlorate be in my milk too? And if so, what exactly would that mean?

The following day, I madly performed Internet searches looking for information about perchlorate, as well as other chemical contaminants that might be found in breast milk. What came back were stories about pesticides, solvents, and flame retardants, many of which can affect the body's endocrine system and can interfere with reproductive, physical, and mental development.

Once the shock subsided, I felt an overwhelming sense of outrage. How dare these chemicals invade my body and my daughter's body without our consent? I saw these chemicals as trespassers on the sacred—not to mention hard-won—nursing relationship between my daughter and me. Along with three other new moms, I co-founded Making Our Milk Safe (MOMS), an organization dedicated to eliminating the presence of toxic chemicals in our environment, our bodies, and our breast milk.

Be assured, however, that despite the presence of toxic chemicals in breast milk, it continues to be the superior food choice it always was. But still, industrial toxins shouldn't be there. And it's time we all joined together to give them the boot.

It's true, there are personal choices we can make before, during, and after pregnancy to minimize the presence of chemicals in our bodies and breast milk. We can eat organic to avoid pesticides, filter out lead and perchlorate in our water, use green cleaning supplies and safer cosmetics.

But perhaps the most effective thing we can do to is to raise our collective voices and say, "No toxic chemicals! Not in our bodies. Not in our babies." Just like the Grand Canyon, it's going to be an uphill climb.

By the way, despite our rough beginning, I ended up nursing my daughter for nearly three years, and it was worth every minute.

Mary Brune is a co-founder and director of Making Our Milk Safe (MOMS). As a mother, she is an outspoken advocate for children's health and has written about toxic chemicals for The Huffington Post *and* Mothering *magazine. She has appeared on local and national media speaking out against the contamination of our environment and our bodies, and has been profiled in two books:* The Virtuous Consumer *by Leslie Garrett and* Not Just a Pretty Face: The Ugly Side of the Beauty Industry *by Stacy Malkan. MOMS has members in forty-three states and in Canada.*

PBDEs in Breast Milk

Polybrominated diphenyl ethers (PBDEs) are flame retardants. They have been and are added to electronics and household products to protect against the risk of fire. For more information on PBDEs, see Chapter 3.

PBDEs accumulate in fatty tissues and then are transmitted with breast milk. The concentrations in the breast milk of North American women indicate that our body burden is the highest in the world, as much as twenty times greater than the highest levels reported for Sweden. The body burden of PBDEs in Americans ranges from 30 to more than 100 ng/g lwt in Americans, whereas the body burden in Europe and Japan is less than 10 ng/g lwt. About 5 percent of Americans have PBDE levels considered high based upon samples of blood and breast milk from 2,000 women.

We are exposed to PBDES primarily by household dust, and concentrations of PBDEs in breast milk are correlated with PBDEs in household dust and diet. A study of first-time mothers in Massachusetts found a statistically significant, positive association between PBDE concentrations in breast milk and house dust, as well as with reported dietary habits, particularly the consumption of dairy products and meat.[30]

The health effects associated with exposure to PBDEs from breast milk are not known. PBDEs appear to disrupt the thyroid hormone system, which is critical for brain development. Laboratory animal studies have shown that low doses of PBDEs can disrupt brain growth and alter estrogen hormones, affecting male fertility and ovary development. Animal studies have associated very low-level PBDE exposures with impaired memory, learning deficits, and affected behavior. PBDEs have also been associated with a variety of cancers in rodents and non-Hodgkin's lymphoma in humans.

For tips on reducing exposure to PBDEs, see Chapter 3.

DDT in Breast Milk

DDT is an organochlorine insecticide used on agricultural crops to control insects, and to control insects that carry malaria and typhus. DDT has been banned in the United States since 1972, but it is still used in some countries.

DDT persists in the environment, along with two of its breakdown (or daughter) products, DDE and DDD. DDT degrades in the air, but it is persistent in soil and water. DDT bioaccumulates, meaning it builds up in plants and in the fatty tissues of fish, birds, and other animals. It concentrates up the food chain.

We are exposed to DDT primarily through eating contaminated food products. Food can be contaminated with bioaccumulated residues of DDT and its metabolites DDE or DDD, or obtained from areas where DDT is still used. Other possible, although less likely, routes of exposure include inhaling contaminated air, drinking contaminated water, and breathing or ingesting contaminated dust or soil, generally near waste sites. DDT is present at some waste sites, and releases from these sites could result in exposure. Residents living near a DDT-containing pesticide dump site in Aberdeen, North Carolina, were found to have higher mean levels of DDE (a metabolite of DDT) in their blood as compared with residents of neighboring communities (4.05 versus 2.85 ppb).[31]

Short-term exposure to high levels of DDT affects the nervous system. Animal studies have shown that short-term oral exposure to DDT may adversely affect reproduction. Long-term levels to small amounts of DDT impact the liver. Also, the EPA has identified DDT, DDD, and DDE as having probable human carcinogens. Studies in rats have shown that DDT and DDE can mimic the action of natural hormones and affect the development of the reproductive and nervous systems.[32]

The good news is that studies of DDT's presence in the breast milk of American women shows a continuous decrease. The bad news? DDT is still found in our breast milk, more than thirty-five years after it was banned.

When I think about the fact that DDT is still in our breast milk, I get angry. But I also always remember how I felt reading Rachel Carson's *Silent Spring.* Her detailed catalogue of DDT's persistence in the environment and her prophetic conclusion that DDT and other pesticides had irrevocably harmed birds and animals and had contaminated the entire world food supply inspired me to become active in the environmental field. I don't think I will ever forget her depiction of a nameless American town where all life—from fish to birds to apple blossoms to human children—was silenced by DDT.

DDT in Breast Milk: Smart Mama's Simple Steps to Reduce Exposure

Be selective about your fish. Certain fish have higher concentrations of DDT. Those with high levels include bluefish, wild striped bass, American eel, and Atlantic salmon.

Check wildlife and fish advisories. Always check advisories for DDT before eating any sport-caught fish or wildlife. If the warning indicates that the fish or wildlife may contain high levels of DDT, don't eat it.

Prepare fish to remove DDT. Since DDT accumulates in the fat tissues, you can prepare your fish to reduce exposure. To prepare the fish, clean and gut the fish you catch before cooking it because some chemicals, including PCBs and DDT, tend to concentrate in the organs, particularly in the liver. Trim the fat, remove the skin, and fillet the fish before cooking. Use a cooking method, such as baking or grilling, that allows the juices to drain away, and then discard the cooking juices.[33]

Go lean. When it comes to meat, choose lean meat cuts, and buy organic meats if possible. Cut off visible fat before cooking meat and choose lower-fat cooking methods: broiling, grilling, roasting, or pressure-cooking. Avoid frying meat in lard, bacon grease, or butter.

Cook the fish. Studies indicate that cooking fish reduces the amount of DDT in fish.

Wash fruits and vegetables. Washing fruit and vegetables may remove DDT from their surface. It is recommended that you wash leafy greens, beans, root vegetables, and fruits and berries to remove DDT or DDE from the surface.

Mercury in Breast Milk

Mercury passes through breast milk, but the amount in breast milk is not as significant an exposure as that during pregnancy. A mother's mercury blood level is usually three times the level found in her breast milk. Keep in mind that most of a baby's mercury exposure from the mother occurs during pregnancy, not from breast-feeding.

Mercury is a developmental neurotoxicant, meaning that it may directly interfere with the processes required for normal brain development. Since brain development continues through infancy, mercury exposure remains of concern.

With all the information about the negative health effects from eating mercury-contaminated fish and shellfish, you may decide to avoid eating fish to eliminate mercury exposure. But, as discussed earlier, there is a benefit in eating fish as well. Fish are a source of beneficial omega-3 fatty acids. We cannot synthesize a sufficient quantity of omega-3 fatty acids to meet our nutritional needs. Omega-3 fatty acids, including DHA, are also important to an infant's developing brain. DHA and another fatty acid, linoleic acid, make up more than a third of the fatty acids in the brain and the retina.

So to balance the benefits and the risks, the simple step to reduce exposure is to choose your fish carefully. You may also want to seek omega-3 fatty acids from other sources.

There is good news. Two long-term studies of children exposed to mercury via breast milk have not documented any adverse health effects. It seems that the benefits of breast-feeding significantly outweigh the adverse health effects associated with exposure to mercury in breast milk.

You can follow the same tips in the "Mercury" section earlier in this chapter to reduce mercury in your breast milk.

Lead in Breast Milk

With all of the concern about fetal and infant exposure to lead, you might be relieved, and surprised, to find out that lead concentrations in breast milk are relatively low. Considerably less lead passes into breast milk as compared to across the placenta. It is believed that lead concentrations in breast milk correlate more closely with lead concentrations in plasma, as opposed to blood lead concentrations. Plasma lead concentrations are around 3 percent of the whole blood lead concentration. Thus, lead concentrations in breast milk will be low.[34]

Nevertheless, uncertainty does exist as to how much lead is passed by breast milk because much of the lead in breast milk comes from the lead stored in the mother's bones. Lactation is a period of intense calcium need. If a nursing mother is deficient in calcium, the body will pull calcium, and along with it lead, from bone stores. Thus, a simple way to reduce the amount of lead being passed to your baby is to maintain a calcium-adequate diet.

And don't think that infant formula is any better than breast milk in terms of lead. Infant formula may also contain lead. It is believed that breast-feeding will expose your baby to slightly less lead than if you didn't breast-feed, assuming that you don't have elevated BLLs for some reason.[35] Finally, a little bit of good news!

Lead in Breast Milk: Smart Mama's Simple Steps to Reduce Exposure

Follow recommendations in other chapters. See Smart Mama's Simple Steps in Chapter 4 to reduce exposure to lead at home and in the workplace.

Got calcium? Make sure you have sufficient calcium intake. If you have adequate calcium intake, your body won't need to extract calcium from your bones and won't release the lead stored in your bones.

Perchlorate in Breast Milk

Perchlorates are the various salts derived from perchloric acid, such as magnesium perchlorate and ammonium perchlorate. Technically, perchlorate refers to the soluble anion associated with the perchloric acid's solid salts.

Perchlorate occurs naturally and is manufactured. In the United States, it is used as the primary ingredient in solid rocket propellant. It is also used in airbags, fireworks, and road flares. Perchlorate has made its way into our drinking water supplies and is present in our irrigated crops. It is estimated that the drinking water supplies of more than 11 million people have perchlorate concentrations in excess of 4 parts per billion (ppb). The EPA states that perchlorate releases have been confirmed in at least twenty-five states in the U.S.

Sometimes perchlorate's presence in drinking water and groundwater supplies is associated with nearby industrial sites that used or manufactured it, or is a result of irrigation with perchlorate-contaminated water. Its presence in fruits, vegetables, and grains is linked to irrigation with perchlorate-contaminated water or plants grown in soil containing perchlorate, either naturally occurring or as a result of exposure to perchlorate-containing water or fertilizer. Milk is linked to the cow's ingestion of perchlorate-containing feed and water. Other times there is no obvious source of perchlorate contamination. Perchlorate may be present because it is naturally occurring or due to the historical application of Chilean fertilizers. No federal standard for perchlorate in drinking water exists, but California has a maximum contaminant level of 6 ppb and Massachusetts has a standard of 2 ppb.

It appears that perchlorate interferes with the thyroid by inhibiting the ability of a specific protein to transport iodine to the thyroid and blocking the thyroid gland from taking up perchlorate.[36, 37] Without iodine, the thyroid may be unable to produce sufficient thyroid hormone, resulting in an underactive thyroid. Underactive thyroid can result in weight gain, fatigue, depression, infertility, and miscarriage, and may contribute to heart disease.

Perchlorate exposure appears widespread. A representative survey of 2,820 Americans, ages six years and older, found detectable levels of perchlorate in all 2,820 urine samples tested.[38] The study found significantly higher levels in children than in adults. However, exposures for babies and infants were not included because no samples were collected from children under the age of six years.

Infants may be especially susceptible to exposure to perchlorate. As noted, perchlorate interferes with the thyroid, and thyroid hormones are necessary for infants' normal growth and development. Short-term thyroid hormone deficits in infants can result in permanent neurological harm. In adult women with lower iodine levels (almost 40 percent of women), perchlorate exposure below the EPA's current safe reference dose of 0.7 micrograms perchlorate per kilogram body weight per day significantly reduced thyroid hormones.[39] The amount of perchlorate necessary to impair an infant's growth is unknown, but the fact that perchlorate affects the thyroid, and thyroid hormones are critical to infant development, suggests a need for caution.

Perchlorate has been detected in breast milk. One small study found perchlorate present in all thirty-six samples of breast milk analyzed, with an average concentration of 10 ppb.

Perchlorate: Smart Mama's Simple Steps to Reduce Exposure

Make sure you are not iodine deficient. Almost four out of every ten women in the United States have an iodine deficiency. Protect your thyroid by taking a vitamin with an appropriate amount of iodine. Talk to your doctor—too much iodine can aggravate hypothyroidism and thyroid conditions. Adequate iodine is necessary to ensure that if your breast-feeding infant is exposed to perchlorate, your baby nevertheless gets sufficient iodine to counteract the effects of perchlorate.

Know your water. If you are on a municipal system, find out whether perchlorate is present. The information should be available from your water provider. If the level is elevated, you may want to consider a filter designed to remove perchlorate.

Perchlorate and well water. If you live near a hazardous waste site or other area where perchlorates have been found and you use well water, you may want to consider an alternative drinking water source to reduce the risk to your family.

Follow workplace safety guidelines. If you work in a factory that makes or uses perchlorates, make sure you follow all recommendations to reduce exposure. You can carry perchlorate dust from work on your clothing, skin, or hair and transfer the perchlorate dust to your car, home, or other locations where family members might be exposed. If you can, change your clothes before getting into your car or coming home. Also, if you can, take a shower to remove any perchlorate dust from your skin or hair.

Eat a wide variety of fruits, vegetables, and grains. Perchlorate has been detected in fruits, vegetables, grains, and milk. Surveys of food products do not suggest a way to limit perchlorate intake from food products because of the wide variability in concentrations. The best solution is to eat a wide variety so that contamination from any one particular food source is not dominant in the diet.

Infant Formula

You may use formula in place of or in addition to breast milk. There are lots of reasons why formula may be used. But, if you can, breast-feed, even if you express the milk and bottle-feed. As discussed, breast milk is best for babies. Formula, despite the marketing claims of formula manufacturers, cannot duplicate breast milk.

Infant formula is regulated under the federal Food, Drug and Cosmetic Act and falls under the jurisdiction of the U.S. Food and Drug Administration (FDA). All infant formulas marketed in the United States must meet the FDA's nutrient specifications, although some child health advocates contend that the nutrition requirements are out of date. In any event, this means that while infant formula manufacturers may have their own combination of ingredients, formula must contain at least the minimum levels of nutrients specified without exceeding any maximum levels. Although manufacturers must notify the FDA prior to marketing a new formula, the FDA does not approve infant formulas before they can be marketed.

DHA and ARA

DHA and ARA are fatty acids that accumulate in the fetal brain and eyes during pregnancy, especially in the last trimester, and are found in breast milk. Blood levels of DHA and ARA are typically higher in breast-fed infants than in infants fed formulas not containing these fatty acids. Because of the perceived benefits of DHA and ARA, many infant formula manufacturers are now marketing formulas containing DHA and ARA. The scientific evidence is mixed on whether adding DHA and ARA to infant formulas has any benefit. Some studies in infants suggest that including these fatty acids may have positive effects on visual function and neural development over the short term, while other studies do not confirm these benefits.

One issue with the addition of DHA and ARA to infant formula may be the source of these acids. Some of the infant formulas contain DHA and ARA that is extracted from laboratory-grown fermented algae and fungus and processed with hexane. These are known as DHASCO and ARASCO (although they are not identified as such on the list of ingredients. DHASCO and ARASCO are structurally different from the DHA and ARA found in breast milk). There have been reports of adverse reactions from some infants consuming infant formula with DHASCO and ARASCO such as diarrhea, bloating, vomiting, jaundice, apnea, flatulence, and other gastrointestinal problems. If your formula-fed infant is experiencing any of these symptoms, you might want to consider trying a formula without added DHA and ARA to see if it helps, or find out from the formula manufacturer the source of the DHA and ARA in the formula. Of course, always follow the advice of your child's doctor.

Go Organic?

If you are concerned about toxic chemical exposure, you may want to choose organic formula. Dairy-based baby formula includes cow's milk and lactose. Certified organic baby formula is made with organic milk products. This means that the milk and lactose used in the formula will come from cows that have not been fed with pesticide-sprayed feeds or injected with growth hormones to increase milk production.

Soy-Based Formula

Soy-based formulas may pose a problem because of the presence of phytoestrogens. Phytoestrogens are plant-derived compounds with biological properties similar to the hormone estrogen. Soy infant formula contains isoflavones (a class of phytoestrogens). Although isoflavones are weak estrogens, the concentration of isoflavones is extremely high. Estimates of an infant's daily estrogenic dose on a body-weight basis from consuming soy-based formula are the equivalent to 0.01 to more than 1 hormonal contraceptive pill per day.[40] An evaluation by the National Toxicology Program found insufficient data to determine whether infant soy formula was a developmental or reproductive toxicant.[41] The report noted that one large study found no adverse effect, yet expressed concern because other studies presented findings that did indicate effects from soy formula, including a study that found soy formula a risk factor for premature breast development.

Melamine in Infant Formula

Following the tragic deaths and illness of many infants in China from melamine-contaminated formula, the FDA has instituted testing of U.S.-made infant formula. In China, melamine was intentionally added to milk products because, like protein, it is rich in nitrogen. When inspectors check to see if milk and milk products have been diluted (lowering protein concentrations), the inspectors measure nitrogen content. Melamine will fool this test.

In the U.S., melamine concentration levels are well below the levels found in Chinese milk products. In its first round of testing involving seventy-four samples, the FDA found low levels of melamine and cyanuric acid in some U.S. infant formulas. As of December 2008, the FDA has found melamine levels at 0.137 ppm and 0.140 ppm in Good Start Supreme Infant Formula with Iron from Nestlé, and found cyanuric acid in Mead Johnson's infant formula powder, Enfamil Lipil with Iron, in the 12.9-ounce can at 0.247, 0.245, and 0.249 ppm.

Melamine causes kidney problems when it is present along with cyanuric acid. In the U.S., none of the samples tested to date have shown both melamine and cyanuric acid.

With the U.S. infant formula, the presence of melamine appears to be a result of contact during processing, not intentional addition, which is prohibited in the U.S. Melamine is used in the manufacturing of dishes, plastic resins, flame-retardant fibers, components of paper and paperboard, and industrial compounds. So melamine may come from rubbing off from these surfaces. Also, trichloromelamine is approved as a sanitizer for food-processing equipment and utensils, except for milk containers and equipment. Trichloromelamine easily breaks down into melamine when it is used as a sanitizer. This could also be a source.

The FDA set a supposedly "safe" level of melamine in infant formulas in December 2008. The FDA has concluded that melamine alone or cyanuric acid alone at or below 1 part per million (ppm) is safe. The levels found in the U.S. infant formula are below this safe level.

Water Used to Make Up Formula

Powdered infant formulas must be made up with drinking water. Any contaminant present in the drinking water will then be present in the made-up infant formula.

Of course, our drinking water can be contaminated with various parasites and bacteria. An infant is at an increased risk because his immune system is not developed. Therefore, it is important to pay attention to any drinking water warnings.

As for contaminants, they include all of those we've previously discussed. For example, lead in drinking water can expose your infant to lead. Babies who drink formula prepared with lead-contaminated water are at a higher risk for adverse health effects because of the large volume of water they consume relative to their body size.

In agricultural areas, nitrates can be present, particularly in private drinking water supplies. Infants who are exposed to elevated levels of nitrates in drinking water have an increased risk of developing methemoglobinemia or "blue baby syndrome." Blue baby syndrome occurs when certain bacteria in the infant digestive system convert nitrates to nitrites. Nitrites oxidize hemoglobin, thus reducing its ability to carry oxygen. Infants under the age of four months are at greatest risk. Blue baby syndrome can be fatal.

Approximately 13 million households use private water wells to supply their drinking water. In agricultural areas, nitrates from fertilizer runoff may contaminate drinking water supplies. According to the United States Geological Survey, more than 8,200 wells nationwide were contaminated with nitrate levels above the EPA's drinking water standard of 10 ppm. The EPA estimates that approximately 1.2 percent of community water wells and 2.4 percent of private wells exceed the nitrate standard.

Formula and Drinking Water: Smart Mama's Simple Steps to Reduce Exposure

Lead in drinking water. See Chapter 4, "Getting the Lead Out."

Test your water. If your water source is a private well, test your water. If you have high levels of nitrates, get water from an alternate source until you can make arrangements to treat the water.

Never boil. Don't boil water to make up formula. Boiling will concentrate nitrates and lead.

Bisphenol A from Formula Containers

With formula, you have an additional concern based upon the container in which the formula is sold. Unfortunately, the container may leach bisphenol A (BPA) into the formula. (See the section on BPA in Chapter 5 for more information.) BPA is found in epoxy-based enamels used to line metal cans. Why? Metal cans require a lining to prevent interaction between the food and the can, especially in cans that undergo heat treatment to ensure commercial sterility.

The Environmental Working Group (EWG) investigated the potential leaching of BPA into infant formula and found BPA present in formula. Liquid formulas in metal cans had higher concentrations of BPA than powdered formula. In fact, the EWG concluded that liquid formulas have the potential to leach at a rate of eight to twenty times higher than powdered formula in metal cans.

The EWG's study tested six liquid formulas. The U.S. Food and Drug Administration (FDA) has also tested liquid formulas. Both studies found an average of 5 parts per billion BPA, with four samples above 10 ppb.[42]

The FDA has approved the use of epoxy resins containing BPA in items that contact foods, including formula. The FDA maintains that the use of BPA-containing enamels for infant formula containers is safe. In its response to a congressional investigation into the use of BPA-containing enamels for infant formula, the FDA stated, "FDA has compared the 'no observed effect' levels of the data reviewed to the estimated daily intake values and considers that an adequate margin of exposure exists for the conclusion of reasonable certainty of no harm under the intended conditions of use."[43] But the response to the congressional inquiry stated that FDA's determination is based on two studies,[44] both of which were reportedly funded by the American Plastics Council, and both of which have been criticized. One study was never published in a peer-reviewed journal, and the other used a certain type of rat that responds to estrogen only at high doses, not low. This study did not use any positive control, which means that it cannot be determined whether the study was capable of finding any health effects from BPA.

The FDA's letter relies on the conclusion that 7 ug/infant/day is safe. But, according to the Environmental Working Group, "a baby of average size would exceed FDA's worst-case dose if he or she drank more than 2.5 bottles (20 ounces) contaminated with BPA at the maximum levels measured in the 20 total samples tested to date in FDA and EWG testing programs."[45] The Environmental Working Group also criticized the BPA migration study cited by the FDA. The BPA migration study used a level of detection of 100 ppb, a level of detection too high to detect the low levels of BPA leaching, and also well above the level of detection used by the FDA in other migration studies.

It is clear that infant formula containers can leach BPA into infant formula, but whether the rate of leaching of BPA results in a risk of harm is subject to debate. Currently, the position of regulatory agencies is that the levels are not at a point that will cause concern.[46] However, over 100 published animal studies indicate adverse health effects at low levels, especially in infants. Many BPA experts believe that due to the adverse health effects shown in animals at low doses of BPA, there is no reason to think that such effects would not also occur in humans. Coupled with the fact that infants do not metabolize BPA at the same rate as adults, you may choose to use formula that does not have BPA in it from the can lining.

Bisphenol A in Formula: Smart Mama's Simple Steps to Reduce Exposure

Choose glass. If you are using liquid formula, choose glass containers over metal cans.

Choose powdered over liquid. BPA leaching appears to occur at a greater rate in liquid stored in metal cans compared to powdered formula stored in metal cans. So pick powdered over liquid if they are both stored in metal cans.

Choose the infant formula container with the smallest surface area coated with BPA-containing enamel. According to the infant formula manufacturers' responses to the congressional inquiry into the use of BPA-containing enamels used to line infant formula containers, all of the manufacturers used BPA-containing enamels in their metal cans. But some coat a smaller surface area of the can with the BPA-containing enamel. The smaller the surface area, the less area is available to leach BPA. According to its response to the FDA congressional inquiry, the Hain Celestial Group states that only the top end of the can is coated with an epoxy-based resin. This means that the cans for its powdered infant formulas (Earth's Best Organic Infant

Formula with Iron, Earth's Best Organic Infant Formula with Iron with DHA & ARA, and Earth's Best Organic Soy Infant Formula with Iron with DHA & ARA) should leach less BPA than cans with more surface area covered by BPA-containing enamel (all other factors being equal). The EWG states that the Enfamil and Similac powdered infant formulas are sold in containers with only the metal top and bottom being lined with a BPA-containing enamel. PBM's infant formula cans (which are most of the store-brand formulas) are entirely metal, and PBM did not provide the congressional panel with any information as to which portions of the can are lined.

Chapter 7

Rock-a-Bye Baby: Baby's Nursery

How much time and effort do we invest in creating the perfect nursery, selecting a color scheme, choosing the perfect bedding, or agonizing over the crib mobile? It seems that if we just get the nursery right, everything else will fall into place. Yet, while most of us invest substantial time and effort in creating a bright, happy, inviting, and safe haven, we don't stop to think about toxic chemical exposures. That fresh coat of paint could expose you and your baby to potentially harmful volatile organic compounds (VOCs). That distinctive new carpet smell? Usually 4–phenylcyclohexane off-gassing, among a host of other potentially toxic chemicals.[1] The chemicals in paints, floor coverings, furniture, window coverings, bedding, crib mattresses, and changing pads can create a toxic soup of chemicals, formaldehyde, phthalates, toluene, and methylene chloride, to mention just a few!

Not the safe haven most of us envisioned.

Before you start feeling overwhelmed, keep in mind that the nursery is a great place to start eliminating or reducing toxic chemical exposures in the home. You can create a relatively toxin-free environment with some simple steps. And, since most of us decorate the nursery while we're pregnant, these steps will also reduce the exposure to you and your fetus.

SMART MAMA WARNING

Do not disturb lead paint or varnish. No matter how strong the urge to nest becomes, stop before engaging in destructive renovations. Do not open or tear down walls or disturb, sand, scrape, or remove old paint or varnish until you determine whether it contains lead. Lead can cross the placenta. (See Chapter 4, "Getting the Lead Out".)

The five simple steps to a non-toxic nursery are:

1. Non-toxic paint or wall coverings.
2. Non-toxic floor coverings.
3. A formaldehyde-free crib with a non-toxic coating.
4. A flame-retardant free mattress.
5. Organic bedding.

We'll now review each of these steps in more detail.

Paint

Making a new space for the baby usually involves applying a fresh coat of paint or hanging wallpaper. Paint holds unlimited possibilities. A fairy-filled forest. Dancing pink elephants. Bright cheery dots. A field of stars. Freshly painted walls seem to be the perfect start for a baby nursery.

Unfortunately, paint can contain a wide variety of toxic chemicals. And those toxic chemicals can off-gas and expose you and your baby. Some of the chemicals can cross the placenta and expose a baby in utero if mom is exposed while pregnant. Others continue to off-gas after application, impacting indoor air quality and potentially exposing occupants.

What Is Off-Gassing?

Off-gassing is the release of gases as material ages and degrades. Off-gassing sounds complicated, but it isn't. You're already familiar with it. That new-car smell is caused by off-gassing from the car's plastic interior. That greasy film that forms on the inside of a new car's windows is also the result of off-gassing.

Studies have shown that concentrations of VOCs are consistently higher indoors than outdoors, with some VOC concentrations up to ten times higher indoors.[2] Some scientists believe that indoor pollutants are 1,000 times more likely to be inhaled compared to outdoor pollutants because we spend about 90 percent of our time indoors, our activities put us near sources of indoor air pollutants, and indoor emissions are partially trapped inside buildings.[3]

Paints and coatings contribute to indoor air pollution. Although emissions from paints and coatings are highest during and immediately after application, low levels of toxic emissions are released into the air for years after application. Some paint-related activities can dramatically increase indoor air concentrations of VOCs. For example, during and for several hours after stripping paint, indoor air concentrations of certain VOCs may be 1,000 times background outdoor levels.[4]

A basic science lesson: a paint consists of a resin (or binder), a carrier, and pigments that give the paint its color. Once the paint is applied to a surface, the carrier evaporates, leaving behind the solid coating. The carrier is usually a VOC.

What are VOCs? VOCs are chemicals that contain at least one carbon atom that easily evaporate at ambient temperature. They are emitted as gases from certain liquids and solids into the air we breathe. You are familiar with VOCs. The smell of gasoline? VOCs evaporating. The scent of a freshly mowed lawn? VOCs evaporating. In fact, isoprene and monoterpenes are two of the most common VOCs emitted from vegetation.[5] Monoterpenes (VOCs) give us pine, lemon, and many floral scents.[6]

The term "VOC" is often used in a precise regulatory context, and the definition is determined by laws. From a regulatory perspective, VOCs are usually of concern because they evaporate at room temperature and then react in sunlight to help form ground-level ozone, an integral component of photochemical smog. These VOCs are referred to as smog precursors. Smog is that green haze that hangs over many large cities that we are working to eliminate.

But you are probably more concerned with VOCs because they have health effects. VOCs can cause respiratory distress; skin and eye irritation; headaches; nausea; muscle weakness; and even more serious ailments and diseases. For example, formaldehyde, a VOC commonly found in paint, is considered a probable carcinogen by the EPA. It is listed on California's Proposition 65 list of chemicals known to the state of California

SMART MAMA SCARY FACT

The EPA reports that paints, stains, and other architectural coatings produce about 9 percent of the VOC emissions from consumer and commercial products, making them the second-largest source of VOC emissions after automobiles.

to cause cancer, is genotoxic (damaging to genetic material), and also causes eye, nose, and throat irritation.[7, 8]

If you are trying to reduce toxic chemical exposures, understanding the regulatory framework is important. Let's say you buy a paint labeled "low VOC." That usually means the paint has low VOC content based upon the definition of VOC under the federal Clean Air Act. But the Clean Air Act defines VOCs in terms of photochemical reactivity (ability to form ozone), and not toxicity.[9] In the regulatory context, certain VOCs are exempt from regulation because they are not photochemically reactive (they are not smog precursors). However, these VOCs may be toxic. For example, methylene chloride and 1,1,1-trichloroethane are not considered photochemically reactive, so they are exempt,[10] but they are associated with adverse health effects.

Methylene chloride is irritating to the skin, eyes, and respiratory tract and is identified as a probable carcinogen by the EPA.[11] 1,1,1-trichloroethane is not classifiable as to its carcinogencity in humans, but animal studies have shown that 1,1,1-TCA can pass through the placenta. Babies of pregnant mice exposed to high concentrations of TCA developed more slowly and demonstrated behavioral problems.[12] So even if the paint is low VOC, you may still want to skip it. In addition, the term "low" refers only to the amount of VOCs in the base coating. The colorant added to the paint may have VOCs as well, so you need to consider the VOC content of the base plus colorant.

How do you find the right paint? Conventional paints are generally classified into two categories: latex (or water based) paints (in which the carrier is water), and oil-based paints (in which the carrier is an organic solvent). When you use oil-based paints, the organic solvent VOC evaporates after application and pollutes the air. Latex paints use water instead of solvents as the primary carrier, so VOC emissions are minimized. Conclusion: Latex paints are usually a better choise over oil-based paints to reduce toxic chemical exposures. However, latex paints aren't risk free because they may use solvents to mix the binder, which are emitted after application.

Paints labeled as "low VOCs" or "zero VOCs" may have fewer toxins than conventional paints.[13] However, remember from the earlier discussion that "low" or "zero" VOC paint refers to photochemical reactivity (whether or not it is a smog precursor) and/or odor, not the amount of toxins. While these paints are environmentally friendly—and I am all for reducing smog—they may still have some toxic chemicals. Look for the VOC content in grams per liter on the paint label—choose one with the lowest number. Generally speaking, and keeping in mind that VOC content is not regulated for health effects, a paint that says "Maximum VOC Content: 45 grams/liter" is preferable to one with a higher number.

In addition to VOCs, you should look out for other potentially toxic ingredients, like ammonia, crystalline silica, fungicides, and biocides like copper, arsenic disulfide, phenol, and formaldehyde. Almost all paints contain toxic preservatives. The amounts are relatively low, but you may want to consider specialty biocide-free paints. Also check the pigment used to make the color. For both the paint and the pigment, ask the manufacturer or supplier for the Material Safety Data Sheet (MSDS) (or get it off the Web), which should identify the ingredients and offer information on health effects.

Another option is natural-based paints and finishes. These paints are made from natural raw ingredients such as plant oils, plant dyes, clay, chalk, milk casein, and beeswax. Natural paints typically use linseed and soy oils as binders, pine- and balsam-derived terpenes or citrus oils as carriers, minerals and sometimes plant-derived compounds as pigments, and lime and chalk as thickeners. These paints are preserved by linseed oil or other natural ingredients. Although natural paints and finishes do not contain petroleum products, they may still emit VOCs from ingredients like citrus-based solvents. Certain natural oil paints emit odors or compounds, such as those from citrus oil, which chemically sensitive people may find hard to tolerate. Mineral, lime, and milk paints are generally well tolerated and are the least toxic paints available. But always check the ingredient list or MSDS. Not all "natural" materials are safe. Cadmium may be used as a bright yellow pigment, but cadmium is toxic.

Paint: Smart Mama's Simple Steps to Reduce Exposure

Get the lead out. If your home was built before 1978, read the chapter on lead first.

Lean on others. Take advantage of anybody who offers to help you. This is the time to forget any concept that you are superwoman, and get help. If you are pregnant, do not paint the room yourself. Many of the chemicals can cross the placenta. Fight the nesting instinct and have someone else handle the project.

Do projects early. If you must paint, paint at least a month before the baby's due date to allow any VOCs to dissipate. Although VOCs can off-gas for years, the off-gassing is highest at the initial application and decreases thereafter.

Ventilate. Make sure you ventilate the space adequately. Keep windows open as much as possible. If you can, paint during a dry spell so you can keep the windows open for at least three days.

Read the label. Always read the label. Labels work as follows: the first item should be the signal word, such as DANGER, WARNING, or CAUTION. Directly following will be a statement of the principal hazard (such as "Vapor Harmful"), followed by any other hazards associated with the product's ingredients. This should be followed by any necessary precautions to take (such as "Open all doors and windows during use"). Stay away from products that indicate the presence of neurotoxins. A paint with neurotoxins may have a label that says something like "May affect the brain or nervous system." Labels may not provide you with sufficient information. If you need more, ask the supplier or manufacturer for the product's Material Safety Data Sheet (MSDS). The MSDS should include a discussion of health effects associated with the product. You may not even have to call the manufacturer—many manufacturers have their MSDSs available on their Web sites.

Choose water-based over oil-based conventional paints. Water-based or latex paints have significantly less VOCs than oil-based paints because water is used as the carrier as opposed to an organic solvent.

Even better, choose environmentally friendly paints. Look for paints labeled low VOC or zero VOC. Just keep in mind that these paints are low or zero in terms of smog formation.

Look for the Green Seal certification for low- and no-VOC paints. The Green Seal certification allows only 50 grams VOC per liter in flat paints, and also does not allow the use of methylene chloride, 1,1,1-trichloroethane, benzene, toluene (methylbenzene), ethylbenzene, vinyl chloride, naphthalene, 1,2-dichlorobenzene, certain phthalates, isophorone, antimony, cadmium, hexavalent chromium, lead, mercury, formaldehyde, methyl ethyl ketone, methyl isobutyl ketone, acrolein, and acrylonitrile.[14] If you are going to use a low- or zero-VOC paint, the Green Seal Certificate provides some assurance that the paint doesn't contain many chemicals.

Best choice if you paint: choose natural-based paints and finishes. Mineral, lime, and milk paints are the least toxic paints available and are generally well tolerated.

Checklist of Paint Ingredients to Avoid

- 1,2-dichlorobenzene
- 1,1,1-trichloroethane
- Acrolein
- Acrylonitrile
- Ammonia
- Antimony
- Arsenic disulfide
- Benzene
- Cadmium
- Copper
- Crystalline silica
- Ethylbenzene
- Formaldehyde
- Fungicides (usually indicated on product label)
- Hexavalent chromium
- Isophorone
- Lead
- Mercury
- Methylene chloride

Methyl ethyl ketone	Phenol
Methyl isobutyl ketone	Toluene (methylbenzene)
Naphthalene	Vinyl chloride

Wall Coverings

Instead of paint, you may want to decorate your baby's nursery with wallpaper. Although it's called "paper," the funny thing is that today, wallpaper usually isn't made of paper. Traditional wallpaper has been largely replaced by wall coverings coated with or made from polyvinyl chloride or some other plastic. Conventional wallpapers and their adhesives are potential sources of VOCs, phthalates, flame retardants, and other chemicals.

We've talked about VOCs, but what the heck are phthalates? Phthalates are a class of widely used industrial compounds known technically as dialkyl or alkyl aryl esters of 1,2-benzenedicarboxylic acid. (And you thought that the technical name would be easier to say?) Phthalates are plasticizers added to a wide variety of consumer products, from plastics to cosmetics. They are added to polyvinyl chloride (PVC) plastic to make it soft and flexible, but they do not form a chemical bond with the plastic and can migrate out of the PVC polymer under certain conditions.[15]

Phthalates are hormone disruptors. For more detail on the health risks associated with phthalates, see Chapter 9.

Vinyl wall coverings can contribute to phthalate exposure. Several studies have also found elevated levels of phthalates in household dust. While the presence of elevated levels of phthalates in dust does not necessarily translate into a health risk, you may want to choose another option.

Further, wallpapers can include chemicals in their binders, inks, dyes, fungicides, pesticides, and flame retardants, all of which may include chemicals that off-gas into the indoor air.

Lead may also be present in PVC wall coverings because it is used to stabilize PVC plastic. Today, other compounds have been substituted as a stabilizer in place of lead in most building products, but lead may be present in older PVC wall coverings. Lead is not bound up in the plastic polymer, and may migrate to the surface, where it can be picked up as lead dust.

It is difficult to get information on the VOC content of conventional wallpapers, but you should be able to determine whether it is made of or coated with PVC. If you can't get the VOC content, ask the supplier or manufacturer whether the wallpaper contains or gives off VOCs or other toxins.

The adhesive used to attach the wallpaper to the wall may also emit VOCs. Conventional wallpaper adhesives are petroleum based. Adhesives usually off-gas most strongly during and immediately after initial application, but they can off-gas for some time after initial application. If the adhesive does not have sufficient information on its label, ask for the Material Safety Data Sheet (MSDS). Of course, a variety of less-toxic alternate adhesives are available on the market.

Also, don't forget about the chemicals used to remove old wallpaper. Many of these contain potentially toxic chemicals. Again, a variety of less-toxic alternates are available.

Wall Coverings: Smart Mama's Simple Steps to Reduce Exposure

Skip PVC wall coverings. A number of alternative wall coverings are available that are not made of PVC, so you can skip the potential exposure to phthalates and lead by skipping PVC or vinyl. There are wall coverings made of bamboo, raffia, rice papers, flax, and recycled paper, among others. An added bonus: many of the alternates are also eco-friendly.

Use low- or no-VOC adhesive. Check the VOC content of the covering and the adhesive used to apply the covering.

Flooring

You may consider installing new flooring in the baby's nursery. Your flooring choice will be based upon a whole host of factors: your design sensibility, cost, ease of cleaning, etc. But you may also want to factor into your decision your baby's exposure to toxic chemicals. Trust me, you and your children will spend an awful lot of time on that floor.

Carpeting

New carpets tend to emit high levels of VOCs. New synthetic carpets can off-gas more than 150 chemicals, although some of the chemicals are emitted in very low concentrations. Researchers have documented emissions of acetaldehyde, benzene, 2-butoxyethanol, carbon disulfide, 1,4-dichlorobenzene, dichloromethane, formaldehyde, styrene, toluene, and trichloroethane. Which chemicals are emitted, and for how long, depends on the carpet, the chemicals added to the carpet (such as pesticides or fungicides or stain or soil repellents), the material used for the carpet's backing, the material used for the carpet padding, and the adhesive used to glue it to the padding and the subflooring.

But translating the results of carpet-emission research into household indoor air concentration, and determining potential health effects, is complex. In fact, health effects associated with carpeting has been a subject of debate, much of it political.[16] Fortunately, the burgeoning green building movement has made more lower-emission alternatives available.

Some research suggests that VOC emissions are highest just after initial installation, and decrease rapidly after seventy-two hours, although other researchers have reported elevated VOC emissions from carpets that are more than ten years old. Other toxic chemicals also pose a problem, including semi-volatile organic compounds, flame retardants, and perfluorocarbons. These may not be emitted until some time has passed after installation, so emissions of these compounds, unlike VOCs, may increase rather than decrease with time, and then remain stable for a long period.[17]

Another problem with carpets is that they trap pollutants, both those that settle from the air and those tracked into the house. This trapped dust can contain lead, pesticides, and other toxic chemicals. Lead-contaminated dust can pose a significant hazard for infants (see Chapter 4, "Getting the Lead Out"). Aside from the potential lead exposure, dust in the carpet may not pose much of a problem when children play and crawl around on carpeting. Although a frightening number of chemicals have been detected in household dust, studies suggest that surface dust on carpeting—that available for pickup—is not any greater than that present on smooth floors. One study reported that only about 1 percent of the bulk loading of dust in the carpet was actually available for pickup at the surface. On the other hand, allergens and asthma triggers, including cat dander and dust mites, may be present at much higher concentrations in carpets than on smooth floors. If your family is prone to allergies or asthma, you may want to skip carpeting.

Wood Flooring

Many believe that wood flooring is better than carpet because it doesn't trap dust like carpet and is easy to clean. In fact, one study examining the amount of dust in grams per square meter found that bare floors had 0.1 grams dust per square meter as compared with a rug that had 26 grams per square meter.[18]

But chemicals such as VOCs and semi-VOCs, including formaldehyde, can be found in the wood product, in any finishing materials, and in any adhesives used during installation. VOCs and semi-VOCs, including formaldehyde, can off-gas during and after installation, contaminating indoor air.

Formaldehyde is identified as a probable carcinogen. It also causes short-term irritant effects, such as eye and nose irritation, coughing, stuffy nose, and sore throat. Some people report headaches, nausea, and fatigue after exposure to formaldehyde. Formaldehyde is also a strong sensitizer, meaning that it can induce an allergic reaction. Skin rashes are the most common form of formaldehyde allergy. Formaldehyde can also cause worsening of asthma symptoms. In an investigation of indoor sources of formaldehyde, the California Air

Resources Board found the highest formaldehyde emission rates from a wet wood-floor finish.[19]

When considering purchasing a wood flooring product, find out about its composition. If the wood flooring is composite (made of wood or manufactured wood, with a veneer glued to a less costly base material) or laminate (plastic laminate surface glued to a manufactured wood product), it may off-gas chemicals used to hold the flooring together. Often composite or laminate flooring is made with formaldehyde-based glue, although formaldehyde-free glues are available. Ask for documentation to support claims of low or no formaldehyde.

Another potential emissions source is the product used to finish the floor. Always ask about the finishing or coating materials. Solid and laminate wood floors can be finished with a urea-formaldehyde based coating. This type of finish is known as an acid-catalyzed urea-formaldehyde coating and can emit high levels of formaldehyde when new. Look for wood flooring made and treated with water-based and non-toxic finishes.

Vinyl Flooring

Vinyl flooring, like vinyl wall coverings, may release a host of potentially problematic chemicals, including phthalates. Vinyl flooring off-gasses chemicals itself. Additionally, it is almost always applied with adhesives, which are a source of VOCs.

Sheet vinyl flooring has plasticizers—phthalates—added to make it soft and flexible. Vinyl tiles generally do not have plasticizers added, although they may have other additives. As noted earlier, phthalates are endocrine disruptors. They have been linked to a host of health effects in laboratory animals and have been associated with various health effects in humans.

Studies suggest that breathing in air and dust containing phthalates that have escaped from vinyl flooring also adds to the amount of phthalates in our systems. Phthalates escaping from vinyl flooring may particularly impact children since they spend a lot of time indoors breathing close to the floor. In fact, an initial study conducted in Norway reported a higher incidence of bronchial obstruction in children living in houses with vinyl, as opposed to wood, floors. Phthalates being released into the air may be the link between these two observations.

Although the debate continues, since there are so many alternative flooring options, it seems prudent to steer away from vinyl flooring.

Toxic Chemicals in Flooring: Smart Mama's Simple Steps to Reduce Exposure

Leave it be. Consider leaving carpeting in good condition in place. Older carpets probably have completed their off-gassing, although they may be harboring a great deal of dust. If you want to change the decor, try a natural-fiber throw rug over the existing carpeting.

Go natural. If you want new carpet, consider some of the natural-fiber options available, such as wool, cotton, hemp, jute, etc., instead of synthetic. Just be careful about how the carpet is treated, which can add chemicals to your natural carpet. Ask about how the carpet was colored. You want undyed or vegetable-dyed fibers. Also ask about treatments for resisting pests (such as mothproofing) or soil or stain fighting. Wool carpet is a great choice because it is durable, naturally flame resistant, and repels stains and liquid. However, wool, as you probably know, is susceptible to moths and carpet beetles, so wool carpets may be treated with mothproofing chemicals. Also, wool carpets may be treated with stain repellent, even though wool is naturally stain resistant. I can attest that it is resistant, but not stain proof. You can ask for untreated carpet.

Go certified. If you are going to buy synthetic carpet, get a carpet that is California Secton 01350 compliant. Its criteria have been adopted by other programs, including Greenguard and Green Label Plus. Compliance with the Section 01350 standard will give you comfort that the carpet meets emission standards for the eighty VOCs covered by the program. But the Section 01350 label does have some limitations. It only covers eighty VOCs, and it does not cover flame retardants or the perfluorocarbons (stain repellents). You also want to make sure there is no added formaldehyde.

Carpet backing. A natural backing such as jute is preferable to a synthetic backing. A sewn-on back is preferable to a glued-on backing. A glued-on backing with no or low VOCs is preferable to an adhesive with a high VOC content. Just ask.

Tack it down. Skip adhesive use by having carpets tacked down or having them cut and finished to fit in rooms. This will eliminate one potential source of VOCs.

Use low-VOC or water-based adhesives. If you cannot tack it down or have it cut, ask for a no- or low-VOC adhesive.

Let it breathe. Ask installers to unwrap, unroll, and air out your carpet for at least three days before installation. If your installer or carpet supplier can't do this, consider taking at least a seventy-two-hour vacation after installation of a new carpet and ventilating the area.

Ventilate. Ventilate well during and after new carpet installation. Leave windows open for at least three days if you can.

Choose natural padding. Also consider padding made from cotton, felt, hemp, or jute, or conventional carpet pads made of foam and synthetic rubber.

Wood is good. Wood flooring is a good option because it doesn't have the same ability to trap dust particles as carpet and is easy to clean. But wood flooring has its share of problems, too. If being green is important to you, look for FSC-certified wood. FSC-certified wood is harvested from a sustainably managed forest. If you are using a composite wood product or a laminate wood, pick one that is formaldehyde free.

Check out how the wood is manufactured. Wood flooring finished with petroleum-based stains, waxes, or coatings, or treated with pesticides, can also off-gas VOCs. If you are going to invest in wood flooring and the wood is finished at the manufacturing plant, make sure you ask about how the wood flooring was made.

Ask for a no- or low-VOC water-based finish. If the wood is finished onsite, make sure the finish is no or low VOC and water based. Although there are some great ones on the market, ask your installer for recommendations. When we remodeled our house, I asked the contractor to use a no-VOC finish I had found. To make a long story short, about five days after being applied, it bubbled up and didn't adhere well to the wood. We had to redo it and go with the one he had recommended and used before.

Use water-based adhesives. If adhesives are used to install the wood flooring, use water-based adhesives.

Check out green options. Some of the eco-friendly options also result in lower exposures to toxic chemicals. Bamboo is an option, although you need to investigate how it is finished and how it is installed. Opt for low-VOC and no-VOC finishes and adhesives. Other possible options include cork and paper.

Furniture

The furniture you choose for your baby's nursery is a matter of your style and your personal taste. It seems that most of us buy or borrow a crib and a changing table, some storage, and perhaps a chair or rocker. You may not have a crib if you are using a co-sleeper or the family bed. You may use a dresser instead of a changing table. You may skip the rocker.

Whatever you choose to put in the nursery, it should be safe for the baby. Keep in mind that your baby will probably touch or chew on most of it, so you want to make sure the furniture is as free of toxic chemicals as it can be. Also, off-gassing chemicals contribute to poor indoor air quality and can cause a number of adverse health effects.

Formaldehyde can be off-gassed from furniture and shelving made of composite wood. Typically, formaldehyde-based glues are used to make composite wood products used in furniture, cabinetry, countertops, moldings, and shelving systems. Composite wood products are wood-based panels made of particles or fibers bound together with a resin or adhesive, and include hardwood plywood, particleboard, and medium-density fiberboard. Hardwood plywood is commonly used in furniture and cabinets, and medium-density fiberboard is used for drawer fronts, cabinets, and furniture tops.

Composite wood products containing urea-formaldehyde resins emit higher amounts of formaldehyde than phenol-formaldehyde resins. Urea-formaldehyde resins are commonly used in indoor wood products such as particleboard, hardwood plywood paneling, and medium-density fiberboard (MDF). Phenol-formaldehyde resins emit formaldehyde at a lower rate than urea-formaldehyde resins, but such products are typically used for exterior construction work.

So if you buy furniture that contains formaldehyde-based glues, they can off-gas formaldehyde. Formaldehyde can also off-gas from coatings and sealants.

The California Air Resources Board reports that formaldehyde from pressed wood products can off-gas for years, although emissions are highest in the first month after manufacture. Formaldehyde is released from unreacted formaldehyde present in the resin and as a result of chemical degradation over time.[20] Also, porous materials and furnishings, such as upholstered furniture, carpets, walls, and window coverings, can absorb formaldehyde and then re-emit it later.[21]

Low levels of formaldehyde can cause irritation of the eyes, nose, throat, and skin. It is possible that people with asthma may be more sensitive to the effects of inhaled formaldehyde. It can also cause headaches, fatigue, and respiratory irritation. The U.S. Department of Health and Human Services has listed formaldehyde as reasonably anticipated to be a carcinogen.

The United States has no federal formaldehyde emissions regulation for composite wood products, although many manufacturers voluntarily follow the U.S. Housing and Urban Development's standard that only applies to manufactured homes. California has enacted a formaldehyde emissions regulation for certain composite wood products.

You may want to skip furniture made with composite wood, or look for composite wood pieces that don't use formaldehyde-based adhesives. Or you can look for Greenguard-certified furniture. Greenguard certification means that the furniture is meeting specified criteria.

In addition to formaldehyde, wood furniture may be treated with clear coatings and sealants designed to protect against water, scratches, and stains. Some finishes may release volatile organic compounds into indoor air. VOCs vary greatly in their safety. One common VOC is d-limonene, which is derived from orange peel oil. It sounds like it would be safe, right? D-limonene can irritate skin and eyes, and may be a reproductive hazard.

If you are using hand-me-down or vintage pieces, make sure they were not painted with a lead-based paint. Lead-based paint for household furniture was not banned until 1978, so earlier pieces may have been painted with it. I had a client who was trying to put together a green nursery by repurposing and using thrift-shop and antique-shop finds. She hired me to test her house using a Niton XRF analyzer right before the birth of her baby. The furniture was mostly weathered looking, with available flakes of paint. I found that all but one of the vintage, shabby-chic pieces had elevated lead, ranging between 90,000 and 195,000 ppm lead. The current federal standard is 600 ppm, and that will drop to 90 ppm in August 2009.

Furniture: Smart Mama's Simple Steps to Reduce Exposure

Go for non-toxic finishes. If you are buying wood furniture, make sure the coating is non-toxic. Look for natural finishes made with plant oils (other than d-limonene), tree resins, minerals, and beeswax, or low- or no-VOC finishes.

Just say no to formaldehyde. If you are buying furniture made with manufactured wood products, look for formaldehyde-free products. Avoid bare, uncoated urea-formaldehyde pressed-wood products that can emit relatively high amounts of formaldehyde.

Let it off-gas outside. Buying green can be expensive, and green products are sometimes difficult to find. If you can't find formaldehyde-free particleboard, let the furniture off-gas as long as you can outside of the nursery, and preferably outside the home, before bringing the furniture inside. Formaldehyde emissions are highest the first month after manufacture, and then gradually decline over several years. Make sure that the area you leave it in has fresh air passing by.

Control climate. The amount of formaldehyde released is increased with increasing temperature and humidity. Keep the humidity and temperature low, and you can reduce the amount of formaldehyde released.

Make sure hand-me-downs meet current standards. If you are using hand-me-downs, make sure that they meet the current safety standards. Cribs manufactured before 1990 may not meet current safety standards. Importantly, the distance between crib slats should not exceed 2 3/8 inches. If the hand-me-downs are painted, make sure the paint is lead free. Lead-based paints were banned from residential furniture and children's toys in 1978, but you should always test hand-me-downs. (See Chapter 4, "Getting the Lead Out," for testing information.)

Seal bare urea-formaldehyde wood products with multiples layers of water-resistant sealants. Research indicates that sealing bare urea-formaldehyde wood products can reduce formaldehyde emissions for months to years after application. Seal all unfinished edges of finished furniture. Of course, the sealants themselves may release other VOCs, so check labels carefully. Use a no- or low-VOC sealant.

Ventilate. Since babies spend 90 percent of their time indoors, make sure to keep the home well ventilated. Opening windows and using fans to move and circulate the air will lower formaldehyde levels inside.

Go green (literally). Some plants have shown an ability to remove pollutants from the air based upon a study by NASA to maintain air quality in confined spaces. Plants shown to remove formaldehyde are those with large leaf surface areas, including azalea, aloe vera, bamboo palm, Boston fern, corn plant, Chinese evergreen, chrysanthemum, date palm, dieffenbachia, golden pothos, mini-schefflera, peace lily, peperomia, mother-in-law's tongue, philodendron (heart-leaf, lacy tree, or elephant ear), poinsettia, snake plant, and spider plant. But I would consider avoiding plants considered poisonous to infants. Also, indoor plants can be problematic. Mold can grow in potted soils and release spores into the air. Houseplants add moisture, thereby fostering the growth of mold and dust mites. No study confirms that houseplants remove significant quantities of pollutants in the home environment, but they may help remove some.

Mattresses

If you have a newborn and are sleep deprived, you may not believe it, but babies may spend as much as twenty hours sleeping. Of course, except for a few lucky, obviously blessed parents, it never seems that babies sleep for any considerable consecutive period of time, and definitely never, ever at night. On average, infants and toddlers spend ten to fourteen hours a day sleeping, most likely on a baby or crib mattress.

A sleeping baby inhales air no more than six inches away from his mattress and, consequently, inhales any chemicals present in that mattress. For the first few years of a child's life, his crib mattress may be the single most prominent object in his environment.

What could be harmful in a mattress? Well, unfortunately, a lot. Conventional baby mattresses are usually filled with polyurethane foam. Polyurethane foam can off-gas toluene and other toxic chemicals. Toluene affects the central nervous system, causing headaches, nausea, dizziness, clumsiness, and drowsiness.[22] It is a respiratory and skin irritant. It is on California's Proposition 65 list of chemicals known to cause reproductive harm or other birth defects.

Other chemicals off-gas as well. A study of three polyurethane mattresses found a number of VOCs emitted from the mattresses, including styrene, ethyl benzene, 1,3-dichlorobenzene, and isopropylbenzene.[23] The study also looked at how the off-gassing affected mice, and reported that mice experienced sensory irritation, pulmonary irritation, and airflow limitation as a result of emissions from the mattresses.[24] However, this study has been criticized because its results were not replicated by a subsequent study.

Polyurethane foam is highly flammable, and is usually treated with chemical fire retardants. We've previously talked about chemical flame retardants known as polybrominated diphenyl ethers (PBDEs). (See Chapter 3.) PBDEs are added to mattresses (and other consumer products) to meet flammability standards.

As of 2004, because of concerns related to PBDEs' persistence in the environment, toxicity, and ability to bioaccumulate, penta-BDE and octa-BDE were voluntarily phased out of production in the United States.[25] But let me caution you: the cessation of manufacturing was not a federal ban on products containing penta-BDE and octa-BDE. Therefore, imported products may contain PBDEs, although some states do have limited bans against PBDEs in consumer products.

And deca-BDE remains in use, although it may be on its way out, too.[26] In 2007, Washington banned the manufacture, distribution, or sale of mattresses made with deca-BDE effective January 1, 2008. Industry maintains that deca-BDE is safe for use and is environmentally stable. Recent data challenges industry's assertions, suggesting instead that deca-BDE breaks down into more toxic compounds and is also more persistent in the environment than believed.

PBDEs were added to mattresses to meet a standard that prevented a cigarette from setting the mattress on fire.[27] However, a new national standard went into effect in 2007, which appears to be encouraging the use of methods other than the addition of chemical flame retardants.[28] This new standard is performance based. It does not dictate how a manufacturer must comply with the standard, only that a mattress must meet the specified performance criteria. Some mattress manufacturers are using barrier methods to meet the new standard, such as using a barrier material that is inherently nonflammable. But other mattress manufacturers continue to use chemical fire retardants, including barrier methods that contain chemical fire retardants. Of course, as always, some of the new methods haven't been thoroughly investigated for long-term health effects. For example, nanomaterials—materials with nanoparticles added to impact certain functions, such as flame resistance—are being developed. There is always a potential for harm when new technologies have not been thoroughly evaluated.

In developing the new mattress-ignition standard, the U.S. Consumer Product Safety Commission (CPSC) evaluated the potential health effects associated with exposure to certain chemicals it believed were likely to be used to meet the standard: antimony trioxide, boric acid/zinc borate, decabromodiphenyl oxide (or deca-BDE), melamine, and vinylidene chloride.[29] The risk-assessment evaluation included migration studies to assess how much of these chemicals were released when used in mattresses. Although antimony trioxide, boric acid/zinc borate, and deca-BDE were found to be released,[30] the CPSC risk assessment concluded that all five chemicals could be used and were not expected to pose any appreciable risk of health effects to consumers who sleep on treated mattresses.

However, the risk-assessment admitted that there were data gaps and that assumptions were made in the risk-assessment process. One problematic assumption was the skin absorption rate for antimony. Since one was not available, one was assumed, but it may not be accurate.[31] Some consumers have reported adverse health effects from mattresses treated with antimony as well as borate. Another more significant limitation for assessing exposure for infants is that the risk assessment did not include any evaluation of exposures for children under the age of five years. The risk assessment assumed that because children under the age of five would sleep on a mattress with polyvinyl chloride (PVC) barrier for bed-wetting purposes, they would be protected from any released fire-retardant chemicals. But there was no factual support cited to this assumption that PVC barriers would prevent exposure to the fire retardants. This, of course, assumes that you are using a PVC barrier—a problem in itself given the presence of phthalates and lead.

The CPSC does seem uncomfortable with the conclusion that fire-retardant chemicals are safe. In her statement voting to approve a notice of proposed rulemaking addressing the flammability of upholstered furniture, acting chairperson of the CPSC Nancy Nord stated, "I am pleased that the [Notice of Proposed Rulemaking] (NPR) addresses upholstered furniture fires without requiring the use of fire retardant ("FR") chemicals. I was concerned that a previous proposal would require extensive use of FR chemicals and the health effects of some of these chemicals are not well-understood. Therefore I directed the staff to try to address the fire risk associated with upholstered furniture without encouraging the use of FR chemicals."[32]

As previously mentioned, conventional crib mattresses are usually covered with polyvinyl chloride (PVC), which may release phthalates and may also contain lead. Phthalates and lead are both associated with adverse health effects. Certain phthalates are endocrine disruptors. Lead can cause a host of problems. Finally, the mattress covering may be treated with flame retardants and stain and water repellents, all of which may off-gas chemicals.

When shopping for a mattress, it is extremely difficult to get information from conventional mattress manufacturers as to the exact technology they are using to meet the flammability standards. When I was recently shopping for a new mattress, only one salesperson out of the eight "conventional" showrooms I visited could answer my questions. I was told at several stores that it is impossible to buy a mattress without flame retardants (not true). When I asked for a natural or organic mattress, several stores steered me to a latex mattress but could not tell me whether the latex was natural.

By the way, unless you have extremely well-mannered children (and if you do, goody for you), don't take your kids mattress shopping with you. Most mattress showrooms have the mattresses laid out like beds, without any bedding, stretching across the showroom. Perfectly reasonable—the layout allows shoppers to stretch out and feel the mattresses. But what do all those beds look like to a two-year-old and a five-year-old? Disneyland! Whoo-hoo! As my darling children leaped gleefully and maniacally from one mattress to the next, it was difficult to get any sales associate to take my pointed questions about flame retardants seriously.

Mattresses: Smart Mama's Simple Steps to Reduce Exposure

Go natural. Cotton and wool are naturally flame resistant, so chemical fire retardants are not necessary. However, it is my understanding that a 100 percent cotton mattress will not meet the federal flammability standard. A doctor's note is required (see below) in order to purchase one. Latex is another natural option, but alone it will not pass the flammability test. A combination of cotton and wool can meet the federal flammability standard without the addition of chemical flame retardants, or a combination of wool with natural latex. Choose organic wool and organic cotton to avoid any pesticide residue (and protect our environment, too!). Make sure that the cotton is not finished with chemicals, as well. The term "organic cotton" refers just to how the cotton is grown, not how it is treated. Always ask how the cotton fabric is finished.

Look for the Organic Trade Association's seal. With that seal, you can be sure that the processing to produce the finished cotton was organic.

Get a doctor's note. Federal regulations provide that with a doctor's written prescription, a mattress can be sold that doesn't meet the federal flammability standards.[33] Several sources have organic cotton mattresses available upon presentation of a doctor's prescription.

Be persistent. Always ask what is used to meet the federal flammability standard. I admit, it is hard to get information from most retailers regarding what is actually in the mattress. But retailers who know in detail how their mattresses meet the flammability standards are more likely to carry mattresses that don't have added flame-retardant chemicals.

Let it off-gas outside. If you do purchase a conventional crib mattress, let it off-gas outside before bringing it inside for a minimum of three days, even longer if you can.

Skip PVC. Skip the PVC waterproof cover. If you want a waterproof cover, choose polyethylene instead. Just keep in mind that polyethylene is a plastic—so it isn't organic, obviously. Some Web sites urge you to skip polyethylene because of phthalates. Even though polyethylene terephthalate (the plastic) seems like it may contain phthalates, it is not the same as "phthalates" (the additives). They are chemically dissimilar. PET is not considered a phthalate and PET does not require the use of softening additives like PVC plastic.

> **SMART MAMA TIP**
>
> There seems to be a lot of confusion about latex, so here's a primer. Natural latex is made from the sap of the rubber tree. Traditionally, it was manufactured using the Dunlop process. One problem with the Dunlop process is that it is difficult to produce long-lasting soft latex. Blended latex combines natural and synthetic latex using the Dunlop process. But synthetic latex is man-made from chemicals and petroleum. There is also blended latex using the Talalay process, often called "Talalay latex," which is usually natural and synthetic latex blended together. The Talalay manufacturing process produces long-lasting latex in a range of firmness. However, 100 percent natural latex manufactured using the Talalay process exists. If a retailer tells you that a mattress is 100 percent Talalay latex and you want it to be all-natural latex, you need to confirm that it is 100 percent natural latex produced with the Talalay process.

Children's Bedding

When you select your child's bedding, you may want to go with organic cotton or another natural fiber. Conventional cotton is one of the most pesticide-dependent crops. It is reported that 25 percent of the world's insecticides are used to grow conventional cotton, and some of the pesticides may be found as residues. Pesticides are linked to a number of adverse health effects.

For children, you really don't need a lot of bedding, so you may want to spring for organic cotton or other natural fibers.

When choosing bedding, keep in mind that formaldehyde is often used to treat fabrics, including cotton, to give them all sorts of easy-care properties. We like our fabrics to be permanent press or durable press. We also like anti-cling, anti-static, anti-wrinkle, and anti-shrink (especially shrink-proof wool); waterproof and stain resistant (especially for suede and chamois); perspiration proof; mothproof; mildew resistant, and color fast. And how do you think fabrics get that way? Chemicals. The most common baby-bedding materials are polyester-and-cotton blends, polyester, or cotton. All of these materials can be finished to create the easy-care fabrics desired by consumers, and they usually are. As a result, conventional baby-bedding materials are usually finished with a formaldehyde derivative, even if the fabric is organic cotton.

Formaldehyde is a carcinogen, irritant, and strong sensitizer. Exposure to formaldehyde in dry products, such as permanent-press fabric, can cause allergic skin reactions. Some children (and adults) experience contact dermatitis as a result of formaldehyde released from fabrics. Researchers believe that sweat may increase the release of formaldehyde from treated fabrics. Because of advances in fabric finishing, the amount of formaldehyde in products has been reduced over the last several years. Information from the American Chemical Society indicates that formaldehyde released from fabric has been reduced from 3,000 parts per million to about 250 parts per million.[34]

If you don't want to be exposed to formaldehyde, steer clear of easy-care fabrics. And this applies to organic cotton as well. On organic cotton baby bedding, look for labeling indicating that the material is formaldehyde free. If the label doesn't indicate this, you may be able to get the information from the sales staff or the manufacturing company. Many companies claim that their materials are "natural fiber," but this doesn't mean chemical free. Natural-fiber bedding (and clothing too) simply designates that the fabric is made from fibers found in nature, such as cotton, wool, or hemp. It doesn't mean that they were grown without pesticides, nor does it mean that they weren't treated with chemicals. You can look for the "Global Organic Trade Certification—Organic" designation on the label, which means that the fiber was organically grown and processed without harsh chemicals.

Some fabrics are naturally wrinkle resistant, such as bamboo fabric, which resists wrinkling without the addition of formaldehyde. And most bamboo is environmentally friendly to boot, although some bamboo processing is not environmentally friendly.

You also want to skip fabrics treated to be stain resistant. Stain-resistant fabrics are usually treated with a fluorotelomer compounds. These compounds can break down into potentially toxic compounds in the body, although the mechanisms for exposure and how these compounds behave are just being understood.

Also skip antibacterial fabrics. You don't need them, and the long-term health effects of exposure to triclosan, the chemical that makes the fabric antibacterial, is not understood. It has been shown to disrupt development of frogs, and it has been shown to be an irritant.

Chemicals in Bedding: Smart Mama's Simple Steps for Reducing Exposure

Got organic? Buy organic children's bedding to eliminate exposure to pesticide residue. Generally, green cotton has not been bleached with chlorine or treated with formaldehyde. Look for "100% Organic" from the Organic Trade Association, or "Global Organic Trade Certification—Organic" for natural fibers grown organically *and* processed without harsh chemicals.

Skip easy care. Avoid bedding advertised as "wrinkle resistant" or "no ironing required," unless it is naturally so, as with bamboo fiber. Such advertising usually signals that the fabric has been treated with formaldehyde.

Wash new treated fabrics. The California Air Resources Board estimates that laundering new fabrics before use can reduce formaldehyde emissions by about 60 percent. However, the fabric treatments are designed to last the fabric's life, so washing will not eliminate all formaldehyde emissions. Launder three times at the hottest temperature the fabric can take to significantly reduce (but not eliminate) formaldehyde emissions.

Make your own. Okay, this probably isn't a "simple" step. But you can usually buy untreated unbleached cotton or cotton flannel at fabric stores to make your own bedding.

Chapter 8

Busy Baby, Busy Mom: The Playroom and Baby Gear

It really is unbelievable how something so tiny can have so much stuff. I suppose it is our society, however, more than the baby, that has convinced us that we need all these things to make our parental lives easier: a pack-and-play, a feeding chair, a sleep positioner, toys, rattles, a changing pad, bottle warmer, diaper-wipe warmer, a diaper bag, and on and on.

I have to admit, I was always envious of the one mom who seemed to travel so lightly—just an organic cotton sling and her baby and she was ready to go. And there is always one mom like this in any group. How I envied her freedom and the fact that she was unburdened. She always walked serenely, with a carefree smile and a happily gurgling or sleeping baby. She never seemed to experience an excess of baby spitup (baby-burp towel and necessary changes of clothing—for both me and the baby), or breast-milk leakage (another change of clothing for me), or a diaper blowout (diaper, wipes, and change of clothing), or any of the other disasters for which I planned and regularly experienced. I wish I could say that cosmic karma got her one day and I experienced a sense of satisfaction, but, alas, it never happened.

In any event, most of us need stuff. Or at least we think we need stuff. And most of that stuff has chemicals in it.

Sleep Positioners

In an effort to prevent sudden infant death syndrome, parents are urged to keep their babies sleeping on their backs. To accomplish this, some parents use sleep positioners. They are also helpful for babies who spit up frequently. But sleep positioners are often made of polyurethane foam and are covered with PVC, so they may off-gas polybrominated diphenyl ethers (PBDEs) and VOCs, and may also expose your baby to phthalates.

As we've talked about before, a PBDE or another chlorinated or brominated flame retardant may be added to polyurethane foam to make it less flammable. Exposure to PBDEs has been linked to impaired learning and memory, delayed onset of puberty, reproductive effects, impaired immune system, and cancer. Early exposure to PBDEs appears to affect the thyroid hormone system. Thyroid hormone levels are critical for normal brain development in fetuses and through approximately two years of age.[1] Abnormal thyroid hormone levels can disrupt brain development, potentially impairing a child's intelligence and affecting behavior.

A survey conducted by the U.S. PIRG Education Fund and the Environment California Research & Policy Center found PBDEs in the foam material of the First Years' Air Flow Sleep Positioner and Leachco's Sleep 'N Secure 3-in-1 Infant Sleep Positioner. No PBDEs were detected in Dex's Secure Sleeper Ultra 3-in-1 Sleep Positioner.[2]

Polyurethane foam also off-gasses volatile organic compounds (VOCs). VOCs can cause adverse health effects, from irritation to cancer.

Sleep positioners may also be covered with PVC. PVC usually contains hormone-disrupting phthalates and may contain lead. As previously mentioned, the Consumer Product Safety Improvement Act establishes a ban of phthalates in children's toys and child-care articles. The term "child-care articles" includes all products intended for children under the age of three that facilitate sleeping or eating. So after February 10, 2009, sleep positioners should not contain certain phthalates in excess of 0.1 percent. However, compliance may be spotty. The CPSC's opinion that the phthalate ban was not retroactive was reversed by a court challenge only days before the February 10, 2009 deadline, leading to a mad scramble to address existing inventory.

Sleep Positioners: Smart Mama's Simple Steps for Reducing Exposure

Skip polyurethane foam. Get a sleep positioner that is not made of polyurethane foam. This may be hard to find, but you should be able to locate one with a little bit of effort.

Use an alternative. Sleep sacks and swaddling may be just as effective as a sleep positioner. Or, if you need a sleep positioner, you may be able to make your own at home. However, if you elect to do this always keep in mind the guidelines to prevent SIDS: no pillow, stuffed animals, or fluffy bedding in cribs.

Skip vinyl. Just skip it. You don't need it. Choose another covering for any sleep positioner.

Changing Pads

Just like sleep positioners, changing pads may be made of polyurethane foam and coated or covered with polyvinyl chloride. Polyurethane foam can off-gas a number of volatile organic compounds (VOCs) and also may contain chemical flame retardants, most likely a polybrominated diphenyl ether (PBDE). The PBDE can be released from the foam. Thus, changing pads can expose your baby to VOCs and PBDEs.

If the changing pad is covered with polyvinyl chloride (PVC), it may also expose your baby to phthalates and lead. Phthalates are used to soften PVC and make it flexible. They can be found at levels of 30 percent by weight in such products as changing-pad and mattress covers. Lead is used to stabilize PVC. Using my Niton XRF analyzer, I have found elevated concentrations of lead in PVC-covered changing pads. This should be addressed by the CPSIA as of February 10, 2009. However, unlike sleep positioners, changing pads are not child-care articles designed to facilitate sleep or eating, so the phthalate ban in the CPSIA does not aply to changing pads.

Changing Pads: Smart Mama's Simple Steps to Reduce Exposure

Skip the changing pad. You don't really need a changing pad. Trust me, you really don't. A folded towel or blanket can work just as well.

Skip polyurethane foam. You can find changing pads with certified organic cotton filling or other similar natural-fiber filling materials.

Go natural. Look for a changing pad cover that is made of a natural fiber, such as organic cotton. A loop cotton, such as terry, will provide some loft if you desire.

Choose polyethylene. If you must have a waterproof, easy-clean type of covering, choose polyethylene over PVC.

Pack-and-Plays

Pack-and-plays (essentially, portable cribs/play yards) are handy and usually essential travel gear to visit relatives. Yet most pack-and-plays are made from polyvinyl chloride (PVC) plastic, and the cushioning foam at the bottom is usually PVC-plastic-encased polyurethane foam containing chemical flame retardants. PVC may contain lead and may also contains phthalates. Both of these cause adverse health effects.

As we discussed in connection with crib mattresses, polyurethane foam off-gasses a number of potentially harmful chemicals. In addition, polyurethane foam is highly flammable, so it most likely contains a polybrominated diphenyl ether flame retardant or another chlorinated or brominated flame retardant. PBDEs are associated with adverse health effects.

I haven't yet seen an organic, completely non-toxic option for a pack-and-play, but you can find a pack-and-play that doesn't use PVC (or vinyl). And you can replace the cushion with one that doesn't contain flame retardants.

If you have one already, keep it dust free. Wipe it down before your baby uses it to reduce the contaminated dust your baby comes into contact with. You can also use a blanket to line the inside—just make sure that it is tight-fitting to prevent suffocation.

Pack-and-Plays: Smart Mama's Simple Steps to Reduce Exposure

Skip PVC. Look for a pack-and-play that is free of polyvinyl chloride.

Skip polyurethane foam. Look for a pack-and-play that does not have a polyurethane foam pad in the bottom. Or, if it does, take it out and use an organic cotton and wool pad.

Let it breathe. If you can't find a pack-and-play without PVC and polyurethane foam, let it ventilate away from the baby for several days before using. This will reduce your baby's exposure to some of the chemicals, but not all.

Keep it dust free. Reduce your baby's exposure to contaminated dust by keeping the pack-and-play free of dust. Wipe it down with a damp cloth before each use.

Use a blanket. If it makes sense, use a blanket or sheet to cover the bottom. Just make sure it fits snugly.

High Chairs

It is most critical to buy a high chair that is safe. Check out the Consumer Product Safety Commission's Web site first for recalled high chairs before buying or borrowing one. You may want to check *Consumer Reports'* Web site as well. It frequently has information on its tests of various high chairs.

In terms of toxic chemical exposures, foam-padded high chairs may contain polyurethane foam in the cushion. As we've discussed, polyurethane foam off-gasses a number of potentially harmful chemicals and may also contain PBDEs.

High chairs may also have padding covered with polyvinyl chloride (PVC) plastic. PVC plastic is waterproof and easy to clean, but it may also contain lead and does contain phthalates. Both lead and phthalates can cause adverse health effects. High chairs are arguably intended for children under three and facilitate eating. Thus, the CPSIA's ban on phthalates may apply. Cloth-covered high chairs are available, but cloth can be difficult to clean. The cloth may be treated with stain and grease repellents, which are also linked to health effects. Ask questions about the cloth if you can.

Wooden high chairs are available. Some of the more expensive, high-end designs convert to chairs that may prolong their usefulness (and justify their price). Alternatively, you may be able to find an unfinished wood chair and finish it yourself. If you are pregnant, have someone else finish it for you, even if you are using low-toxicity materials. Whichever option you choose, don't forget to consider the finish. The best finish would be a high chair finished with walnut oil, linseed oil, or natural tung oil, or beeswax. Or look for wooden high chairs finished with no-VOC or low-VOC finishes.

Keep in mind that you don't really use a high chair for all that long so you may want to borrow one, which is always a green solution.

High Chairs: Smart Mama's Simple Steps to Reduce Exposure

Skip PVC. Always the best solution. Reduce exposure by skipping PVC.

Skip polyurethane foam. Just skip high chairs padded with polyurethane foam. Or, if the high chair you already have has polyurethane foam, remove it if you can, or let it off-gas outside.

Wood is good. Wood is a great option, as long as the finish is low or no VOC.

Teethers

Soft teethers may expose your baby to phthalates.

The CPSC conducted an assessment of diisononyl phthalate (DINP) in children's products, most notably teethers, to determine whether babies were exposed to levels of concern. The report concluded that they weren't exposed to enough DINP to be considered a problem. But the conclusion wasn't that DINP isn't associated with health effects, or that DINP doesn't leach from plastic teethers. Instead, the conclusion was based primarily on an exposure assessment. And the critical factor in that assessment was the time the children mouthed the phthalate-containing objects. The study used observational studies, where children are observed for a fixed period of time and observations are made of the items they mouth. This method tends to underreport mouthing time by 30 percent or so when compared to studies that use observational reports coupled with recording activities. The observational study looked at activity in ten fifteen-minute periods over two days. The study then eliminated mouthing activities of any item that didn't contain phthalates: wood toys, pacifiers, fingers and toes, etc. The resulting estimates of mouthing times? For children between the ages of three and twelve months, 12.03 minutes per day were spent mouthing vinyl teethers, and for children between the ages of three and twenty-six months, 2.1 minutes per day. Using these mouthing time estimates and applying the DINP leaching factor in the presence of saliva, the report concludes that mouthing teethers isn't a concern.

Say what? I have to object to the methodology. If your child happens to mouth vinyl teethers more than 12.03 minutes per day, you are going to have a significantly greater exposure. At 75 minutes per day, your baby will be exposed to levels consistent with those showing adverse health effects. And this only considers phthalate exposure from teethers, not from any other source. Do vinyl toys carry such warnings? No. When the industry claims that phthalates don't show any health effects from normal use, this is the sort of study the industry uses for support.

The good news is that the CPSIA bans certain phthalates in teethers beginning February 10, 2009. However, there has been a lot of confusion, so it may be some time before all teethers on the market are free of certain banned phthalates.

SMART MAMA TIP

Those soft vinyl teethers look great, but you may not want your baby to get a dose of phthalates (or even lead) while teething. If you are looking for a substitute for a PVC teether, try a small cloth (preferably an organic cloth) with a small corner wetted, crinkled up, and frozen before use. If that doesn't work, natural wood teethers work well. Another solution is a silicone teether.

Toys

Contrary to public perception, up until the Consumer Product Safety Improvement Act of 2008 (CPSIA), the federal Consumer Product Safety Act (CPSA), enforced by the CPSC, did not require any pre-market safety testing of most toys—or of other consumer products, for that matter. Instead, manufacturers were required to ensure that their toys were properly labeled and that they met federal standards. The sweeping changes enacted in August 2008 have changed all of that, and toy manufacturers are now required to provide independent testing.

Other changes in the CPSIA include establishing for the first time a standard for lead (as opposed to lead in paint) in children's products. The term "children's products" is broadly defined and includes all products intended primarily for use by children under the age of twelve. Beginning February 10, 2009, no children's product can contain more than 600 ppm lead. This provision has been interpreted to apply retroactively so that existing inventory must meet this standard. That maximum level of 600 ppm lead will be reduced to 300 ppm on August 14, 2009.

Another change is that certain phthalates are limited to 0.1 percent in children's toys and child-care articles (defined as products intended for children under the age of three that facilitate sleeping or eating). This provision applies to children's toys and child-care articles beginning February 10, 2009. Although the CPSC originally opined that this provision was not retroactive and existing inventory could be sold, that opinion was set aside by a court after a legal challenge.

Toys made out of polyvinyl chloride (PVC) plastic may expose your child to lead and phthalates. PVC is a soft, flexible plastic; think of a yellow raincoat or the lining of a lunch box. Those are both usually PVC.

PVC must be stabilized, otherwise it loses strength. PVC is usually stabilized with a metallic salt, often lead but sometimes cadmium or organotin compounds. Lead and cadmium (if used) are not bound up in the plastic polymer and will migrate to the surface and be available for pickup. This process is enhanced by exposure to friction and heat.

Greenpeace issued a study finding lead in many popular children's toys and products. However, the Consumer Product Safety Commission (CPSC) attempted to replicate Greenpeace's findings, and did not find that hazardous lead levels were released from PVC toys. One problem with the CPSC's efforts? It did not "weather" any of the toys tested because CPSC concluded that children's products would not have prolonged exposures to sunlight and heat in the course of reasonably foreseeable use. I think the people at the CPSC have completely forgotten how kids play with toys.

Another problem with the CPSC's evaluation is that it was completed in 1999, before new studies showed that lower lead levels may result in significant health effects, including a substantial drop in IQ.

As we have discussed, lead is a neurotoxin and can cause a host of adverse health effects. Lead exposure is cumulative, so all the little exposures can add up.

PVC also contain phthalates. Phthalates are added to PVC to soften it and make it flexible. Phthalates are hormone disruptors. Again, although the CPSIA bans certain phthalates in toys, because of confusion regarding the law, it may take time for full compliance.

SMART MAMA WARNING

Yes, unfortunately, those keys, so attractive to baby, contain lead. Home and car keys made of brass typically contain lead. Brass keys generally contain about 2 percent lead. Lead is added to brass to make it easier to cut. When a baby handles brass keys or puts them in his mouth, he can be exposed to lead.

Surprised? Many parents are. It seems that keys are a fail-safe of parents everywhere when a baby acts up and no other soothing devices are on hand. How many of us haven't jangled keys when a baby gets fussy in the supermarket?

In a response to a *Consumer Reports* article about what parents can do to reduce lead exposure, one parent wrote that her daughter was diagnosed with lead poisoning. The source? Her brass office key and brass house key, with which her daughter played.

The California Childcare Health Program advises that children should never be allowed to play with house or car keys, and that pregnant women should minimize their exposure by washing their hands after handling keys.

Are we sure that babies are exposed to lead in brass keys? Yes. In connection with a lawsuit filed by the California attorney general against thirteen manufacturers of brass keys and locks under California's Proposition 65, testing was conducted to determine if enough lead was present to require a Proposition 65 warning. (California's Proposition 65 law requires warnings to consumers before exposing them to certain substances, including lead.) Laboratory tests showed that handling the keys could result in exposure to lead. The highest test results showed exposure at 80 times the Proposition 65 so-called safe level of 0.5 micrograms per day, while the lowest was still above that safe level. As a result, in California, brass keys must carry a Proposition 65 warning if they contain more than 1.5 percent lead.

I don't know about the lead level in brass keys sold in other states, but even the 1.5 percent is too much for me—it is significantly above the lead level allowed in paint (0.06 percent). Of course, I recognize the medium is different. Yet, with no lead level being safe for children, I didn't want my children to get in the habit of chewing on keys.

What can you do? Don't let your children play with your keys. Don't forget to remind other caregivers as well. My mom, despite lots of warnings, still doesn't hesitate to jingle keys to calm my daughter—it's just too ingrained. And make sure you wash your hands after handling your keys and digging in your purse—there's enough lead dust in there to be a significant exposure if you let your keys rattle around loose. This is especially important if you are pregnant or nursing. You might want to think about keeping your keys in a designated pocket. And brass keys that are plated will reduce exposure as compared to unplated keys.

Plastic, wood, glass, or ceramic toys can all be painted or decorated with a paint or coating. That surface coating could contain lead, cadmium, and other toxic chemicals. Federal law limits the amount of lead in paints or other coatings to 600 ppm. But, as we learned in 2007 with the massive recall of toys from popular brands such as Fisher-Price and Disney, that standard isn't always met.

And, prior to the recently enacted CPSIA, no federal standard for lead in toys themselves existed—there were standards only for paints and coatings. Surprising, isn't it? You'd think that there would have been a limit for lead in toys before last August. And quite a few toys that do not have paints or coatings have tested positive for lead. I thought most of our toys were pretty safe—I've been careful with respect to what I've let in the house. I tested some of the toys with a handheld XRF device, which detects the amount of lead in toys. Most toys were pretty good. But then I tested a set of yellow plastic drumsticks; they weren't painted or coated, and the yellow was an integral part of the plastic. The results? 45,000 ppm. Yes, that is right: 45,000 ppm. I was horrified. And then I felt guilty since my daughter had played with them the night before.

Even with the recalls of 2007, testing by the Ecology Center for the 2008 holiday season found lead, cadmium, and other chemicals in about 80 percent of the 1,500 toys it analyzed. The results of the testing:

- 41 percent had low levels of the chemicals of concern;
- 29 percent had medium levels; and
- 9 percent had high concentrations.

We've already talked about the hazards associated with lead, but just to review, lead can harm brain development, resulting in reduced IQ, shorter attention span, and delayed learning. It is widely recognized that there is no safe level of lead. Cadmium, also found in toys, is a carcinogen. It is also associated with developmental deficiencies, including delayed sensory motor development, hormonal effects, and altered behavior.

The risk of lead exposure for toys may be small in comparison to the risk of lead poisoning from lead-based paint and household dust contaminated with lead, but every source of lead exposure matters. As explained by Mary Jean Brown, chief of the CDC's Lead Poisoning Branch, "Every little bit counts because once lead is in the body, it's very difficult to remove."[3] And toys coated with lead add to the risk. "Parents need to know it is not an acute problem," states John Benitez, M.D., director of the Lawrence Poison and Drug Information Center and associate professor of pediatric and environmental medicine at the University of Rochester, New York. "If a kid just touches and plays with a lead painted toy, it is not a problem. But if that child sits and chews on it for weeks and months and absorbs lead—that becomes a risk."

Why worry about lead in toys? Seek out alternates.

Toys: Smart Mama's Simple Steps to Reduce Exposure

Wood is good. Wood toys are a great solution to avoid the risks of plastics. Look for toys colored with vegetable dyes or those finished with walnut oil, linseed oil, pure tung oil (be careful—sometimes "tung oil finish" is used as a generic term to describe a wetted wood finish), or with beeswax. And always look for the Forestry Stewardship's seal.

Cloth is good too. Cloth toys are another solution to avoid PVC plastic toys. Try organic cloth toys that aren't treated with formaldehyde or grown with pesticides.

Check for recalled toys. Keep an eye out for recalls. Regularly check the CPSC's Web site identifying recalled toys.

Use the toy database. You can check out your toys by using the toy database maintained by the Ecology Center at www.healthytoys.org. It even has the capability to use your mobile phone for information while you shop.

Test your toys. You can use the home lead test kits (discussed in Chapter 4) as a screen. But be aware that they check only for lead, not for all chemicals of concern. And they are prone to both false positives and false negatives.

Children's Jewelry

Children's jewelry seems harmless, but it is the opposite. The CPSC states that jewelry containing more than 0.06 percent total lead can result in excess lead exposure if children ingest the jewelry, but there has not been a standard for jewelry up until the enactment of the CPSIA in August 2008.[4] Up until the adoption of the CPSIA, the only standard for lead in children's items was for paints and other surface coatings and a voluntary standard of 0.06 percent.

Lead has been found in unsafe levels in children's jewelry. According to the Center for Environmental Health (CEH), testing performed in advance of a Proposition 65 lawsuit filed by CEH showed that lead levels in PVC cords on children's costume jewelry ranged from 1,400 to 20,000 ppm, and lead levels in a child's bracelet tested at over 165,000 ppm. In tests conducted by the CPSC and others, metal components often tested at over 500,000 ppm, and as high as 950,000, or 95 percent lead. Tragically, a four-year-old boy died after ingesting a charm that was mostly lead. The bracelets were tucked inside a pair of Reebok shoes as a gift with purchase. Parts of the bracelet were more than 99 percent lead. At the time, while federal law bans the amount of lead in paints and coatings used on consumer products, no federal law addressed lead in children's jewelry. The recently adopted Consumer Product Safety Improvement Act sets a standard for all children's products, effective in February 2009, including children's jewelry.

Recalls for lead in children's jewelry have included pieces from big-name retailers, including Limited Too, Juicy Couture, Claire's, and Kmart. And children do get sick from lead in jewelry. Cynthia O. Keeton told the *Tampa Tribune* that she had treated at least four children, although she suspects more, whose lead poisoning was linked to children's jewelry. One child, a three-year-old girl, treasured a Catholic saint charm and kept placing it in her mouth. Blood tests showed that the girl's blood lead level was approaching 20 micrograms per deciliter, or double the so-called "level of concern."[5]

Lead in Children's Jewelry: Smart Mama's Simple Steps to Reduce Exposure

Buy "pure" metals. If you are buying more than costume jewelry, buy sterling silver, gold, or other quality jewelry. Lead is not usually a component of such jewelry.

Check the recall list. Always check the recall list at the CPSC for any recalled items.

Skip PVC cords, cheap metal components, and paint on fake pearls. All of these are commonly found to contain lead.

Test your children's jewelry. The home test lead kits can be used to test children's jewelry. Just keep in mind that they are not foolproof and have been known to give both false positives and false negatives.

Chapter 9

Rub-a-Dub-Dub: The Bathroom

The bathroom is functional and utilitarian. It is where we take care of basic bodily functions. It can also be magical. It holds the promise of great glamour. The bathroom is the repository of all those interesting, mysterious vials, pots, and tubes that hold great promises, promises to make us look, feel, and smell better. I have to admit that I used to love makeup and personal care products. I wasn't particularly adept at applying makeup, but I loved the promise. I believed that if I could find the right moisturizer, my face would look younger and glow. The right shampoo could make my hair shine, and the right conditioner would make it sleek.

Yes, I had been brainwashed. The cosmetic industry spends more money on television advertising than any other industry, and I had bought into the hype. The cosmetic and toiletry industry accounts for between $32 and $60 billion in annual sales (depending on what products you include in the industry figures). The market includes over 1,000 manufacturing companies but is dominated by large companies, with the ten largest accounting for 62 percent of the total sales. All of these companies are vying to make you the best you can be, if you would just use their products. And, of course, it probably goes without saying that the more products you buy, the better they do.

But my desire for those vials and pots faded when I learned what was in them. All of the products contain chemicals—chemicals that we can pass on to our developing babies when we are pregnant, or to our babies if we are nursing or through skin contact. If the products are intended to be used on infants, toddlers, or kids, we put those chemicals directly on our children, where they can be absorbed through the skin. It has been estimated that the skin absorbs more than 60 percent of what is put on it.

Just think about how many different cosmetics and personal care products you have that you use (we won't talk about all of those products hidden in the back of the cabinet or buried at the bottom of the drawers that didn't work out for one reason or another). Think about all of them: the shampoos and conditioners, the body wash or bar soap, the shaving cream, moisturizer, body lotion, foundation, sunblock, eye shadow, blush, mascara, perfume, makeup remover, and more. The average person uses nine to fifteen personal care products every day, and applies an average of 126 unique ingredients.

Babies, toddlers, and kids are no exception. They get their supply of personal care products as well. Personal baby-care products are a fast-growing segment of the personal care industry. We apply baby lotions, baby shampoos, baby body washes, massage oils, and diaper creams to our babies. The Environmental Working Group (EWG) found that children used an average of five personal care products every day, and are exposed to an average of *sixty-one* unique ingredients in these products each day![1] An infant is exposed to an average of six products and sixty-seven unique chemicals every week. Of these, the EWG contends that twenty-seven have not been found safe for kids.

Children's exposures to personal care products may put them at a greater risk because they are more susceptible to exposure to toxic chemicals. We've talked about it before in Chapter 2: Kids have a greater skin-surface area than adults. Newborns' skin is 30 percent thinner than an adult's, so products applied to a newborn's skin may be absorbed more readily. Plus, since kids are still developing, they lack some of the protective mechanism that adults have.

The EWG's online survey of more than 3,300 parents and EWG's review of the reported products used found that:

- 82 percent of children are exposed on a weekly basis to one or more ingredients with the potential to harm the brain and nervous system;
- 69 percent of children are exposed on a weekly basis to one or more ingredients that are suspected of disrupting the hormone system; and
- 3.6 percent of children are exposed to ingredients with strong data linking them to cancer, including chemicals classified as known or probable human carcinogens.

The EWG also found that 80 percent of children's products marked as gentle and non-irritating actually contained ingredients linked to allergies and skin or eye irritation.

Most people assume that if a product is sold in the United States, some agency must have determined that the product is safe for use. Some 86 percent of us believe personal care products are safe.[2] Most U.S. consumers believe that if they buy products from trusted household brands, they can be confident in the products' safety and that the products don't contain carcinogens, mutagens, or other toxic agents. But that safety guarantee just isn't true for the most part when it comes to cosmetics.

The FDA is vested with responsibility for cosmetics. Cosmetics are defined as "articles intended to be rubbed, poured, sprinkled, or sprayed on, introduced into, or otherwise applied to the human body or any part thereof for cleansing, beautifying, promoting attractiveness, or altering the appearance." But the FDA's authority over cosmetics is relatively limited. As explained on the FDA's Web site, "FDA's legal authority over cosmetics is different from other products regulated by the agency, such as drugs, biologics, and medical devices." The FDA does not approve cosmetics ingredients before they are placed on the market. In fact, the FDA explains that "[i]n general, except for color additives and those ingredients which are prohibited or restricted from use in cosmetics by regulation, a manufacturer may use *any ingredient* in the formulation of a cosmetic provided that the ingredient and the finished cosmetic are safe, the product is properly labeled, and the use of the ingredient does not otherwise cause the cosmetic to be adulterated or misbranded under the laws that FDA enforces." The list of prohibited or restricted ingredients is amazingly short—the FDA has banned nine ingredients and restricted certain color additives. In comparison, the European Union list of prohibited or restricted chemicals is over 1,100 chemicals, although some of the chemicals would never be found in cosmetics.

Who determines whether a cosmetic is safe? As explained on the FDA's Web site, "Cosmetic firms are responsible for substantiating the safety of their products and ingredients before marketing," and not the FDA. In other words, no independent agency determines whether a product is safe. In fact, the FDA doesn't even define the criteria to determine whether a product is safe. The regulations provide that each ingredient must be adequately substantiated for safety prior to marketing, but the FDA doesn't clearly define the meaning of "adequately substantiated" or "safety" for cosmetics. If cosmetic companies don't adequately substantiate a cosmetic product's safety before marketing it, they are required to include on the label the following statement: "Warning—The safety of this product has not been determined." But if there are no definitions or guidance, how does a company even determine whether a product complies? The Environmental Working Group (EWG) states that it reviewed more than 20,000 cosmetic product labels and did not find a single one with the statement. I've never seen such a statement either.

Approximately 89 percent of the ingredients routinely used in cosmetics have not been assessed by the FDA or the industry.[3] According to the EWG, 98 percent of all personal care products contain one or more ingredients never publicly assessed for safety.[4]

Cosmetic companies may privately conduct their own assessments. The cosmetics industry also relies upon the Cosmetic Ingredient Review (CIR). The CIR was created by the cosmetic industry trade group to police the industry. The CIR is funded by the member companies of the Cosmetic, Toiletry and Fragrance Association and its recommendations regarding safety are just that, recommendations, not requirements, and can be ignored. Also, the CIR's focus is whether a cosmetic ingredient causes irritation or allergic reactions, not carcinogenicity or reproductive or developmental toxicity. One analysis of the CIR's ingredient review found that of the ingredients approved by the CIR for use in cosmetics based upon sensitization, 14 percent also had some data indicating cancer risk. Yet the CIR panel still chose sensitization as the area of concern, not carcinogenic potential.[5] For an illuminating discussion of the CIR and the cosmetics industry, I highly recommend Stacy Malkan's book, *Not Just a Pretty Face.*

What about labels? I hate to disillusion even further, but many of the claims on personal care products are meaningless. Most of the claims aren't regulated and don't have any legal meaning. Don't be fooled by labels.

The claim that a product is "hypoallergenic" is not subject to any federal standard or regulation. The term means what any particular company wants it to mean. Some products labeled as "hypoallergenic" contain known allergens, such as quaternium 15 and propylene glycol.

The claim that a product is "cruelty free" or "not tested on animals" is also not regulated by federal standards or regulation. A company may truthfully claim that the finished cosmetic product has not been tested, although the raw materials may have been tested on laboratory animals. If such a claim is important to you, you need to find out what the cosmetic manufacturer means by the claim.

The claim that a product is "natural" has no legal meaning either. Seventy percent of us believe natural products will improve our health. In one sense of the word, petroleum products are natural, aren't they? Petroleum is naturally occurring, formed from the remains of ancient organic material over time. So it qualifies, right? Some cosmetic manufacturers think so. But it probably is not what you want when you buy a "natural" product. It has become a marketing slogan. And just a reminder: natural doesn't necessarily mean safer, either. Chemicals can be harmful whether naturally occurring or synthetically derived.

If you are looking for some guidance, look for products carrying the USDA certified organic label, which indicates the product meets the requirements of the USDA's National Organics Program (NOP), regulating organic ingredients and approving and excluding processing methods. But make sure it is "certified organic by the USDA." The term "organic" in the product's name doesn't have any regulatory significance, nor does its use without the certification (except for California, which has a state law regulating the use of the term organic). And a caveat: some great personal care products are not certified under NOP because the ingredients may not be "agricultural" products, such as minerals. But it is one of the few regulated tools available to identify personal care products.

You may also want to look for products from companies that have signed the compact started by the Campaign for Safe Cosmetics, a coalition of public and environmental health groups that lobbies companies to sign a pledge to voluntarily eliminate chemicals linked to cancer, mutation, birth defects, and other health problems. The steps for compliance with the compact require global compliance with the European Union's Cosmetic Directive, publication of ingredients, substantiation of ingredients and impurities for safety, development of a substitution plan, and transparency and public reporting. A list of companies that have signed the pledge is available from the Campaign for Safe Cosmetics.

A number of private certifiers have popped up, each with its own requirements for certification. These standards are competing in the marketplace for recognition. Some are not as rigorous as others. The best thing you can do? Read the ingredients. If you recognize the ingredients, then the product may be what you want.

What should you look for in personal care products? What do you want to skip? There are so many different products with so many different ingredients that it is hard to provide specific answers. Every person uses different types of products, but this chapter should provide you with some guidance.

Stacy Malkan, author of *Not Just a Pretty Face,* says that people demand that she just tell them what to buy. And I hear that refrain too, from friends and clients. Most people just want to know what to buy and don't want to decipher labels. I understand. But, unfortunately, with the numerous and varied products on the market, we're going to have to talk about the ingredients so that you can figure out what to buy.

Personal Care Products

Before talking about specific potential problem ingredients, let's talk about some general simple steps to buy safer personal care products. Personal care products are hard to discuss in general because there are so many different products, and each individual has her own needs and desires. But here are a couple of general suggestions to get you started:

Be smart about ingredients. Read ingredient lists and ask questions. Then avoid the problem ingredients we will discuss in this chapter.

Channel your inner skeptic. As discussed in this chapter, most marketing claims on personal care products are not regulated by law and have very little meaning. If a product claims to be "natural," read the ingredient list to see if the claim is supported and means what you think it means.

Skip fragrance. A general rule of thumb is to skip products with synthetic fragrance, which may also be identified as "parfum," because they usually contain hormone-disrupting phthalates.

Use fewer products. Why do we buy into the cosmetic industry's hype that we need twenty different products for every application? The cosmetic industry has a vested interest in getting us to spend our money, but do we really need five different moisturizers? Probably not.

Use cosmetic databases. It is hard to get information. Use the Cosmetic Safety Database maintained by the Environmental Work Group (EWG) on their Web site to look up products. I love the database and it is a fabulous resource. But sometimes products have changed ingredients, so if you have a favorite product and the EWG's database says it isn't good, see if the ingredients match.

Phthalates

Phthalates are a family of chemicals that are used in cosmetics. You may remember them from our discussion about plastics: they make polyvinyl chloride (PVC) plastic soft and flexible. Phthalates are also used in personal care products for a variety of reasons. They are used in lotions to make skin feel soft and to help penetrate the skin, they lubricate the other ingredients in the product and help fragrance to stick to the skin so it lasts. Phthalates are known developmental and reproductive toxicants in laboratory animals. Some of them are also endocrine disruptors, interfering with sexual and reproductive development (see Chapter 5).

We are exposing our children to phthalates when we apply personal care products to them. A study of infant exposure published in *Pediatrics* found use of various baby care products linked to the presence of phthalates in urine.[6]

The researchers collected urine from wet diapers and information regarding infant care products used during the previous twenty-four hours. The collected urine samples were analyzed for nine different phthalate metabolites (the metabolites are indicative of phthalate exposure). The researchers found that all babies had detectable levels of at least one phthalate metabolite. Over 80 percent of the babies had at least seven metabolites. Four metabolites (MEP, MBP, MBzP, and MEOHP) occurred in over 90 percent of the babies sampled.

What products were used on the babies? Products you would expect to be used. Ninety-four percent of mothers reported they had used infant wipes within the previous twenty-four hours, and 54 percent had used infant shampoo. Reported use also included baby lotion (36 percent), diaper cream (33 percent), and baby powder (14 percent). The researchers found statistically significant associations between use of certain baby products and higher levels of phthalate metabolites. Based upon the researchers' finding a strong association between several phthalates and personal care products applied to the skin, the researchers concluded that absorption through the skin is a route of exposure.

More importantly in terms of evaluating what products to use, the researchers found that use of baby lotion, baby powder, and baby shampoo resulted in higher concentrations of mixtures of phthalate metabolites compared to use of diaper cream and baby wipes (although the researchers noted that almost all had reported use of baby wipes, so any contribution might not have shown). Plus, the more products used in the previous twenty-four hours, the higher the concentration of phthalate metabolites.

So how do you find products without phthalates? It is hard, because phthalates are frequently not identified in the ingredient list, except for certain ones in California. But if a product contains "fragrance" or "parfum" and the fragrance is not identified as being from essential oils, it probably contains phthalates.

Phthalates: Smart Mama's Simple Steps to Reduce Exposure

Skip fragrance. Phthalates are frequently included in synthetic fragrance. So you can stay away from products that identify fragrance as an ingredient. In the infant study of phthalate exposure, MEP was detected at the highest concentration in the urine. MEP is a metabolite of the phthalate DEP. DEP is the phthalate commonly used in fragrance. If the fragrance comes solely from essential oils, you don't have this concern.

Look for phthalate-free products. Some products are now advertising themselves as phthalate free. But I urge you to read the ingredients carefully nonetheless.

Fragrance

There is no doubt that scent sells. You can find fragrance in almost every product, from shampoos to lotions to household cleaners to candles to a number of toys such as the line of scented Strawberry Shortcake dolls. But, in addition to skipping synthetic fragrances because of the presence of phthalates, synthetic fragrances can trigger various allergic reactions and respiratory ailments. Chemicals commonly used in synthetic fragrances include: acetone, alpha-pinene, alpha-terpineol, benzyl acetate, benzyl alcohol, benzaldehyde, camphor, ethanol, ethyl acetate, g-terpinene, limonene, and linalool.

Fragrances are the leading cause of cosmetic contact dermatitis, according to the American Academy of Dermatology.

Reactions to fragrance can vary widely, from irritant responses to allergic responses. You may experience headaches, hives, dizziness, watery eyes, or a whole host of other reactions. It is hard to be specific because fragrance can contain so many distinct chemical compounds.

Fragrance: Smart Mama's Simple Steps to Reduce Exposure

Skip fragrance. Look for products that don't have fragrance or parfum identified in the ingredient list. Keep in mind our discussion about labeling. The label "fragrance-free" is not a regulated term. Generally, fragrance-free means only that the product itself doesn't have a noticeable odor. It doesn't mean that masking agents weren't added to hide a bad odor. A better claim is "no fragrance added" to the product.

Look for phthalate-free products. Some products are now phthalate free even if they have synthetic fragrance.

Look for products scented only with essential oils. If you want a good smell, and most of us do, look for products scented with essential oils. Essential oils don't contain phthalates. But some essential oils can trigger allergic and irritant responses. And you may want to skip products applied to the skin that contain tea tree oil or lavender. A very small case note found the use of such products linked with increased breast development in three baby boys. The increased breast development went away when the mothers stopped using lotions and massage oils containing tea tree oil and lavender. However, the case note does not provide the ingredient lists for the products, whether the lavender and tea tree oil were synthetic or natural, or whether the boys had exposure to any other hormone-disrupting chemicals.[7]

Parabens

Parabens are used in personal care products as preservatives. Methyl, ethyl, propyl, and benzyl parabens inhibit the growth of bacteria, yeasts, and mold so that the products have a longer shelf life.

Parabens can cause skin irritation and itchiness. Animal studies have linked parabens to brain and nervous-system effects. But the more problematic health effect is that some of the parabens are suspected hormone disruptors. Individual parabens have shown weak estrogenic activity in some in vitro screening tests. Estrogenic activity is associated with certain forms of breast cancer, and parabens have been found in breast cancer tissues. However, no studies have linked exposure to parabens in personal care products to breast cancer. Nevertheless, it has been hypothesized that excess absorption of parabens from personal care products, perhaps in concert with exposure to other endocrine disruptors, could influence breast tissue.

Are parabens found in personal care products? Yes. Methyl paraben, propyl paraben, ethyl paraben, butyl paraben, and others, are used in shampoos, bubble baths, diaper rash ointment, baby wipes, lotions, and toothpaste. According to the FDA, parabens are usually present in cosmetics at levels ranging from 0.01 to 0.3 percent by weight.

Are we exposed to parabens as a result of using personal care products? Yes. A study found that parabens could be measured in urine hours after a paraben-containing cream was applied to the backs of adult males.

In baby products, the EWG found parabens present in 50 percent of the lotions and moisturizers, 50 percent of the baby wipes, 69 percent of sunscreen, and 30 percent of baby body washes and liquid soaps.

Cosmetic manufacturers believe that preservatives are necessary for many cosmetic products to ensure long shelf life and preserve the quality of the product. There are other preservatives available, but some of those have their own problems and some aren't suitable for particular products. Nonetheless, paraben-free products are readily available.

Parabens: Smart Mama's Simple Steps for Reducing Exposure

Buy paraben-free. Unless the product is labeled paraben-free, you need to read the ingredient list. Look for methyl paraben, propyl paraben, butyl paraben (those are the most common in personal care products) and other ingredients with the word "paraben." Or check the Environmental Working Group's Skin Deep cosmetics safety database.

1,4-Dioxane

The chemical 1,4-dioxane is a probable carcinogen. 1,4-dioxane may also cause eye and nose irritation and can affect the liver and kidneys. It is unknown whether infants are more susceptible to exposure to 1,4-dioxane. However, the EPA has determined that early life exposures to carcinogens (exposures in the first two years) are more significant, and multiply the risk by a factor of ten.

1,4-dioxane is not used as a cosmetic ingredient. It is an impurity present in personal care products. Ethylene oxide is added to make certain ingredients mild, and a by-product of this process is 1,4-dioxane. 1,4-dioxane can be removed from the product by vacuum stripping, but it is virtually impossible to tell if this step has been done by reading the product's packaging materials.

The Environmental Working Group found that 97 percent of hair relaxers, 57 percent of baby soaps, and 34 percent of body lotions were contaminated with 1,4-dioxane.

Buying so-called natural products doesn't protect you. A study by the Organic Consumers Association found 1,4-dioxane present in a number of leading so-called natural products. In fact, about 50 percent of the products tested had 1,4-dioxane present.

1,4-dioxane readily penetrates the skin. So you may want to skip 1,4-dioxane-contaminated personal care products for you and for your baby.

1,4-Dioxane: Smart Mama's Simple Steps to Reduce Exposure

Skip certain ingredients. You can avoid 1,4-dioxane by skipping products with ingredients that have myreth, oleth, laureth, ceteareth, or any other "eth-" as a prefix or "-oxynol" as a suffix. Also skip products with PEG, polyethylene, polyethylene glycol, or polyoxyethylene. Polysorbate 60 and polysorbate 80 may be contaminated with 1,4-dioxane, but some products with these ingredients do not have 1,4-dioxane. The manufacturer may have processed the product to remove the 1,4-dioxane.

Buy certified organic. USDA-certified 100 percent organic products do not contain 1,4-dioxane.

DEA, TEA, and MEA

These three ingredients—diethanolamine (DEA), triethanolamine (TEA), and monoethanolamine (MEA)—have been identified as suspect, and several organizations warn about using products containing these ingredients. A 1998 study by the U.S. National Toxicology Program found that these compounds might be carcinogenic. As a result, the FDA issued a warning about them.

However, further research explained the findings, indicating that they might not be relevant to humans.

DEA, TEA, and MEA are used in personal care products to improve the consistency of lotions and creams. DEA and TEA are also used in shampoos to generate a rich lather.

In studies with mice, repeated skin application of DEA was found to cause liver and kidney damage. The study also discovered that when absorbed through the skin, DEA accumulated in organs. However, the damage appears to be caused by DEA's ability to inhibit choline uptake. Choline is necessary for brain development.

Research has shown that pregnant mice deprived of choline had babies that weren't as smart as those born to mice with choline-rich diets. So if DEA interferes with choline uptake, it could potentially affect your fetus. That being said, the doses given the animals were significantly higher than you would expect from washing your hair. And humans are resistant to the development of choline deficiency, unlike mice. Plus, as compared with mice, humans have a slower dermal uptake of DEA, though DEA can also irritate eyes and skin.

TEA may also cause contact dermatitis in some individuals. TEA has been shown to cause liver tumors in female mice, but the mechanism is again interference with choline uptake, to which humans are resistant. Moreover, the levels of TEA that caused the response are higher than those for DEA that caused adverse health effects.[8]

Another problem with DEA, TEA, and MEA is that they can combine with nitrates to form cancer-causing nitrosamines. If a product contains nitrites (used as a preservative, or present as a contaminant but not listed), a chemical reaction may occur resulting in the formation of nitrosamines. Unfortunately, you can't tell whether a product contains nitrosamines. However, the potential for DEA and TEA to form nitrosamines appears to be low. DEA is more likely to form nitrosamines than TEA, but even DEA has been shown not to form nitrosamines when laboratory animals are fed DEA and nitrating agents.

These are the ingredients to look out for that contain DEA, TEA, or MEA:

- Cocamide DEA
- Cocamide MEA
- DEA-Cetyl Phosphate
- DEA Oleth-3 Phosphate
- Lauramide DEA
- Linoleamide MEA
- Myristamide DEA
- Oleamide DEA
- Stearamide MEA
- TEA-Lauryl Sulfate
- Triethanolamine

DEA, TEA, and MEA: Smart Mama's Simple Steps to Reduce Exposure

Skip DEA. If you are concerned, read the ingredients, or use one of the product databases online to check your products. Try EWG's Skin Deep cosmetic safety database or the National Institutes of Health's Household Products Database. You may want to skip DEA.

TEA. If the ingredients identify TEA, you may want to skip it too. However, in a rinse-off product, the exposure levels are relatively low and the mechanism of risk doesn't appear to apply to humans. However, since it can be irritating, you may elect not to use it.

Lanolin

Lanolin is derived from sheep's wool and is found in many "natural" products and also in some nursing nipple creams. Lanolin is highly touted by some as a great natural solution for nursing moms. It is also recommended for babies. But you should be cautious about lanolin because it may contain pesticide residues used to control external parasites if the sheep are dipped. Lanolin is also a common allergen and because of this has been replaced in many products. If you like lanolin, make sure you buy certified organic products. Such products will not have pesticide-contaminated lanolin. Lanolin oil, a more refined product, has been found to have little insecticide residue.

Lanolin: Smart Mama's Simple Steps to Reduce Exposure

Buy organic. I used lanolin on my nipples when I first started nursing, but I bought organic to reduce any risk of pesticide exposure.

Talc

Talc is a mineral, produced by mining talc rocks, which are then processed by crushing, drying, and milling. Processing eliminates a number of trace minerals from the talc, but does not separate minute fibers that are very similar to asbestos.

Talc is found in many personal care products. The products that pose the most serious health risks are body powders, including baby powders, medicated powders, perfumed powders, and designer perfumed body powders.

Talc is toxic. In animal studies, after exposure to cosmetic-grade talc, researchers found some evidence of carcinogenic activity in male rats and clear evidence of carcinogenic activity of talc in female rats.[9] Clearly, talc poses a health risk when exposed to the lungs. The common household hazard posed by talc is inhalation of baby powder by infants. Since the early 1980s, records show that several thousand infants each year have died or become seriously ill following accidental inhalation of baby powder.

Researchers have also found a strong link between frequent use of talc in the female genital area and ovarian cancer. Talc particles are able to move through the reproductive system and become imbedded in the lining of the ovary. Researchers have found talc particles in ovarian tumors and have found that women with ovarian cancer have used talcum powder in their genital area more frequently than healthy women.

Talc: Smart Mama's Simple Steps for Reducing Exposure

Skip talc. If you feel you need a powder, use cornstarch or a powder that does not contain talc instead.

Make sure care providers and day cares have a no-talc policy. Just ask. And if they use it, recommend an alternate product such as cornstarch or a non-talc powder.

Do not apply talc to your genitals, underwear, or sanitary pads.

Dyes in Personal Care Products

Dyes are used as coloring agents in personal care products. Individual dyes have different chemical properties and different potential health effects. Some dyes have been linked to cancer, and others may be developmental toxicants.

Dyes: Smart Mama's Simple Steps to Reduce Exposure

Read ingredients. Again, read the ingredient list. Skip the following ingredients: D&C Violet 2, EXT D&C Violet 2, FD&C Blue 1, FD&C Green 3, D&C Red 4, and FD&C Yellow 5.

DMDM Hydantoin

DMDM hydantoin is a preservative that may cause an allergic response. But the more significant problem is that degradation of DMDM hydantoin may result in the formation of formaldehyde, a carcinogen, which is why you may want to avoid it.

Nonylphenol and Nonylphenol Ethoxylates

Nonylphenol and nonylphenol ethoxylates are estrogen mimics present in shampoos, shaving creams, and hair colors. Nonylphenol ethoxylates may be listed as octoxynol or nonoxynol in personal care products. They are persistent in the environment and bioaccumulate. Many European countries are phasing them out because of their persistence in the environment.

Research suggests that nonylphenols reduce male fertility, testicular size, and sperm quality. Nonylphenols are yet another class of compounds that are endocrine disruptors, and when you combine exposure with other endocrine disruptors, they may have a significant adverse health effect. Avoid personal care products containing nonylphenol ethoxylates.

Quaternary Ammonium Compounds

Quaternary ammonium compounds may be found in personal care products. They are identified benzalkonium chloride, cetrimonium bromide, quaternium-15, and quaternium 1-29. These compounds are caustic and can irritate the eyes. Quaternium-15 is the number-one cause of preservative-related contact dermatitis. Quaternium-15 also may result in the presence of formaldehyde, a carcinogen, because it works as a preservative by releasing formaldehyde.

Another concern with these compounds is that they are sensitizers, meaning that they can cause you to develop allergic reactions after repeated exposure. For about 5 percent of people, these compounds are extreme sensitizers and can cause a variety of asthma-like symptoms. When they are used with hot running water, steam increases the inhalation of vapors.

Choosing Products

Even with all of this information, you may feel frustrated about choosing safer personal care products. The information is a bit overwhelming. And who really has time to read all of those ingredient labels. So let's just try out a common baby product and see how you do.

Let's look at a sample label from a popular conventional baby wash, Johnson's Ultimate Baby Wash. This information was pulled directly off the manufacturer's Web site. This product was marketed as hypoallergenic, allergy and dermatologist tested, and gentle to the eyes.

> Ingredients: Water, Cocamidopropyl Betaine, PEG-80 Sorbitan Laurate, Sodium Laureth Sulfate, PEG-150 Distearate, Tetrasodium EDTA, Sodium Chloride, Polyquaternium-10, Fragrance, Quaternium-15, Citric Acid.

So let's look at one of the last ingredients: fragrance. What is in synthetic fragrance usually? Hormone-disrupting phthalates.

What about the other ingredients? Sodium laureth sulfate and PEG-150 distearate. The "-eth" should clue you in. These ingredients may result in 1,4-dioxane, a carcinogen, being present in the product.

In this case, according to the manufacturer's Web site for this product, "Some of the ingredients in our products may contain 1,4-dioxane as an incidental ingredient at extremely low levels. This trace ingredient is common in the personal care industry, and results from a process that makes products mild for even the most delicate skin. . . . Test results recently released by these groups state that some shampoos and bath products contain trace amounts of 1,4-dioxane. We are unclear as to the testing methodology used by these groups and cannot verify the data that was listed in their press release."

And, as you may recall, sodium laureth sulfate "may induce eye and skin irritation."[10]

So far, we have an endocrine disruptor and a carcinogen, and also an ingredient that may induce eye and skin irritation. What else? Another ingredient, quaternium-15, is known to cause allergic responses and skin irritation, and may release formaldehyde, a known carcinogen. Is that what you expect in a baby body wash advertised as mild and gentler than water?

Let's try another. Desitin diaper cream is a basic staple for most parents. The ingredients are zinc oxide 40 percent, BHA, cod liver oil, fragrance, lanolin, methylparaben, petrolatum, talc.

Any problems?

First, BHA is known to cause cancer in animals. It has shown to be a hormone disruptor in laboratory animals. It has been banned from cosmetics in the EU. We also have fragrance. And we know that synthetic fragrance probably has hormone-disrupting phthalates. Another issue is methylparaben. Methylparaben is a paraben, and parabens have been shown to be hormone disruptors. They have been found in breast cancer tumors, but no direct link has been established between parabens and breast cancer development. A small percentage of the population is also allergic to parabens, resulting in contact dermatitis reactions.

So you may be feeling even more frustrated—who really has time to go through this analysis when shopping, especially if you have kids pulling at you? Doing your research beforehand is a big help. But you will find after a little bit that you can quickly identify ingredients you don't want. And, as for diaper cream, I really like Earth Mama Angel Baby's Angel Baby Bottom Balm.

Antibacterial Products

We seem to love our antibacterial products, and that means that manufacturers are now putting them in everything. You can find antibacterial soaps, shampoos, household cleaners, clothing, and toothpaste. We even have antibacterial-impregnated shopping carts now—at least at Target. It seems that we are deathly afraid of germs. And why shouldn't we do everything we can to protect ourselves from those pesky microbes? Because we may be doing more harm than good, especially when antibacterial products have not been shown to have any significant benefit except to the immune compromised.

Triclosan or its close chemical cousin triclocarban are the chemicals commonly used to give a product antibacterial properties. Triclosan is a chlorinated antimicrobial and antifungal pesticide. It is found in at least 60 percent of our streams and rivers. According to the United States Geological Survey (USGS), triclosan is one of the most detected chemicals in surface waters in the United States. And it disrupts the aquatic environment. A study found triclosan harmful to the development of frogs, disrupting the transition from tadpole to frog. People assume that the antibacterial products they wash down the drain are treated by the wastewater treatment plant. Unfortunately, our wastewater treatment plants are having a difficult time handling the heavy triclosan loads because triclosan impacts the beneficial bacteria needed for the water treatment process.

And what are we doing to ourselves? Triclosan and its degradation products (the chemicals that it breaks down into) bioaccumulate in humans. A Swedish study found triclosan in human breast milk in three out of five women.

To date, agencies have found triclosan to be safe. Triclosan's regulatory status is a little complicated because products containing triclosan are regulated by three separate agencies, depending on the application. The EPA is responsible for regulating triclosan as a pesticide. The FDA is responsible for triclosan as a food packaging chemical, hospital disinfectant, and ingredient in personal care products. The CPSC covers consumer products containing triclosan that do not make a claim for antimicrobial action. The EPA is undertaking a re-registration evaluation of the pesticide, but it states in its risk assessment that it is evaluating all the exposure pathways.

Environmental health-advocacy organizations have disagreed with the EPA's risk assessment. The Environmental Working Group (EWG) and Beyond Pesticides contend that the draft risk assessment finding triclosan safe is inadequate.[11] The EWG contends that the draft risk assessment fails to take into account critical routes of exposure for infants and young children, including breast milk, children's personal care products, toys, and clothing.[12]

Triclosan's disruptive effects shown in frogs have not been established in humans. But triclosan's chemical structure is similar to certain estrogens. Because it has a similar structure to certain estrogens, triclosan has the ability to act as an endocrine disruptor. Studies have shown that triclosan has adrogenic and estrogenic activity. Laboratory animal studies demonstrate that triclosan may affect the central nervous system and the immune system. In addition, triclosan can result in contact dermatitis, skin irritation, and photoallergic contact dermatitis.

More problematic is that triclosan has been shown to react with chlorine, used to disinfect our water, and form chloroform, a known carcinogen. Virginia Polytechnic Institute scientists found that use of antibacterial soaps could result in an exposure to chloroform 10 to 40 percent above the EPA's safe limit for tap water as compared with regular soaps. Whether this reaction could occur in a home has not been demonstrated.

Another potential downside to using antibacterial products is that they may contribute to the risk of drug-resistant bacteria. According to Beyond Pesticides, "Evidence is mounting that links the use of triclosan-containing products with the promotion of bacteria resistant to antibiotic medications and antibacterial products."

Why do triclosan-containing products contribute, as opposed to soap or alcohol-based cleaners? Antibacterial products leave surface residues, creating conditions that may foster the development of resistant bacteria. Basically, triclosan works by targeting a certain enzyme that bacteria need to live. Apply triclosan, and bacteria die. But the bacteria that survive are those that are resistant to that targeting, and they create more bacteria resistant to triclosan.

Jay Feldman, executive director of Beyond Pesticides, states that "[t]he nonmedical uses of triclosan are frivolous and dangerous, creating serious direct health and environmental hazards and long-term health problems associated with the creation of resistant strains of bacteria."

The science is still developing, and whether any human health effects result from triclosan exposure is subject to debate. The real question is, Are we getting any benefit from the plethora of antibacterial products? Not really. Studies have shown that antibacterial products provide no added benefit over using soap. Soap works by loosening and lifting dirt, oil, and microbes from surfaces so that they can be easily rinsed away by water. One study showed that regular soap and water killed 99.5 percent of microbes and antibacterial soap killed 99.6 percent.

So if we get no real benefit and there is the potential for adverse effects to the environment and human health, it seems to me it just isn't worth it. I'll skip antibacterial products and use plain soap and water for washing.

It you feel the need to disinfect, or need something for on the go, try an alcohol-based cleaner. Alcohol-based cleaners inflect sweeping damage to cells by demolishing key structures, then evaporate, leaving no residue. If you want to use antibacterial hand cleaner and don't have access to running water, use an alcohol-based hand sanitizer. A word of caution, though: Being alcohol based, you should not let your toddler play with them. There is enough alcohol in them to make him sick if he eats a large quantity. Even better, try some of the natural sanitizers that rely on essential oils.

And just a word to those with a fear of germs: Although viruses and bacteria can survive several hours, even days, on inanimate objects, most do not exist in sufficient quantities to make you sick. For example, even if all the critters on your toilet are *Staphylococcus* bacteria, less than half of those you touch transfer to your hand, and just 1 percent of those get past your mucous membranes (eyes, nose, or mouth) and into your body. Also, it takes 100 million *E. coli* to make you ill, but a single virus particle can give you the flu. Antibacterial products do not kill viruses.

Antibacterial Products: Smart Mama's Simple Steps to Reduce Exposure

Skip antibacterial products. Just skip them altogether. Don't buy antibacterial soaps, body washes, cleaners, or any other products.

Use soap. Just use regular soap, preferably a castile soap, and warm water. Wash hands for twenty seconds. If you need a cheat, just sing "Happy Birthday" two times while washing. And don't forget to conserve water by turning it off while washing.

Use "natural" or alcohol-based sanitizers. If you feel the need to sanitize, try some of the natural sanitizers that rely on essential oils. Or try isopropyl alcohol. And for on the go, use a natural or alcohol-based sanitizer.

Insect Repellents

Insect repellents may be necessary to keep the bugs off, but you may not want to use a product that contains a pesticide such as DEET. DEET's use is controversial. Major regulatory and medical establishments, including the American Academy of Pediatrics, claim that DEET is safe and effective if used properly. However, studies have found that DEET can slow motor skills and impair central-nervous-system function, especially if combined with permethrin (used on some outdoor clothing to repel insects). These studies associated adverse health effects from sustained, regular use of DEET-containing repellants (at least once per day, for five or more days). The reported adverse health effects included skin irritation, headaches, seizures, restlessness, rapid loss of consciousness, and even death.

Another option may be an insect repellent that uses essential oils instead of a product containing a synthetic pesticide. Plants whose essential oils have been reported to have repellent activity include citronella, cedar, verbena, geranium, lavender, pine, cajeput, cinnamon, rosemary, basil, thyme, allspice, garlic, and peppermint. Calendula ointment is also an excellent insect repellent. However, these products tend to give short-lasting protection, usually less than two hours. If you are in an area with insects carrying potentially life-threatening diseases and you need to have long-lasting protection, it may make sense to use an insect repellent with DEET or something similar. And essential oils can be irritating or cause allergic reactions. It is always a good idea to patch-test before applying all over.

Some "natural" insect repellents rely upon eucalyptus lemon essential oil. It is the only plant-based active ingredient for insect repellents so far approved by the CDC. (The CDC has also approved the synthetic version, known as PMD, though I would skip the synthetic version completely.) Eucalyptus lemon essential oil can be toxic if ingested in high concentrations, so only use a product with a low concentration. Also, these products are not recommended for children under three years of age, so I tend to skip them.

As always, prevention is the best solution.

Smart Mama's Simple Steps to Reduce the Need for Insect Repellents

Stay indoors at dawn and dusk. This is when the flying insects are most likely to be out and about looking for you.

If you live near a woods, spread a three-foot-wide swath of wood chips between your lawn and the woods to deter ticks. Ticks aren't able to navigate the chips.

Don't let mosquitoes breed. Eliminate standing water in your yard. And don't forget to clear clogs from gutters—mosquitoes will breed in a very small amount of water.

If you have a birdbath, change the water twice weekly.

Don't forget to change any outdoor water dishes daily.

Plant scented geraniums, lemon thyme, marigold, tansy, citrosa plants, sweet basil, and/or sassafras near your home to repel mosquitoes.

Sunscreens

Children need sunscreen protection. You want a sunscreen that will provide both UVA and UVB protection. A barrier-method sunscreen is preferred over a chemical-based sunscreen. A physical-barrier sunscreen uses titanium dioxide or zinc oxide. Even micronized, these do not penetrate the horny epidermis of the skin, whereas the chemicals in chemical-based sunscreens have been shown to penetrate the skin rapidly. Of course, follow any recommendations of your child's doctor.

Sunscreens: Smart Mama's Simple Steps to Reduce Exposure

Avoid fragrance. Look for a barrier sunscreen without synthetic fragrance to avoid hormone-disrupting phthalates.

Cover up. Like mother always said, prevention is the best solution. Have your child wear adequate protection from the sun.

Chapter 10

Cleanliness and the Pursuit of Perfection

Housework can't kill you, but why take the chance?
—Phyllis Diller

I use this quip often. I read an article that said women do seven more hours of housework a week once they get married as compared to when they were single. That extra seven hours alone is enough to kill you. But even though Phyllis Diller wasn't referring to toxic chemicals in household cleaners, she wasn't far off the mark. And I still use it to defend myself when my husband makes comments about the state of our house, although he isn't referring to cleanliness as much as he is referring to the piles of various objects that tend to accumulate when you have two small children. And my husband likes to think he is neat and clutter free, although he isn't really. But I will freely admit that I am prone to clutter, especially since I never have the time to get the various projects done.

The U.S. household cleaning market is a huge industry recently fueled by our love of disinfectants. We make fun of the obsessively clean, but we also aspire to maintain sparkling clean, pleasantly scented homes. As if it is a sign of being the perfect, got-it-all-together woman, wife, and mom.

But conventional household cleaners contain a number of potentially harmful toxic chemicals that may cause adverse health effects. Possible adverse health effects vary widely—because the chemicals in conventional household cleaners vary widely—ranging from relatively mild irritant responses such as watery eyes or skin irritation to more serious effects. Conventional household cleaners can contain known or suspected carcinogens and reproductive and developmental toxicants.

Have you ever cleaned the shower and then experienced teary eyes, itchy throat, or dizziness? Or have you cleaned the oven and suffered from headaches or nausea? Chemicals commonly found in both shower and oven cleaners could have caused these symptoms, and more.

Conventional household cleaners can affect indoor air quality. And indoor air is important—we spend 90 percent of our time indoors, in homes that are increasingly airtight. Many of the chemicals in conventional household cleaners are volatile organic compounds (VOCs), meaning that they volatilize or evaporate. These VOCs can pollute indoor air. The United States Environmental Protection Agency (EPA) has detected about a dozen common VOCs at levels two to five times higher inside homes than outside concentration levels. Some VOCs have been detected at concentrations in indoor air ten times outdoor air concentrations.

Conventional household cleaners are believed to contribute to the elevated levels of VOCs found indoors. A recent study analyzed the VOCs off-gassing from six consumer products: three air fresheners and three laundry products (cloth dryer sheets, a fabric softener, and a laundry detergent).[1] The results? A total of ninety-eight different VOCs were identified off-gassing from these products, representing fifty-eight unique VOCs. Five of the six products emitted one or more chemicals identified as federal Hazardous Air Pollutants under the Clean Air Act: acetaldehyde, chloromethane, and 1,4-dioxane.

While using products containing VOCs, you can expose yourself and others to very high pollutant levels, and elevated concentrations can persist in the air long after the activity is completed. A study funded by the California Air Resources Board found that a person who cleans a shower stall for fifteen minutes with a cleaning product containing glycol ethers may be exposed to three times the recommended one-hour exposure limit. The same study found that using air freshener in a child's room along with an air purifier that generates ozone can result in the formation of formaldehyde, a known carcinogen, at levels 25 percent higher than the state recommends.

As I said, the potential health effects from exposure vary greatly depending on the product. But a study by the National Cancer Association found that women who work in the home are at a 54 percent higher risk of developing cancer than women who work outside the home, which was attributed in part to the use of common consumer products, including conventional household cleaners.

When shopping, it is hard to keep track of all the problematic ingredients in conventional household cleaners, but you don't need a doctorate in chemistry. A good rule of thumb is to look for the warning label and read it closely. If the label is marked "danger" or "poison," look for a safer product. As a general rule, products that do not have caution, warning, danger, or poison warning labels are safer than those that have caution or warning labels, which are in turn safer than those that have danger or poison warning labels. Another general rule of thumb is that if a product requires you to wear personal protective equipment, you probably want to skip it.

Conventional cleaners may increase the risk of asthma. A study of over 3,500 subjects found that using household cleaning sprays as little as once per week can increase the risk of developing asthma.[2] Air fresheners, furniture cleaners, and glass cleaners were particularly likely to increase the risk of developing asthma. In fact, the risk of developing asthma was 30 to 50 percent higher in those regularly exposed to cleaning sprays, and the risk of developing asthma increased with frequency of cleaning and number of different sprays used. "The relative risk rates of developing adult asthma in relation to exposure to cleaning products could account for as much as 15%, or one in seven of adult asthma cases," said Jan-Paul Zock, Ph.D., of the Centre for Research in Environmental Epidemiology at the Municipal Institute of Medical Research in Barcelona. While this study did not include infants as subjects, the results suggest that use of household cleaners may also increase the risk of developing asthma in infants and children. And a study in the United Kingdom found that the frequent use of household cleaners was associated with persistent wheezing among pre-school-age children.[3]

The most hazardous household cleaners tend to be oven cleaners, metal polishes, and adhesive removers. Metal polishes and adhesive removers typically contain petroleum distillates. These can cause temporary eye clouding. Long-term exposure can damage the nervous system, skin, kidneys, and eyes.

Disinfectants typically contain phenol and cresol. Phenol and cresol can cause diarrhea, fainting, dizziness, and kidney and liver damage.

Furniture and floor polishes can contain nitrobenzene. Nitrobenzene can cause skin discoloration, shallow breathing, vomiting, and death, and is associated with cancer and birth defects.

Carpet cleaners, room deodorizers, laundry softeners, spot removers, and other products may contain perchloroethylene (PCE). PCE can cause liver and kidney damage if ingested, and PCE is an animal carcinogen and a suspected human carcinogen.

Spray starch may contain formaldehyde, phenol, and pentachlorophenol.

The list of potentially hazardous compounds and their associated adverse health effects is long, so let's just talk about simple steps to reduce exposure.

Cleaning Products: Smart Mama's Simple Steps to Reduce Exposure

Ditch conventional cleaners. Try some of the "natural" cleaning products. Labeling claims aren't well regulated for household cleaners, but look at the ingredient list. Generally, avoid petroleum-based solvents (look for petroleum distillates, Stoddard solvent, toluene, benzene, or similar ingredients), glycol ethers, and phenol. Some brands you may want to try include Seventh Generation, Method, eCover, and Planet.

Read warning labels. As a general rule, products that do not have caution, warning, danger, or poison warning labels are safest. Products with caution or warning labels are generally safer than those that have danger or poison warning labels.

Look for specific claims. If "green" is important to you, products labeled organic and biodegradable are generally the safest. Look for specific claims. Biodegradable means that the product can be broken down by microbial action. The rate at which the product breaks down is important. Ingredients that biodegrade slowly or incompletely can threaten the environment.

Try castile soap. My favorite, a mild liquid soap, great for lots of applications. Castile soap traditionally meant made from olive oil, but other vegetable oils can be used.

Homemade Cleaning

If you are ambitious, you can make your own household cleaners. The benefit is that you will know exactly what is in the cleaner. I make up mine in a series of spray bottles I've labeled. An added bonus? You'll be fabulously green! You'll reduce energy consumption since you won't be buying new containers, and reduce trash, too.

To make your own household cleaners, you need only rummage through your pantry:

Baking soda (sodium bicarbonate) is a great cleaner and deodorizer. You can buy baking soda at the local grocery store—you probably have some in your pantry already. You can use baking soda to polish by making a paste with water. Baking soda will polish aluminum, chrome, and tin; soften fabrics; remove certain stains; and can be used as underarm deodorant and toothpaste.

Lemon juice can be used to clean glass; remove stains from aluminum, clothes, and porcelain; and lighten or bleach if used with sunlight.

Washing soda (SAL soda, sodium carbonate decahydrate) will cut stubborn grease on grills, broiler pans, and ovens.

Vinegar (distilled white) will dissolve mineral deposits; remove grease, traces of soap, or wax buildup; polish some metals; and deodorize.

Borax can be used as a deodorizer; inhibits mold growth; boosts the cleaning power of soap or detergent; removes stains; and kills cockroaches when used with an attractant such as sugar.

Celery absorbs odors when rubbed on a cutting board.

Citrus peel disinfects, deodorizes, adds fragrance, and freshens air.

Cream of tartar is a non-abrasive cleaner for porcelain, drains, and metals.

Salt is an abrasive, non-scratching cleaner usable on most surfaces with antibacterial qualities.

For homemade cleaning recipes, try the following:

Air freshener	To absorb odors, use bowls of vinegar or baking soda and place where needed. To scent air, boil herbs or spices (cloves, cinnamon, oranges, etc.) until the heat causes the release of odors, let cool, and put out in a bowl. Add a little salt to discourage fungus growth.
All-purpose cleaner	Combine 2 cups white vinegar with 2 cups water in a spray bottle. Add a few drops of your favorite essential oil. Spray where needed. Do not use this all-purpose cleaner on marble. Vinegar will strip the marble's finish.
Alternate all-purpose cleaner	Dissolve 3 tablespoons of baking soda in 1 quart warm water. You can make this up and keep in spray bottle. Warm water is best so that the baking soda dissolves easily.
Alternate all-purpose cleaner	1 quart warm water, 1 teaspoon liquid soap, 1 teaspoon Borax, and 1/4 cup undiluted white vinegar. Put in spray bottle or squirt bottle.
All-purpose disinfectant	Mix 1/2 cup Borax into 1 gallon hot water to disinfect and deodorize. Isopropyl alcohol is also a good disinfectant, but use gloves and keep it away from children. For a disinfecting spray, add 2 teaspoons tea tree oil to 12 ounces of water in a spray bottle.
Brass	Slather on some ketchup. Or cut a lemon in half, and sprinkle lemon with salt. Rub lemon with salt wherever the item needs to be polished.
Car odors	To freshen your car's interior, drop any scent you like in a traveling coffee mug with boiling water and uncover when safely in a cupholder in your car. Try pine needles, cinnamon sticks, peppermint candies, orange peels, whatever you like.
Carpet cleaner	For big spills, spread cornmeal over the spill. Wait 15 minutes, then vacuum. For stains, combine 1/4 cup biodegradable soap with 1/3 cup water in a blender to make foam (or stir by hand), then apply to the stain.
Carpet deodorizer	To get rid of odors in carpet, sprinkle baking soda or cornstarch, let sit 30 minutes or so, and vacuum.
Cat hair	Place a damp rubber dishwashing glove on your hand and lightly run over affected surfaces. The cat hair will stick to it.
Copper	Slowly, add vinegar to salt in a bowl until you get a paste, then apply to copper. Or cut a lemon in half and sprinkle with salt. Rub lemon with the salt wherever the item needs to be polished.
Diaper pail	Sprinkle 1/2 cup baking soda or Borax in bottom of pail to freshen and inhibit mold and bacteria growth.

Drain cleaner	Prevent clogs by using hair and food traps. Also try pouring boiling water down drains once per week as preventive maintenance. To keep drains from slowing, pour 1/2 cup baking soda down sink, followed by a cup of white vinegar. Let fizz and then flush with hot water. For clogged drains, use a plunger first. You can try the baking soda/vinegar recipe, but it does not work well on clogged drains with water in the sink bowl. When rising with hot water, add some salt with the boiling water. **Warning:** Do not use this method after trying a commercial drain cleaner. The vinegar can react with the drain cleaner and create dangerous fumes.
Dust	Wear an old sock on your hand to pick up dust. Just wash with your rags when you are done!
Floor cleaner	A few drops of vinegar in 3 to 4 cups of water will remove soap traces. For vinyl or linoleum, add a capful of baby oil to the water to preserve and polish. For wood floors, apply a thin coat of 1:1 oil and vinegar and rub well. For painted wood floors, mix 1 teaspoon washing soda in 1 gallon hot water. For brick and stone tiles, use 1 cup white vinegar in 1 gallon water and rinse with clear water. Do not use vinegar on marble floors.
Garbage disposal odors	To eliminate sink odors, you can put lemon, lime, orange, or grapefruit peels in the disposal and run. Or freeze some vinegar in ice cube trays and drop a couple in the disposal. Use 1 cup vinegar in an ice tray and fill with water, then freeze.
Kitchen cleaner	Baking soda on non-scratch surfaces and vinegar/water mixture on other surfaces. Apply to rag or directly to countertop for cleaning.
Laundry detergent	Choose a biodegradable, phosphate-free brand. To reduce the amount of commercial detergent, add baking soda. If you are using liquid detergent, add about 1/2 cup baking soda at the beginning of the wash. If you are using powdered detergent, add ½ cup of baking soda during the rinse cycle. The baking soda softens the water, thus increasing the potency of the detergent.
Microwave cleaner	Place lemon slices in a microwave-safe cup with at least 8 oz. of water. Heat on high for 3 minutes. Let sit for 3 minutes without opening the door, then safely remove cup and wipe down inside of microwave. The steam and lemon should allow you to remove any baked-on food particles and leave your microwave smelling great.
Moths	Instead of using mothballs (which contain naphthalene), use a sachet of pennyroyal, cedar chips, lavender, and eucalyptus.
Onions	To remove onion smell from hands, rub vinegar on hands before and after slicing.
Oven cleaner	Make paste of baking soda, salt, and hot water. Alternate: 1 quart warm water, 2 teaspoons Borax, and 2 tablespoons liquid soap. Mix ingredients, spray on, wait 20 minutes, then clean.

Red wine stains	Try a dab of foaming shaving cream directly on the stain. Pat gently.
Rust remover	Mix cream of tartar with water or hydrogen peroxide to form a thick paste. Apply and rub with a cloth.
Scouring powder	3 parts baking soda to 1 part Borax. Keep in wide-mouth jar and apply dry. Use a damp cloth to scour. You can add a couple of drops of your favorite essential oil. I keep baking soda with a little Borax in a red-pepper-flake shaker jar with a couple of drops of orange essential oil at my kitchen sink.
Stainless steel cleaner—dirt	Use dishwashing liquid and hot water. Apply to cloth and wipe stainless steel. Follow with a soft cloth and polish with the "grain" of the stainless steel.
Stainless steel cleaner—fingerprints	Fingerprints can be removed by gentle rubbing with a paste of soda ash and water applied with a soft rag, followed by a thorough warm water rinse. Glass cleaner will work too (4 tablespoons lemon juice in one gallon water).
Tea stains	Use a paste of baking soda and water to remove tea stains from teacups and teapots. Make up enough paste to cover stain, apply, let sit ten or so minutes, then wash.
Tile and tub cleanser	Mix 1 and 2/3 cups baking soda, 1/2 cup liquid soap, 1/2 cup water. Add 2 tablespoons vinegar (add after soap and water because it will react with the baking soda if added too early).
Toilet bowl cleaner	Sprinkle in some baking soda, let sit, and then clean with toilet brush. If needed, before cleaning with toilet brush, you can try letting white vinegar sit in the bowl. Or you can use Borax and lemon juice.
Wax on fabric	Place a brown paper bag (or a paper towel) over the wax and press with an iron on low heat. The paper will absorb the wax.
Window cleaner	Add 3 tablespoons vinegar per 1 quart water to spray bottle.

Chapter 11

The Ants Go Marching: Pesticides

We love pesticides. We use them to kill bugs in our homes and keep our gardens green and thriving. Home lawns and gardens consume up to ten times per acre the amount of pesticides farmers use on their crops. Many different chemicals are used as pesticides, and they have a range of health effects. However, for simplicity, this chapter discusses pesticides as a group of chemicals.

Pesticides are used to prevent or destroy insects, fungus, weeds, or any other pests. Pesticides are sprayed on agricultural crops (with residue remaining on the food we eat), in our communities (for example, to reduce mosquitoes), and in our homes. Household products such as foggers to control insects, rat poison, flea and insect control products for pets, ant and cockroach sprays, and those that we use on our lawns and in our gardens are all pesticides, and are also used in public places, including day cares and schools. The U.S. Environmental Protection Agency (EPA) estimates that 80 percent of our pesticide exposure comes from our diet, and the remaining 20 percent comes from pesticides in our drinking water and those used in and around our homes. I'm not sure that this is accurate—it seems that use in the home may account for a greater amount of exposure.

More than one billion pounds of pesticides are used each year in the United

States, with more than 700 million pounds used annually in agriculture. Studies have documented widespread pesticide exposures for the U.S. population, including pregnant women and children. Several studies suggest that resident farm families and farm workers have higher exposures than do other populations.

Concern over pesticide exposure has focused on agricultural and occupational exposure but, as the many uses above show, pesticides are routinely encountered in the home. One study found that 90 percent of us use pesticides. Another found that 80 percent of families used pesticides, even when a woman in the household was pregnant.

The California Birth Defects Monitoring Program interviewed over 2,000 women and found that 75 percent reported being exposed to pesticides while pregnant, and 15 percent reported being exposed to three or more sources of pesticides. The program found that household exposure to pesticides was frequent. The women reported that approximately half of the homes were treated for pests, using pesticides applied by the mother, a professional, or others. Almost half of the households reported pets with flea collars or other treatments to manage fleas. Almost one in five reported gardening using weed killers or insecticides. Occupational exposure was relatively rare, with only 5 percent of the mothers having jobs involving contact with pesticides. But almost one in four of the women indicated that they lived within a quarter-mile of agricultural crops, including orchards and commercial flower fields.

According to Beyond Pesticides, herbicides are the most-used pesticide in our homes and gardens, with over 90 million pounds applied on lawns and gardens per year.[1] In fact, Beyond Pesticides reports that suburban lawns and gardens receive more pesticide applications per acre (3.2–9.8 lbs) than agriculture (2.7 lbs per acre on average).

Pesticides and Pregnancy

Biomonitoring studies find that pesticides pass from mother to child through umbilical-cord blood and breast milk. Fetal exposure has also been linked with neurological and reproductive disorders, low birth weight, and higher rates of miscarriages. Of the thirty commonly used lawn pesticides, nineteen have studies indicating that they may have carcinogenic effects, thirteen are linked with birth defects, twenty-one have reproductive effects, fifteen are neurotoxicants, and eleven have the potential to disrupt the endocrine system.[2] According to Kids for Saving the Earth, twenty-four pesticides on the market, including 2,4-D, lindane, and atrazine, are known endocrine disruptors.

Some studies indicate that the greatest risk of exposure to pesticides is during the first three to eight weeks of the first trimester when the neural tube development is occurring.

Pesticides and Children

An EPA study found that indoor household air had at least five pesticides present, at concentrations more than ten times those found in outside air. Our children take in more pesticides relative to their body weight than we do as adults, and they are more susceptible to exposure because their systems are still developing. We talked in Chapter 2 about how children breathe in a different zone than adults. That zone has a higher concentration of pesticides after household application, especially since pesticide residues collect on plush toys, carpets, and upholstered furniture and then are re-emitted for two or more weeks, exposing children. The National Academy of Sciences estimates that 50 percent of lifetime pesticide exposure occurs during the first five years of life. Exposure to herbicides before the age of one appears to cause a four-fold increase in the risk of childhood asthma.

SMART MAMA SCARY FACT

Some common household pesticides cause lifelong hyperactivity in rodents exposed to a single small amount on a critical day of brain development.[3]

Children ages six to eleven have higher levels of lawn chemicals in their blood than all other age categories. Scientists have found that children who are exposed to indoor pesticides are at an elevated risk of leukemia (cancer of the blood cells). One study found that the risk is significantly increased when the exposure occurs in utero, and also when professional pest control services are used in the home from one year before pregnancy to three years after birth.[4] Parental use of pesticides in the home or garden may increase the risk of childhood leukemia by a factor of three to nine times. Other studies have supported this study, including one that showed an increased risk of acute childhood leukemia associated with household pesticide use. The researchers concluded that "the consistency of the findings with previous studies on acute leukemia raises the question of the advisability of preventing pesticide use by pregnant women."[5] Approximately 27 percent of all childhood cancers are leukemia.

Proximity to agricultural fields sprayed with pesticides may be a significant risk factor for autism. A recent small study found that women who live near farm fields sprayed with organochlorine pesticides may be more likely to give birth to autistic children. In a relatively small study, scientists found that the rate of autism was six times greater in women who lived within 500 meters of fields sprayed with the organochlorine pesticides endosulfan and dicofol during their first trimester of pregnancy.[6]

Pesticides: Smart Mama's Simple Steps to Reduce Exposure

Skip pesticides. While you are pregnant, do not use any pesticide products in or around the home. This means no indoor foggers, ant sprays, roach sprays, flea and tick pet products, and no weed killers, herbicides, or any other pesticide on the lawn or in the garden.

Ventilate and wipe. If you have to use a pesticide to treat the home or garden, have someone else do it and then make sure that the area is well ventilated and that all surfaces are wiped down using liquid castile soap or another mild cleaner. Make sure not to re-contaminate surfaces.

Got organic? Switch to organic foods certified as organic by the USDA. Organic means that the food is grown without the use of pesticides, synthetic fertilizers, sewage sludge, genetically modified organisms, or ionizing radiation. Pesticides are so ubiquitous in our environment that even organic foods may have some pesticide residues, but not from being sprayed on the crop. You can lower your pesticide exposure from your foods by going organic. In fact, a study found that in children, switching to an organic diet reduced pesticide metabolites in urine significantly in a mere five days.[7]

Wash your food. Washing your food with water and a brush or washcloth can reduce pesticide residue on the food's surface. It cannot reduce those residues absorbed in the food. Although no scientific study has shown this to be more effective at removing pesticide residue than scrubbing, you may want to use baking soda to help clean your fruits and vegetables. Sprinkle on a clean, damp sponge, scrub, and rinse. This may help you do a thorough job of washing your fruits and vegetables, and that would help remove pesticide residue.

Eat a varied diet. By eating a wide variety of foods you eliminate the risk of overexposure to a pesticide residue found in any one food.

Use a doormat. Don't track in pesticides. Use a good-quality doormat to avoid tracking in dirt contaminated with pesticides and other compounds.

Take off your shoes. Better yet, take off your shoes before coming inside. This will avoid tracking in pesticides and other compounds.

Smart Mama's Simple Steps to Pest Control without Pesticides

Block entrances. Block pest entrances by caulking holes, using door sweeps, and keeping window screens in good repair. Ninety percent of all insect infestations migrate into the home from the outside.

Eliminate moisture and food sources. For example, for pet food served outside, you can place the food bowl inside a larger bowl of soapy water so your pet can reach the food but ants can't.

Use non-toxic, pesticide-free products. A poison non-toxic to humans can be mixed with a food that insects find attractive, such as oatmeal (attractive) with plaster-of-Paris (poison); cocoa powder and flour (attractive) with Borax (poison).

- For ants, try sprinkling red chili powder, paprika, dried peppermint, peppermint essential oil, or Borax (Borax may be harmful to humans when ingested, so don't do this where your baby can get it) where the ants are entering.
- For fleas, try feeding your pet brewer's yeast in powder mixed with food or by tablets.
- For both ants and fleas, spray a mixture of 4 ounces of natural soap in 1 gallon of water. You can also sprinkle powdered soap around your home's foundation to keep ants out.
- For weeds, boil 1/2 gallon of water. Add 1/2 cup of salt and 1/2 cup plus 2 tablespoons of white vinegar. Pour directly on weeds in the driveway, pathway, sidewalks, etc., while still hot.
- Soap makes a great all-purpose pesticide. It kills pests by dehydrating them. Mix 1 to 2 tablespoons liquid soap with 1 gallon of water. Spray infested plants. Don't add more soap than 2 tablespoons because it will dry out the leaves.
- My favorite? Two tablespoons of liquid peppermint castile soap added to 1 gallon water. Spray where you have infestations. Do not rinse. Flies, ants, fleas, and mice avoid peppermint.

Got pests? Go natural. Encourage natural predators such as ladybugs, lacewings, toads, dragonflies, and praying mantises in your garden. Grow plants that will attract these natural predators. You may also want to buy these predators from your local garden shop. My kids loved hatching praying mantis eggs, although we only caught the emerging babies due to luck.

Pet fleas? As part of an overall flea-control strategy, put an herbal sachet with insect-repellent herbs in your dog's bedding. Make a large sachet (about the size of a piece of paper) and fill with any of these repellent herbs: rose geranium, rue, camphor, feverfew, lavender, rosemary, sage, eucalyptus, black walnut tree leaves, or neem.

Some dogs can be irritated by herbal pillows. If this is the case, try a non-toxic flea powder for your dog. Mix 1/2 cup baking soda and 1/2 teaspoon orange oil. Blend. Dust onto your dog and work into the fur. You can also make your own flea collar. Just place a few drops of repellent essential oil on a cloth collar and repeat weekly. Try orange oil, cedar, or eucalyptus. Keep in mind that essential oils can be irritating so use only a few drops, and don't try this if your dog has sensitive skin.

Appendix A: Smart Mama's Day-Care Questions

I know that in some areas day cares and care providers are difficult to find, and long waiting lists exist. But you should still find out what your children may be exposed to while away from you. Here are some questions you might want to ask:

1. Do you serve organic food? Can I bring my own?
2. What cleaning products do you use? Do you have a cleaning service? What products does the service use? Is the vacuum used on the carpets equipped with a HEPA filter?
3. How do you sanitize the changing pad? What do you use for diaper changes?
4. How do you control pests? (If the day care rents the location, ask what pest-management methods the landlord uses.)
5. Do you have a lead survey? (Look at the condition of the paint and whether dust is collected around windowsills. If the facility was constructed before 1978, ask about lead and whether wet wiping is used.)

6. Are scented products used?

7. Does the facility use PVC toys? How does the facility check for recalled toys? Have the toys been tested for lead? (You should also check out the toys to see if they are in good condition.)

8. What do you use to feed the children? Are the dishes, bottles, etc., made of polycarbonate plastic? What detergent is used to clean bottles? Is it mild or abrasive?

9. Are the indoor areas where children play a shoe-free zone? (Check to see if the floor in this area is clean.)

10. If there is an outdoor playground structure or wood deck, were they constructed with CCA-treated lumber?

11. Is vinyl present on the crib mattresses? Diaper changing pads? Any other surfaces, such as floor coverings or mini-blinds?

12. Is ventilation adequate? Does the facility experience moisture problems? Musty odors?

13. What is the drinking water source? Are the pipes free of lead? If bottled water is used, is the storage bottle free of BPA?

Appendix B: Common Acronyms and Abbreviations

ACRONYM	STANDS FOR
ADHD	Attention Deficit Hyperactivity Disorder
ASD	Autism Spectrum Disorders
BLL	Blood Lead Level
BPA	Bisphenol A
BFR	Brominated Flame Retardants
CARB	California Air Resources Board
CCA	Chromated Copper Arsenate
CDC	Centers for Disease Control and Prevention
CERCLA	Comprehensive Environmental Response, Compensation and Liability Act
CFR	Code of Federal Regulations, also Chlorinated Flame Retardant
CPSC	Consumer Product Safety Commission
DHA	Docosahexaenoic acid
DHHS	U. S. Department of Health and Human Services

dL	Deciliter
EPA	U.S. Environmental Protection Agency
EWG	Environmental Working Group
FDA	U.S. Food and Drug Administration
GRAS	Generally Recognized as Safe
HEPA	High-Efficiency Particulate Air
HUD	U.S. Department of Housing and Urban Development
Kg	Kilogram
mg	Milligram
mVOCs	Microbial Volatile Organic Compounds
NAS	National Academy of Sciences
NCI	National Cancer Institute
NHANES	National Health and Nutrition Examination Survey
NOP	National Organic Program
NSF	National Science Foundation
OSHA	Occupational Safety and Health Administration
PAH	Polyaromatic Hydrocarbon
PCBs	Polychlorinated biphenyls
pCi	PicoCurie
ppb	Parts per billion
ppm	Parts per million
PVC	Polyvinyl chloride
SIDS	Sudden infant death syndrome
TSCA	Toxic Substances Control Act
TSP	Trisodium phosphate
ug	Microgram
USDA	United States Department of Agriculture
VOC	Volatile Organic Compound

Endnotes

Chapter 1

1 Environmental Working Group, "BodyBurden: The Pollution in People," 2003, found at http://archive.ewg.org/reports/bodyburden1/es.php.

2 E-mail communication with Charlotte Brody, June 15, 2008.

3 M. Cone, "Common Chemicals Are Linked to Breast Cancer," *Los Angeles Times,* May 14, 2007.

4 Memo to Interested Parties, from Fairbank, Maslin, Maullin & Associates, "Regarding Key Findings of Recent Maine Survey on Persistent Toxic Chemicals," dated April 15, 2003.

5 TSCA, 15 U.S.C. §§ 2601–2692.

6 This is the number of chemical substances, as identified under TSCA, currently listed on the TSCA inventory. General Accounting Office, "Chemical Regulation: Comparison of U.S. and Recently Enacted European Union Approaches to Protect against the Risk of Toxic Chemicals."

7 "Chemical Regulation: Actions Are Needed to Improve the Effectiveness of EPA's Chemical Review Program," Statement of John B. Stephenson, Director, Natural Resources & Environment, Government Accountability Office, GAO-06-1032T.

8 15 U.S.C. § 1605(a) and § 1605(c)(1).

9 *Corrosion Proof Fittings v. EPA,* 947 F.2d 1201 (Fifth Circuit, 1991).

10 General Accounting Office, "Toxic Substances Control Act: Legislative Changes Could Make the Act More Effective," 9/26/94, GAO/RCED-94-103.

11 21 CFR § 170.3(i).
12 7 CFR § 205.2

Chapter 2

1 This stems from a statement made by a Swiss doctor in the 1500s: "All things are poison and nothing is without poison, only the dose permits something not to be poisonous." *Von der Besucht,* Paracelsus, 1567.
2 S. G. Gilbert, *A Small Dose of Toxicology: The Health Effects of Common Chemicals,* p. 27, 2004.
3 Environmental Working Group, "BodyBurden: The Pollution in Newborns," July 14, 2005.
4 Greenpeace and World Wildlife Fund, "A Present for Life: Hazardous Chemicals in Umbilical Cord Blood," September 2005.
5 C. Lu, K. Toepel, R. Irish, R. A. Fenske, D. B. Barr, and R. Bravo, "Organic Diets Significantly Lower Children's Dietary Exposure to Organophosphorous Pesticides," *Environmental Health Perspectives,* vol. 114, no. 2, February 2006.
6 G. Daston, E. Faustman, G. Ginsberg, P. Fenner-Crisp, S. Olin, B. Sonwane, J. Bruckner, and W. Breslin, "A Framework for Assessing Risks to Children from Exposure to Environmental Agents," *Environmental Health Perspectives,* vol. 112, no. 2, February 2004, 238–256.
7 "Developmental Origins of Environmentally Induced Disease and Dysfunction," International Conference on Foetal Programming and Developmental Toxicity, Torshavn, Faroe Islands, May 20–24, 2007.
8 International Programme on Chemical Safety, "Principles for Evaluating Health Risks to Progeny Associated with Exposure to Chemicals during Pregnancy."
9 Ibid.
10 The Faroes Statement, International Conference on Fetal Programming and Developmental Toxicity, Torshavn, Faroe Islands, issued May 24, 2007.
11 "Developmental Origins of Environmentally Induced Disease and Dysfunction," International Conference on Foetal Programming and Developmental Toxicity, Torshavn, Faroe Islands, May 20–24, 2007.
12 T. Schettler, "Developmental Disabilities — Impairment of Children's Brain Development and Function: The Role of Environmental Factors," The Collaborative on Health and the Environment, February 8, 2003.
13 S. G. Selevan, C. A. Kimmel, and P. Mendola, "Identifying Critical Windows of Exposure for Children's Health," *Environmental Health Perspectives Supplements,* vol. 108, no. S3, June 2008.
14 World Health Organization, "Children's Health and the Environment: Children Are Not Little Adults," WHO Training Package for the Health Sector, July 2008.
15 National Research Council, *Pesticides in the Diets of Infants and Children,* National Academy Press, 1993.
16 "Pediatric Environmental Health — The Child as Susceptible Host: A Developmental Approach to Pediatric Environmental Medicine, Case Studies in Environ-

mental Medicine," Agency for Toxic Substances & Disease Registry, Department of Health and Human Services.
17 National Research Council, *Pesticides in the Diets of Infants and Children,* National Academy Press, pp. 30–31, 1993.
18 Ibid., 9.
19 U.S. Environmental Protection Agency, "America's Children and the Environment, Measure D5: Cancer Incidence and Mortality," located at http://www.epa.gov/envirohealth/children/child_illness/d5-graph.htm.
20 M. Xiaomei, P. A. Buffler, R. B. Gunier, G. Dahl, M. T. Smith, K. Reinier, and P. Reynolds, "Critical Windows of Exposure to Household Pesticides and Risk of Childhood Leukemia," *Environmental Health Perspectives,* vol. 110, no. 9, September 2002.
21 U.S. Environmental Protection Agency, *America's Children and the Environment,* EPA 240-R-00-006, p. 9, December 2000.
22 American Lung Association, Childhood Asthma Overview, October 2007, located at http://www.lungusa.org/site/pp.asp?c=dvLUK9O0AE&b=22782.
23 U.S. EPA, *Supplemental Guidance for Assessing Susceptibility from Early-Life Exposure to Carcinogens,* EPA 630/R-03/003F, March 2005, p. 32.
24 Ibid.
25 Ibid., 33–34.

Chapter 3

1 Radon is actually not responsible for the health effects. Radon decays to isotopes of polonium, bismuth, and lead. These decay products are known as "radon progeny." Two of the radon progeny are of most concern: polonium-218 and polonium-214. They are minute particles that, once inhaled, are retained in the lungs and emit their radiation.
2 U.S. Environmental Protection Agency, "Health Risks: Exposure to Radon Causes Lung Cancer in Non-Smokers and Smokers Alike," found at http://www.epa.gov/radon/healthrisks.html (accessed 2/19/08).
3 Radioactive elements seek a more stable energy state. This process is known as radioactive decay. Uranium is the first in a chain of radioactive elements that decay until the element is reached (the stable element). Radon's immediate parent is radium.
4 A Curie is the standard measurement for radioactivity. It is the rate of decay for a gram of radium, and is equivalent to 37 billion decays per second. A pCi/L corresponds to one decay every 27 seconds in a volume of one liter, or 0.037 decays per second in every liter of air.
5 U.S. Environmental Protection Agency, "Health Risks: Exposure to Radon Causes Lung Cancer in Non-Smokers and Smokers Alike," found at http://www.epa.gov/radon/healthrisks.html (accessed 2/19/08).
6 Ibid.
7 U.S. Environmental Protection Agency, *A Citizen's Guide to Radon: The Guide to Protecting Yourself and Your Family from Radon,* US EPA, EPA 402-K-07-009, Revised May 2007.

8 U.S. Environmental Protection Agency, *EPA Assessment of Risks from Radon in Homes,* EPA 402-R-03-003, June 2003.

9 Committee on Environmental Hazards, "Radon Exposure: A Hazard to Children," American Academy of Pediatrics, found at http://www.medem.com/search/article_display.cfm?path=n:&mstr=/ZZZZ9IZ4NAC.html&soc=AAP&srch_typ=NAV_SERCH (accessed 2/19/08).

10 U.S. Environmental Protection Agency, *Consumer's Guide to Radon Reduction,* EPA 402-K-06-094, Revised, December 2006, http://www.epa.gov/radon/pubs/consguid.html#howenters.

11 H. A. Jones-Otazo, J. P. Clarke, M. L. Diamond, J. A. Archbold, G. Ferguson, T. Harner, G. M. Richardson, J. J. Ryan, and B. Wilford, "Is House Dust the Missing Exposure Pathway for PBDEs? An Analysis of the Urban Fate and Human Exposure to PBDEs," *Environmental Science & Technology,* vol. 39, issue 14, 5121–5130, July 15, 2005.

12 P. Costner, B. Thorpe, and A. McPherson, *Sick of Dust: Chemicals in Common Products—A Needless Health Risk in Our Homes,* Safer Products Project, Clean Production Action, March 2005.

13 S. Janssen, "Brominated Flame Retardants: Rising Levels of Concern," *Health Care Without Harm,* Winter 2005.

14 M. Lorber, "Exposure of Americans to Polybrominated Diphenyl Ethers," *Journal of Exposure Science and Environmental Epidemiology,* vol. 18, no. 1, pp. 2–19 (2008).

15 D. A. Butler, *Damp Indoor Spaces and Health,* Institute of Medicine, National Academy of Sciences, 2004.

16 W. J. Fisk, Q. Lei-Gomez, and M. J. Mendell, "Meta-Analyses of the Associations of Respiratory Health Effects with Dampness and Mold in Homes," *Indoor Air,* vol. 17, issue 4, pp. 284–296, August 2007.

17 D. Mudarri and W. J. Fisk, "Public Health and Economic Impact of Dampness and Mold," *Indoor Air,* vol. 17, issue 3, pp. 225–235, June 2007.

18 Minnesota Department of Health, "Mold in Homes," found at http://www.health.state.mn.us/divs/eh/indoorair/mold/index.html.

19 P. C. Stark, H. A. Burge, L. M. Ryan, D. K. Milton, and D. R. Gold, "Fungal Levels in the Home and Lower Respiratory Tract Illnesses in the First Year of Life," *American Journal of Respiratory and Critical Care Medicine,* vol. 168, pp. 232–237, 2003.

20 K. Belanger, W. Beckett, E. Triche, M. B. Bracken, T. Holdford, P. Red, J. McSharry, D. R. Gold, T. A. E. Platts-Mills, and B. P. Leaderer, "Symptoms of Wheeze and Persistent Cough in the First Year of Life: Associations with Indoor Allergens, Air Contaminants, and Maternal History of Asthma," *American Journal of Epidemiology,* 158: 195–202, 2003.

21 J. J. K. Jaakkola, B. F. Hwang, and N. Jaakkola, "Home Dampness and Molds, Parental Atopy and Asthma in Childhood: A Six-Year Population-Based Cohort Study," *Environmental Health Perspectives,* vol. 113, no. 3, March 2005.

22 S. C. Redd, State of the Science on Molds and Human Health, Statement for the Record before the Subcommittees on Oversight and Investigations and Housing and Community Opportunity, Committee on Financial Services, United States House of Representatives.

23 American Academy of Pediatrics, Committee on Environmental Health, Policy Statement, "Spectrum of Noninfectious Health Effects from Molds."
24 U.S. Environmental Protection Agency, "Health Effects of Exposure to Secondhand Smoke," found at http://www.epa.gov/smokefree/healtheffects.html.
25 U.S. Department of Health and Human Services, "The Health Consequences of Involuntary Exposure to Tobacco Smoke: A Report of the Surgeon General, 6 Major Conclusions of the Surgeon General Report," found at http://www.surgeongeneral.gov/library/secondhandsmoke/factsheets/factsheet6.html.
26 The National Survey on Environmental Management of Asthma and Children's Exposure to Environmental Tobacco Smoke.
27 U.S. Environmental Protection Agency, "The National Survey on Environmental Management of Asthma and Children's Exposure to Environmental Tobacco Smoke," 2004.
28 U.S. Department of Health and Human Services, "The Health Consequences of Involuntary Exposure to Tobacco Smoke: A Report of the Surgeon General, 6 Major Conclusions of the Surgeon General Report," http://www.surgeongeneral.gov/library/secondhandsmoke/factsheets/factsheet6.html.
29 U.S. Department of Health and Human Services, *The Health Consequences of Involuntary Exposure to Tobacco Smoke: A Report of the Surgeon General.* Atlanta, GA. U.S. Department of Health and Human Services, Centers for Disease Control and Prevention, Coordinating Center for Health Promotion, National Center for Chronic Disease Prevention and Health Promotion, Office on Smoking and Health, p. 13, 2006.
30 California Environmental Protection Agency, "Proposed Identification of Environmental Tobacco Smoke as a Toxic Air Contaminant," ES-5, as approved by the Scientific Review Panel, June 24, 2005.
31 California Environmental Protection Agency, "Proposed Identification of Environmental Tobacco Smoke as a Toxic Air Contaminant," ES-7, as approved by the Scientific Review Panel, June 24, 2005.
32 California Environmental Protection Agency, "Proposed Identification of Environmental Tobacco Smoke as a Toxic Air Contaminant," ES-5, as approved by the Scientific Review Panel, June 24, 2005.
33 California Environmental Protection Agency, Office of Environmental Health Hazard Assessment, *Health Effects of Exposure to Environmental Tobacco Smoke,* 1997.
34 Global Environment & Technology Foundation, "Report of Findings and Recommendations on the Use and Management of Asbestos," May 16, 2003.
35 The EPA issued a rule under TSCA on July 12, 1989, entitled the "Asbestos Ban and Phase Out Rule." That rule purported to ban certain asbestos-containing products. However, following a legal challenge to the EPA's authority to issue the rule under TSCA, the rule was mostly vacated by the U.S. Circuit Court of Appeals in 1991.
36 51 Fed. Reg. 185, *Labeling of Asbestos-Containing Household Products; Enforcement Policy,* p. 33910, September 24, 1986.
37 See http://www.cpsc.gov/CPSCPUB/PREREL/prhtml80/80021.html.
38 U.S. Environmental Protection Agency, "Asbestos in Your Home," found at http://www.epa.gov/asbestos/pubs/ashome.html#2.

39 C. Jakober and T. Phillips, "Evaluation of Ozone Emissions from Portable Indoor Air Cleaners; Electrostatic Precipitators and Ionizers," Staff Technical Report, California Environmental Protection Agency, California Air Resources Board, February 2008.

40 Ibid.

41 E. Kwon, H. Zhang, Z. Wang, G. S. Jhangri, X. Lu, N. Fok, S. Gabos, X. Li, and X. C. Le, "Arsenic on the Hands of Children after Playing in Playgrounds," *Environmental Health Perspectives,* vol. 112, no. 14, October 2004.

Chapter 4

1 *Measuring Lead Exposure in Infants, Children, and Other Sensitive Populations,* National Academy Press, 1993, p. 3.

2 J. M. Braun, R. S. Kahn, T. Froehlich, P. Auinger, and B. P. Lanphear, "Exposures to Environmental Toxicants and Attention Deficit Hyperactivity Disorder in U.S. Children," *Environmental Health Perspectives,* vol. 114, 1904–1909, 2006.

3 P. M. Lutz, T. J. Wilson, A. L. Jones, J. S. Gorman, N. L. Gale, J. C. Johnson, and J. E. Hewett, "Elevated Immunoglobin E (IgE) Levels with Exposure to Environmental Lead," *Toxicology,* 134.63–78.

4 D. Gao, T. K. Modal, and D. A. Lawrence, "Lead Effects on Development and Function of Bone-Marrow Derived Dendritic Cells Promotes ThZ Immune Responses, Toxicology and Applied Pharmacology," vol. 222, 69–79, 2007.

5 *Children's Health and the Environment in North America,* Commission for Environmental Cooperation, 2006.

6 S. Tong, Y. E. von Schirnding, and T. Prapamontol, *Environmental Lead Exposure: A Public Health Problem of Global Dimensions,* Bulletin of the World Health Organization.

7 Testimony of Dana Best, M.D., M.P.H., F.A.A.P., on behalf of the American Academy of Pediatrics to the Energy and Commerce Subcommittee on Commerce, Trade, Consumer Protection, "Protecting Children from Lead-Tainted Imports," September 20, 2007.

8 N. Graber and J. Forman, *Guidelines for the Identification and Management of Pregnant Women with Elevated Lead Levels in New York City, Recommendations from a Peer Review Panel,* New York City Department of Health and Mental Hygiene and the Mount Sinai Center for Children's Health and the Environment, October 4, 2004.

9 B. L. Gulson, K. J. Mizon, M. J. Korsch, J. M. Palmer, and J. B. Donnelly, "Mobilization of Lead from Human Bone Tissue during Pregnancy and Lactation — A Summary of Long-Term Research," *Science of the Total Environment,* vol. 303, issues 1–2, pp. 79–104, February 2003.

10 American Academy of Pediatrics, "Lead Exposure in Children: Prevention, Detection, and Management, American Academy of Pediatrics," Committee on Environmental Health, *Pediatrics,* vol. 116, no. 4, 1036–1046, October 2005.

11 H. Hu, M. M. Tellez-Rojo, D. Bellinger, D. Smith, A. S. Ettinger, H. Lamadrid-Figueroa, J. Schwartz, L. Schnaas, A. Mercado-Garcia, and M. Hernandez-Avila, "Fetal Lead Exposure at Each Stage of Pregnancy as a Predictor of Infant Mental

Development," *Environmental Health Perspectives,* vol. 114, no. 11, 1730–1735, Nov. 2006.

12 J. Moya, C. F. Bearer, and R. A. Etzel, "Children's Behavior and Physiology and How It Affects Exposure to Environmental Contaminants," *Pediatrics,* vol. 113, no. 4, 996–1006, April 2004.

13 H. Loukmas, S. Boese, and M. McCoy, "Unwanted Exposure: Preventing Environmental Threats to the Health of New York State's Children," Summary of Children's Environmental Health Leadership on October 12, 2006, Albany, New York, p. 9, summary of comments of David O. Carpenter, M.D., professor at the Environmental Health and Toxicology Division, School of Public Health at the University of Albany, New York.

14 R. Levin, M. J. Brown, M. E. Kashtock, D. E. Jacobs, E. A. Whelan, J. Rodman, M. R. Schock, A. Padilla, and T. Sinks, "U.S. Children's Lead Exposures, 2008: Implications for Prevention," *Environmental Health Perspectives,* vol. 116, no. 10, 1285–1293, Oct. 2008.

15 L. Schneitzer, "Lead Poisoning in Adults from Renovation of an Older Home," *Annals of Emergency Medicine,* 19 (April 1990), 415–420.

16 Endpoint devices—those devices intended to dispense water for human consumption—must also meet a performance standard under Section 1417(e) of the federal Safe Drinking Water Act. The performance standard ensures that the endpoint devices, but not in-line piping, leach no more than eleven (11) parts per billion lead. Endpoint devices include kitchen and bar faucets, water dispensers, drinking fountains, water coolers, residential refrigerator ice makers, etc.

17 "Elevated Blood Lead Levels in Refugee Children: New Hampshire," 2003–2004 (lead exposure occurred in the United States), *Morbidity and Mortality Weekly Report* 54:42–46.

18 Complaint filed in the case *State of Rhode Island v. Lead Industries Association, Inc., et al.*

19 "Child Lead Poisoning and the Lead Industry," Web site, available at http://www.sueleadindustry.homestead.com/index.html.

20 *The Dutch Boy's Hobby: A Paint Book for Girls and Boys,* National Lead Company, personal collection of author.

21 Memo of Bernhard Mautz reprinted in decision of the Court of Appeals of the State of Wisconsin, District I, in the case entitled *City of Milwaukee v. NL Industries, Inc., et al.,* case no. 01CV003066, Appeal No. 03-2786, November 9, 2004, available at http://www.wisbar.org/res/capp/2004p/03-2786.pdf.

22 B. Anderson, "Chipping Away at a Deadly Problem," *The Fresno Bee,* May 29, 2007.

23 Ibid.

24 J. M. Gaitens, S. L. Dixon, D. E. Jacobs, J. Nagaraja, W. Strauss, J. W. Wilson, and P. J. Ashley, "U.S. Children's Exposure to Residential Dust Lead, 1994–2004: I. Housing and Demographic Factors," *Environmental Health Perspectives,* DOI: 10.1289/ehp.11917, November 14, 2008.

25 H. Holmes, *The Secret Life of Dust,* p. 178.

26 D. J. DeNoon, "Lead Poisoning and Kids, Lead Poisoning: What It Is, How to Test, What to Do," WebMD, August 15, 2007.

27 N. Graber and J. Forman, *Guidelines for the Identification and Management of Pregnant Women with Elevated Lead Levels in New York City, Recommendations from a Peer Review Panel,* New York City Department of Health and Mental Hygiene and the Mount Sinai Center for Children's Health and the Environment, p. 49, October 4, 2004.
28 M. Rhor, "Folk Medicines Contain Lead," Associated Press, 2008.
29 M. Rhor, "Folk Medicines Pose Poison Risk: Immigrants' Traditional Remedies Laden with Dangerous Lead Levels, U.S. Health Officials Say," *San Francisco Chronicle, SFGate,* January 23, 2008.
30 Centers for Disease Control and Prevention, MMWR, 53 (26): 582–584, July 9, 2004.
31 Ibid.
32 "CPSC Finds Lead Poisoning Hazard for Young Children in Imported Vinyl Miniblinds," Press Release 96-150, U.S. Consumer Product Safety Commission, June 25, 1996.
33 "Survey Data on Lead in Women's and Children's Vitamins," CFSAN/Office of Regulatory Science, U.S. Food and Drug Administration, August, 2008, found at http://www.cfsan.fda.gov/~dms/pbvitami.html (accessed 12/8/08).

Chapter 5

1 "Opinion of the Scientific Panel on Food Additives, Flavourings, Processing Aids and Materials in Contact with Food," on a request from the Commission related to 2,2-bis(4-hydroxyphenyl)propane (Bisphenol A), Question Number EFSA-Q-2005-100, *The EFSA Journal,* 428, adopted November 29, 2006.
2 Ibid.
3 A. M. Calafat, X. Ye, L-Y Wong, J. A. Reidy, and L. L. Needham, "Exposure of the U.S. Population to Bisphenol A and 4-Tertiary-octylphenol: 2003–2004," *Environmental Health Perspectives,* vol. 116, no. 1, 39–44, Jan. 2008.
4 N. Lubick, "U.S. Baseline for Bisphenol A," *Science News,* November 7, 2007.
5 Ibid.
6 H. Takada, T. Isobe, N. Nakada, H. Nishiyama, T. Iguchi, H. Irie, and C. Mori, "Bisphenol A and Nonylphenols in Human Umbilical Cords." Poster presentation at International Conference at Monte Verita, Ascone, March 7–9, 1999.
7 *Baby's Toxic Bottle: Bisphenol A Leaching from Popular Baby Bottles,* The Work Group for Safe Markets, February 2008.
8 A study cited on an industry Web site, the Bisphenol A Information Web site, claims to have looked at "real world" use of baby bottles and BPA migration and states that use does not increase migration. The Bisphenol A Information Web site is sponsored by the Polycarbonate/BPA Global Group, which includes members of the American Chemistry Council, PlasticsEurope, and the Japan Chemical Industry Association. The "real world" activities included cleaning in a dishwasher or with a brush, sterilization with boiling water and temperature of migration. The study confirmed increased BPA leaching with temperature, and did not find any increase with use. However, the "use" was twelve cycles of use, which for most of us would be two weeks of bottle washing, not particularly reflective of the "real world" use of baby bottles

by most parents. See N. C. Maragou, A. Makri, E. N. Lampi, N. S. Thomaidis, and M. A. Koupparis, "Migration of Bisphenol A from Polycarbonate Baby Bottles under Real Use Conditions," *Food Additives & Contaminants*, vol. 25, no. 3, 373–383 (2008).

9 C. Brede, P. Fjeldal, I. Skjevrak, and H. Herikstad, "Increased Migration Levels of Bisphenol A from Polycarbonate Baby Bottles after Dishwashing, Boiling and Brushing," *Food Additives and Contaminants*, vol. 20, no. 7, pp. 684–689 (2007). In this study, the researchers looked at new and used polycarbonate plastic baby bottles. The used polycarbonate bottles were subjected to simulated use of dishwashing 51 times and 169 times, respectively. The bottle with simulated use equivalent to dishwashing 51 times had the highest mean level of BPA leaching. The bottles with simulated use showed significantly higher levels than the brand-new bottle.

10 Environmental Working Group, "Bisphenol A: Toxic Plastics Chemical in Canned Food," March 5, 2007, available at http://www.ewg.org.

11 A. Zsarnovszky, H. H. Le, H. S. Wang, and S. M. Belcher, "Ontogeny of Rapid Estrogen-Mediated Extracellula Signal-Regulated Kinase Signaling in the Rat Cerebellar Cortex: Potent Nongenomic Agonist and Endocrine Disrupting Activity of the Xenoestrogen Bisphenol A," *Endocrinology*, 146: 5388–5396, December 2005.

12 Centers for Disease Control, "DES Update: Consumers, About DES," found at http://www.cdc.gov/DES/consumers/about/effects.html (accessed 2/18/08).

13 E. Grossman, "Two Words: Bad Plastic," *Salon.com News*, August 2, 2007.

14 Ibid.

15 O. Takahaski and S. Oishi, "Disposition of Orally Administered 2,2-Bis (4-hydroxyphenyl) propane (Bisphenol A) in Pregnant Rats and the Placental Transfer to Fetuses," *Environmental Health Perspectives*, vol. 108, no. 10, 931–935, October 2000.

16 P. A. Hunt, K. E. Koehler, M. Susiarjo, C. A. Hodges, A. Ilagan, R. C. Voiget, S. Thomas, B. F. Thomas, and T. J. Hassold, "Bisphenol A Exposure Causes Meiotic Aneuploidy in the Female Mouse," *Current Biology*, 13, 546–553, 2003.

17 L. N. Vandenberg, M. V. Maffini, P. R. Wadia, C. Sonnenschein, B. S. Rubin, and A. M. Soto, "Exposure to Environmentally Relevant Doses of the Xenoestrogen Bisphenol-A Alters Development of the Fetal Mouse Mammary Gland," *Endocrinology*, 148(1):116–27.

18 R. R. Newbold, W. R. Jefferson, and E. P. Banks, "Long-Term Adverse Effects of Neonatal Exposure to Bisphenol A on the Murine Female Reproductive Tract," *Reproductive Toxicology*, vol. 24, no. 2, 253–258, August–September 2007.

19 The National Toxicology Program (NTP) Center for the Evaluation of Risks to Human Reproduction (CERHR) convened an expert panel to evaluate BPA. The report has been subject to extensive criticism because many believe the authors were unduly influenced by industry. Critics charge that the panel weighted studies funded by industry over other studies. The panel rejected studies that used non-oral routes of administration. In doing so, the panel rejected large numbers of peer-reviewed studies that found health effects at low doses of exposure. A study conducted by a lead critic found no difference in the route of administration of BPA.

In any event, as a result of the complaints, the National Institute of Health's National Toxicology Program is undertaking a review of the report. But what is telling is that even the industry-friendly report found concern:

— For pregnant women and fetuses:

- Some concern that the exposure to BPA in utero causes neural and behavioral effects;
- Minimal concern that exposure to BPA in utero causes effects on the prostate and accelerations in puberty;
- Negligible concern that exposure to BPA in utero produces birth defects and malformations

— For infants and children:

- Some concern that exposure to BPA causes neural and behavioral effects
- Minimal concern that exposure to BPA potentially causes accelerations in puberty

20 This stems from a statement made by a Swiss doctor in the 1500s: "All substances are poisons; there is none which is not a poison. The right dose differentiates a poison from a remedy." *Von der Besucht,* Paracelsus, 1567.

21 E-mail communication with Scott M. Belcher.

22 R. Elsby, J. L. Maggs, J. Ashby, and B. K. Park, "Comparison of the Modulatory Effects of Human and Rat Liver Microsomal Metabolism on the Estrogenicity of Bisphenol A: Implications for Extrapolation to Humans," *The Journal of Pharmacology and Experimental Therapeutics,* 297: 103–113 (2001).

23 M. W. H. Coughtrie, B. Burchell, J. E. A. Leakey, and R. Hume, "The Inadequacy of Perinatal Glucuronidation: Immunoblot Analysis of the Developmental Expression of Individual UDP-Glucuronosyltransferase Isoenzymes in Rate and Human Liver Microsomes," *Mol. Pharmacol.,* 34: 729–735.

24 CPG 7117.11, FDA Compliance Policy Guide § 500.450.

25 Consumer Product Safety Commission, Press Release: "CPSC Warns about Worn Vinyl Baby Bibs," U. S. Consumer Product Safety Commission, May 2, 2007, Release No. 07-175.

26 K. H. Lund and J. H. Petersen, "Migration of Formaldehyde and Melamine Monomers from Kitchen and Tableware Made of Melamine Plastic," *Food Additives and Contaminants,* vol. 23, no. 9, 948–955, Sept. 2006.

27 E. L. Bradley, V. Boughtflower, T. L. Smith, D. R. Speck, and L. Castle, "Survey of the Migration of Melamine and Formaldehyde from Melamine Food Contact Articles Available on the UK Market," *Food Additives and Contaminants,* vol. 22, no. 6, 597–600, June 2005.

28 "Childhood Lead Poisoning from Commercially Manufactured French Ceramic Dinnerware—New York City," *Morbidity and Mortality Weekly Report* 53: 584–586.

29 J. Torres, "Could Your Kids' Toys Be Poison," *The Record,* June 3, 2007.

Chapter 6

1 E. Miller and N. Snow, "Safeguarding our Children at Home: Reducing Exposures to Toxic Chemicals and Heavy Metals," *Zero to Three,* 2005.

2 A. Schneider, "Harmful Pesticides Found in Everyday Foods," *Seattle Post-Intelligencer,* January 30, 2008.

3 U.S. Environmental Protection Agency, "Mercury Study Report to Congress," EPA-452/R-97-003, December, 1997, p. 3-3.

4 Mercury Policy Project, "Mercury Pollution," found at http://www.mercury policy.org/emissions/index.shtml (accessed 3/1/08).

5 U.S. Environmental Protection Agency, "Mercury Study Report to Congress," EPA-452/R-97-003, December 1997.

6 K. Murata, P. Weihe, E. Budtz-Jorgensen, P. J. Jorgensen, and P. Grandjean, "Delayed Brainstem Auditory Evoked Potential Latencies in 14-Year-Old Children Exposed to Methylmercury," *Journal of Pediatrics,* 144:177–183.

7 Agency for Toxic Substances & Disease Registry, "Toxicology Profile for Mercury," March 1999, § 2.2.2.6.

8 Committee on the Toxicological Effects of Methylmercury, Board on Environmental Studies and Toxicology, National Research Council, National Academy of Sciences, p. 9, 2000.

9 An open letter to federal and state regulators, departments of health, product manufacturers, businesses, and consumers from over sixty physicians nationwide, December 16, 1998, found at http://www.mercurypolicy.org/emissions/documents/doc_letter.pdf (accessed 3/1/08).

10 T. Schettler, "Developmental Disabilities—Impairment of Children's Brain Development and Function: The Role of Environmental Factors," The Collaborative on Health and the Environment, February 8, 2003.

11 Committee on the Toxicological Effects of Methylmercury, Board on Environmental Studies and Toxicology, National Research Council, National Academy of Sciences, p. 4, 2000.

12 F. Xue, C. Holzman, M. H. Rahbar, K. Trosko, and L. Fischer, "Maternal Fish Consumption, Mercury Levels and Risk of Preterm Delivery," *Environmental Health Perspectives,* vol. 115, no. 1, pp. 42–47, January 2007.

13 CDC, "Blood Mercury Levels in Young Children and Childbearing-Aged Women—United States," 1999–2002, MMWR, 53(43): 1018–1020, November 5, 2004.

14 The United States Environmental Protection Agency reports that approximately 8 percent of women of childbearing age have mercury blood levels above 5.8 ppb. This is based on the NHANES data for 1999–2000. If 8 percent of childbearing-aged women have mercury blood levels above 5.8 ppb, then approximately 320,000 babies born each year have an increased risk of learning disabilities and motor-skill impairment based upon fetal mercury exposure, assuming 4,000,000 births per year. The NHANES data are reported in two-year cycles. The MMWR report updated the 1999–2000 mercury blood estimates, and found a decline for 2001–2002, to 3.9 percent. The MMWR, however, cautions that the apparent decline between the 1999–2000 and 2001–2002 is not statistically significant, and advised that the 1999–2002 data is the most reliable estimate.

15 K. R. Mahaffey, "Methylmercury: Epidemiology Update." Presentation at the National Forum on Contaminants in Fish, San Diego, California, January 28, 2004.

16 T. Schettler, J. Stein, F. Reich, and M. Valenti, *In Harm's Way: Toxic Threats to Child Development,* Greater Boston Physicians for Social Responsibility, May 2000.
17 S. Roe and M. Hawthorne, "How Safe Is Tuna? Federal Regulators and the Tuna Industry Fail to Warn Consumers about the True Health Hazards of an American Favorite," *Chicago Tribune,* December 13, 2005.
18 Ibid.
19 "Imported Herbal Medicine Products Known to Contain Lead, Mercury or Arsenic," The City of New York, Department of Health & Mental Hygiene.
20 International Programme on Chemical Safety, Environmental Health Criteria 101, Methylmercury; United States Environmental Protection Agency, Fact Sheet: "Mercury Update: Impact on Fish Advisories," EPA-823-F-01-011, June 2001.
21 T. W. Hale, "Medications and Mothers' Milk," 2004, p. 528.
22 S. D. Soechitram, M. Athanasiadou, L. Hovander, A. Bergman, and P. J. Jacob Sauer, "Fetal Exposure to PCBs and Their Hydroxylated Metabolites in a Dutch Cohort," *Environmental Health Perspectives,* vol. 112, no. 11, August 2004.
23 California Office of Environmental Health Hazard Assessment, "PCBs in Sport Fish: Answer to Questions on Health Effects," available at http://www.oehha.ca.gov/fish/pcb/index.html.
24 R. D. Williams, "Breast-Feeding Best Bet for Babies," *FDA Consumer Magazine,* U.S. Food and Drug Administration, October 1995.
25 American Academy of Pediatrics, Policy Statement, "Breastfeeding and the Use of Human Milk," *Pediatrics,* vol. 115, no. 2, 496–506.
26 Ibid.
27 P. J. Landrigan, B. Sonawane, D. Mattison, M. McCally, and A. Garg, "Chemical Contaminants in Breast Milk and Their Impacts on Children's Health: An Overview," *Environmental Health Perspectives,* vol. 110, no. 6, June 2002.
28 "Contaminants in Human Milk: Weighing the Risks against the Benefits of Breastfeeding," *Environmental Health Perspectives,* vol. 116, no. 10, October 2008.
29 U.S. Department of Health and Human Services, "HHS Blueprint for Action on Breastfeeding," U.S. DHHS, Office on Women's Health, Appendix 1.
30 N. Wu, T. Herrmann, O. Paepke, J. Tickner, R. Hale, E. Harvey, M. La Guardia, M. D. McClean, and T. F. Webster, "Human Exposure to PBDEs: Associations of PBDE Body Burdens with Food Consumption and House Dust Concentrations," *Environmental Science & Technology,* 41, 6282–6289.
31 U.S. Department of Health and Human Services, "Toxicological Profile for DDT, DDE and DDD," U.S. DHHS, Public Health Service, Agency for Toxic Substances and Disease Registry, September 2002.
32 ATSDR, ToxFAQs for DDT, DDE and DDD, § 2.1, September 2002.
33 California Office of Environmental Health Hazard Assessment, "PCBs in Sport Fish: Answer to Questions on Health Effects," available at http://www.oehha.ca.gov/fish/pcb/index.html.
34 American Academy of Pediatrics, "Lead Exposure in Children: Prevention, Detection, and Management," *Pediatrics,* vol. 116, no. 4, 1036–1046, October 2005.
35 Ibid.

36 O. Dohan, C. Portulano, C. Basquin, A. Reyna-Neyra, L. M. Amzel, and N. Carrasco, "The Na^+/I^- symporter (NIS) mediates electroneural active transport of the environmental pollutant perchlorate." *Proceedings of the National Academy of Science,* vol. 104, no. 51, pp. 20250–20255, December 18, 2007.

37 "CDC Perchlorate Fact Sheet," Department of Health and Human Services, Centers for Disease Control and Prevention, October 5, 2006.

38 B. C. Blount, L. Valentin-Blasini, J. D. Osterloh, J. P. Mauldin, and J. L. Pirkle, "Perchlorate Exposure of the U.S. Population," *Journal of Exposure Science and Environmental Epidemiology,* vol. 10, 1–8, 2006.

39 B. C. Blount, J. L. Pirkle, J. D. Oserloh, L. Valentin-Blasini, and K. L. Caldwell, "Urinary Perchlorate and Thyroid Hormone Levels in Adolescent and Adult Men and Women Living in the United States," *Environmental Health Perspectives,* vol. 114, no. 12, 1865–1871, 2006.

40 J. C. Bernbaum, D. M. Umbach, N. B. Ragan, J. L. Ballard, J. I. Archer, H. Schmidt-Davis, and W. J. Rogan, "Pilot Studies of Estrogen-Related Physical Findings in Infants," *Environmental Health Perspectives,* vol. 116, no. 3, pp. 416–420, March 2008.

41 Center for the Evaluation of Risks to Human Reproduction, "NTP-CERHR Expert Panel Report on the Reproductive and Development Toxicity of Soy Formula," U.S. Department of Health and Human Services, National Toxicology Program, April 2006.

42 J. E. Biles, T. P. McNeal, and T. H. Begley, "Determination of Bisphenol A Migrating from Epoxy Can Coatings to Infant Formula Liquid Concentrates," *Journal of Agricultural and Food Chemistry,* 45: 4697–4700 (1997) (done for the U.S. Food & Drug Administration).

43 Letter to the Honorable John D. Dingell, Chairman, Committee on Energy and Commerce, House of Representatives, from Stephen R. Mason, Acting Assistant Commissioner for Legislation, Food and Drug Administration, Department of Health and Human Services, dated February 25, 2008.

44 The FDA letter to the Committee on Energy and Commerce states that "FDA believes that this level of exposure (referring to 11 ug/person/day and 7 ug/infant/day) is safe as defined in 21 CFR § 170.3 (i). This conclusion is based on our most recently completed reviews of two pivotal multigenerational oral studies performed under applicable regulatory guidelines." Letter to the Honorable John D. Dingell, Chairman, Committee on Energy and Commerce, House of Representatives, from Stephen R. Mason, Acting Assistant Commissioner for Legislation, Food and Drug Administration, Department of Health and Human Services, dated February 25, 2008.

45 "Agency Improperly Relied On Chemical Industry Studies," Environmental Working Group, Statement of Dr. Anila Jacob, M.D., M.P.H, Senior Scientist, Environmental Working Group, March 21, 2008.

46 In 2006, the European Food Safety Authority found that the levels currently used in packaging are safe. The EPA's oral reference dose is 50 micrograms per kilogram body weight per day.

Chapter 7

1 "Carpeting, Indoor Air Quality, and the Environment," *Environmental Building News,* November/December, 1994 (Issue 6).
2 U.S. Environmental Protection Agency, "Indoor Air Quality, Basic Information," http://www.epa.gov/iaq/voc.html.
3 California Air Resources Board, "Report to the California Legislature: Indoor Air Pollution in California," July 2005.
4 U.S. Environmental Protection Agency, "Indoor Air Quality, Basic Information, Levels in Homes," available at http://www.epa.gov/iaq/voc.html (reporting on results from EPA's Total Exposure Assessment Methodology).
5 A. Guenther, T. Karl, P. Harley, C. Wiedinmyer, P. I. Palmer, and C. Geron, "Estimates of Global Terrestrial Isoprene Emissions Using MEGAN (Model of Emissions of Gases and Aerosols from Nature)," *Atmospheric Chemistry and Physics,* 6, 3181–3210, 2006.
6 "About Trees and VOCs," http://instaar.colorado.edu/outreach/trees-and-vocs/index.html.
7 U.S. Environmental Protection Agency, "Integrated Risk Information System, Formaldehyde."
8 California Air Resources Board, "Proposed Airborne Toxic Control Measure to Reduce Formaldehyde Emissions from Composite Wood Products," March 9, 2007, p. 147.
9 40 CFR 51.100(s).
10 40 CFR 51.100(s)(1).
11 Department of Health and Human Services, Agency for Toxic Substances & Disease Registry, ToxFAQs for Methylene Chloride, February 2001; EPA IRIS Dichloromethane. (Dichloromethane is another name for methylene chloride); The U.S. Department of Health and Human Services has identified it as "reasonably anticipated to be a human carcinogen."
12 Department of Health and Human Services, Agency for Toxic Substances & Disease Registry, ToxFAQs for 1,1,1-Trichloroethane, July 2006.
13 A word of warning on "low-VOC" and "no-VOC" labels for paints and coatings: No national definition exists for what constitutes a "low-VOC" and "no-VOC" paint. A low-VOC paint can be a paint that meets the EPA's standard of 250 grams VOC/Liter. However, paints are generally marketed as "low-VOC" paints if they fall below 50 g/L. The Green Seal certified paint meets a standard of no more than 50 g/L for flat paints, and 150 g/L for non-flat paints. As for "no-VOC" paint, it usually means that the paint has 5 g/L or less.
14 Green Seal Standards and Certifications, Paints (GS-11).
15 Polyvinyl chloride consists of long chains of polymers with large strands of molecules. Plasticizers, usually phthalates, are liquids that are added to the polymers. Heat and sometimes pressure are used to force the polymers and liquid plasticizers together. The plasticizers make the PVC more flexible.
16 In the early to mid-1990s, whether VOC emissions from carpeting caused health effects was the subject of a great deal of debate and even the subject of congressional hearings.

17 T. Lent, "Improving Indoor Air Quality with the California 01350 Specification," Healthy Building Network, June 15, 2007.
18 T. Brennan, "Keep It Clean," printed in *The Healthy House*, pp. 236–237.
19 California Environmental Protection Agency, California Air Resource Board, "Research Reports: Indoor Emissions of Formaldehyde and Toluene Diisocyanate," August 1997, No. 97-9.
20 California Air Resources Board, "Proposed Airborne Toxic Control Measure to Reduce Formaldehyde Emissions from Composite Wood Products," March 9, 2007, p. 1.
21 Ibid., p. 30.
22 U.S. Department of Health and Human Services, Agency for Toxic Substances and Disease Registry, Division of Toxicology and Environmental Medicine, "Toluene Toxicity," February 2001.
23 Rosalind C. Anderson and Julius H. Anderson, "Respiratory Toxicity of Mattress Emissions in Mice," *Archives of Environmental Health,* Jan/Feb 2000 (vol. 55, no. 1), pp. 38–43.
24 Ibid., pp. 41–42.
25 No federal law bans the use of PBDEs. The United States Environmental Protection Agency reached an agreement with the only United States manufacturer of penta-BDE and octa-BDE to cease production of these chemicals in 2004. In comparison, the European Union has banned the use of penta-BDE and octa-BDE in all products. Six states have banned or limited octa-BDE and penta-BDE.
26 The three major brominated flame-retardant classes are penta-BDE, octa-BDE and deca-BDE, so named for the number of bromine molecules.
27 40 CFR 1632.
28 40 CFR 1633. California enacted an open-ignition standard effective January 1, 2005, for mattresses sold in California.
29 T. A. Thomas and P. M. Brundage, "Quantitative Assessment of Potential Health Effects from the Use of Fire Retardant (FR) Chemicals in Mattresses," January 9, 2006.
30 Ibid., pp. 23–25.
31 Ibid., p. 18.
32 Statement of the Honorable Nancy A. Nord, Acting Chairman, U.S. Consumer Product Safety Commission, Ballot Vote (NPR Upholstered Furniture), February 1, 2008.
33 16 CFR 1632.33(f) and 1633.13(c).
34 American Chemical Society, National Historic Chemical Landmarks, "Durable Press" found at http://acswebcontent.acs.org/landmarks/landmarks/cotton/press.html.

Chapter 8

1 S. P. Porterfield and C. E. Heindrich, "The Role of Thyroid Hormones in Prenatal and Neonatal Neurological Development—Current Perspectives," *Endocrine Reviews,* vol. 14, no. 1, pp. 94–106, February 1993.
2 M. Purvis and R. Gibson, "The Right Start: The Need to Eliminate Toxic Chemicals from Baby Products," U.S. PIRG Education Fund, October 2005.

3 ConsumerReports.Org, "The Resurgence of Lead," accessed October 30, 2007.
4 Consumer Product Safety Commission, "Advance Notice of Proposed Rulemaking, Children's Jewelry Containing Lead," *Federal Register,* vol. 72, no. 5, pp. 920–922, January 9, 2007.
5 M. Shedden, "Toxic Trinkets—Tribune Investigation Uncovers Lead in Children's Trinkets," *Tampa Tribune,* June 24, 2007.

Chapter 9

1 Environmental Working Group, "Safety Guide to Children's Personal Care Products," November 1, 2007.
2 S. Rorie, "Courting a Double Standard: Organic Labeling for Personal Care, Supplyside," *Inside Cosmeceuticals,* February 26, 2008.
3 Environmental Working Group, "Skin Deep, Cosmetic Safety Database, Why This Matters?," available at http://www.cosmeticdatabase.com/research/whythismatters.php.
4 Letter to Andrew C. von Eschenbach, M.D., Commissioner of Foods and Drugs, U.S. Food and Drug Adminstration, from Richard Wiles, Executive Director, EWG, dated September 26, 2007.
5 T. Little, S. Lewis, and P. Lundquist, "Beneath the Skin: Hidden Liabilities, Market Risk and Drivers of Change in the Cosmetics and Personal Care Products Industry," Investor Environmental Health Network and Rose Foundation for Communities and the Environment, February 2007.
6 S. Sathyanarayana, C. J. Karr, P. Lozano, E. Brown, A. M. Calafat, F. Liu, and S. H. Sawn, "Baby Care Products: Possible Sources of Infant Phthalate Exposure," *Pediatrics,* 121, 260–268, 2008.
7 D. V. Henley, N. Lispon, K. S. Korach, and C. A. Bloch, "Prepuberteal Gynecomastia Linked to Lavender and Tea Tree Oils," *New England Journal of Medicine,* vol. 356, no. 5, 479–485, February 1, 2007.
8 National Toxicology Program, "NTP Technical Report on the Toxicology and Carcinogenesis Studies of Thiethanolamine (CAS No. 102-71-6) in B6C3F Mice (Dermal Study)," National Toxicology Program, U.S. Department of Health and Human Services, NIH Publication 04-4452, May 2004.
9 National Toxicology Program, "NTP Study Report, TR-421, Toxicology and Carcinogenesis Studies of Talc (CAS No. 14807-96-6) (Non-Asbestiform) in F344/N Rats and B6C3F1 Mice (Inhalation Studies)."
10 Cosmetic Ingredient Review, "Ingredient Alerts, SLS (Sodium Lauryl Sulfate), Sodium Laureth Sulfate, and Ammoniam Laureth Sulfate," available at http://www.cir-safety.org/staff_files/alerts.pdf.
11 Letter from Rebecca Sutton, Ph.D., Environmental Working Group, to Office of Pesticide Programs, Regulatory Public Docket, EPA, Regarding Triclosan Risk Assessment, Docket EPA-HQ-OPP-2007-0513, dated July 7, 2008; Letter from Jay Feldman, Executive Director, Beyond Pesticides, to OPP Public Regulatory Docket (7502P), Re Docket Identification No.: EPA-HQ-2007-0513, dated July 7, 2008.

12 Letter from Rebecca Sutton, Ph.D., Environmental Working Group, to Office of Pesticide Programs, Regulatory Public Docket, EPA, Regarding Triclosan Risk Assessment, Docket EPA-HQ-OPP-2007-0513, dated July 7, 2008.

Chapter 10

1 A. C. Steinemann, "Fragranced Consumer Products and Undisclosed Ingredients," *Environmental Impact Assessment Review,* available online July 23, 2008, accessed at http://www.ce.washington.edu/people/faculty/bios/documents/Steinemann2008.pdf.
2 American Thoracic Society, "Even Occasional Use Of Spray Cleaners May Cause Asthma in Adults." *ScienceDaily,* October 14, 2007.
3 A. Sherriff, et al. "Frequent Use of Chemical Household Products Is Associated with Persistent Wheezing in Pre-School Age Children," *Thorax,* 2005; 60:45–49.

Chapter 11

1 "Beyond Pesticides, Lawn Pesticide Facts & Figures," available at http://www.beyondpesticides.org/lawn/factsheets/facts&figures.htm.
2 Ibid.
3 T. Schettler, J. Stein, F. Reich, and M. Valenti, "In Harm's Way: Toxic Threats to Child Development," Greater Boston Physicians for Social Responsibility, May 2000.
4 X. Ma, P. A. Buffler, R. B. Gunier, G. Dahl, M. T. Smith, K. Reinier, and P. Reynolds, "Critical Windows of Exposure to Household Pesticides and Risk of Childhood Leukemia," *Environmental Health Perspectives,* vol. 110, no. 9, September 2002.
5 J. Rudant, F. Menegaux, G. Leverger, A. Baruchel, B. Nelken, Y. Bertrand, C. Patte, H. Pacquement, C. Verite, A. Robert, G. Michel, G. Margueritte, V. Gandemer, D. Hemon, and J. Clavel, "Household Exposure to Pesticides and Risk of Childhood Haematopoietic Malignancies: the ESCALE Study (SFCE)," *Environmental Health Perspectives,* vol. 115, no. 12, 1787–1793, December 2007.
6 M. Cone, "Pesticide Link to Autism Suspected," *Los Angeles Times,* July 30, 2007.
7 C. Lu, K. Toepel, R. Irish, R. A. Fenske, D. B. Barr, and R. Bravo, "Organic Diets Significantly Lower Children's Dietary Exposure to Organosphosphorus Pesticides," *Environmental Health Perspectivies,* vol. 114, no. 2, February 2006.

Index